TIDEWATER TALES

Professor William C. Garnett

Tidewater Tales

Professor William C. Garnett
of Essex

HERITAGE BOOKS
2022

HERITAGE BOOKS
AN IMPRINT OF HERITAGE BOOKS, INC.

Books, CDs, and more—Worldwide

For our listing of thousands of titles see our website
at
www.HeritageBooks.com

A Facsimile Reprint
Published 2022 by
HERITAGE BOOKS, INC.
Publishing Division
5810 Ruatan Street
Berwyn Heights, Md. 20740

Originally printed in the United States of America
by Whittet & Shepperson, Richmond, Va.

International Standard Book Number
Paperbound: 978-0-7884-2615-5

DEDICATION

TO MY WIFE AND CHILDREN, AND TO ALL OTHERS WHO FEEL AN INTEREST IN THE HISTORY OF ESSEX AND OTHER TIDEWATER COUNTIES, ESPECIALLY TO MRS. MARY NEALE CURLETTE, WHOSE ASSISTANCE I ACKNOWLEDGE; TO MISS J. L. C. GARNETT, WHOSE ENCOURAGEMENT HAS BEEN HELPFUL, AND TO THE LATE JUDGE T. R. B. WRIGHT, WHOSE SUGGESTIONS AND INTEREST PROMPTED ME, THIS LITTLE VOLUME OF SKETCHES AND COUNTY HISTORY IS MOST RESPECTFULLY SUBMITTED.

CONTENTS

Dedication.

Introduction.

I. Essex County, *Geographical and Agricultural* 13

II. Essex from 1608 to 1876 18

III. A Trip on the Tidewater Trail . . 40

IV. Educational 64

V. Upright 71

VI. Fragments of History from Dunnsville 75

VII. Bestland and the Road to Essex Mill 82

VIII. Center Cross 88

IX. Dunbrooke 92

X. Paul's Cross Roads 95

XI. The Court Room in Tappahannock, Va. 100

XII. St. Margaret's School in Tappahannock, Va. 104

XIII. The Rise of Chinkapin 110

Sketches

XIV. Major Bob 119

XV. All for Fun 124

XVI. Agriculture in the Public Schools 131

XVII. Charlie B. and His Yarns 138

XVIII. Around the Country-Store Fire . . 145
XIX. Jim Robert Roane Puzzled About Himself 152
XX. Prof. Robert Ryland Bentley . . . 157
XXI. The Ware-Hundley Wedding . . . 167
XXII. A Recipe for Silencing Some Agents 171
XXIII. Bob and the Panther 174
XXIV. Mars Frank 178
XXV. Baylor and the Bull 182
XXVI. Old Uncle Rouzie Grey 187
XXVII. Bob Beazley Shoots at a "Flock" of Dogs 193
XXVIII. A Corn Shucking Before the Civil War 195
XXIX. Arch Johnson, the Noted Fiddler . 202
XXX. The History of the Virginia Mad-Stones 207
XXXI. Sora Shooting on the Piscataway . 211
XXXII. A New Remedy for All Ills . . . 215
XXXIII. A Little Book Talk 217
XXXIV. Just a Line from Dunnsville . . . 221
XXXV. "A Fox Hunt 'fore the Civil War" . 225
XXXVI. Bob's 'Coon Hunt 230
XXXVII. An Address Upon the Death of President McKinley 234
XXXVIII. My Ship—Liberal Verse Poem . . . 238
XXXIX. An Ode to Nature 239

ILLUSTRATIONS

Professor William C. Garnett . . . Frontispiece
The Home of Mr. and Mrs. John Curlette . . 32
"Font Hill," the Home of the Late R. M. T. Hunter 32
"Ben Lomond," the Home of the Late Judge Muscoe Garnett 64
The Home of Wm. G. Rennolds, Superintendent of Schools 64
"Hundley Hall," the Home of Hon. Deane Hundley 96
"Waiting for the Tide" 96
The Old Ritchie Home at Tappahannock . . . 128
The Walnut Tree at Caret 128
The Home of Miss J. L. C. Garnett 160
"Hill and Dale," the Home of the Author . . 160
Prof. Bentley's Method of Teaching Division of Fractions 192
One of My Jewels 192
Ready for School 224
The Youngest and Eldest of a Household . . 224

INTRODUCTION

I THINK it well to make some record of the history, both local and general, of each county in the State, in order that those who may follow us can read with interest and with a considerable degree of pride, and be encouraged to cultivate their own intellects and to promote the welfare of their county.

With this feeling on my part, I am offering this brief history of Essex, beginning in 1608, at the time when Captain John Smith made a voyage of exploration up the Rappahannock River, to a time within the memory of many now living. Besides my own brief sketch of history, I have the pleasure to add an address delivered by the late Henry Wise Garnett, Esq., of Washington City, having as his theme "Essex County." I consider this address of great value, for the data therein required the deepest research and much labor.

Added to this I am presenting some sketches from the various centers of the county involving very local history and some biography which I am encouraged to publish.

Thus, with my brief of the county, the excellent address by Mr. Garnett, and these local sketches, all considered, make a right comprehensive history of the county, though I may add that there is much more that could be written. But I am not offering a complete history—just a brief of what I consider of most interest. Then follow some sketches, some of these being in negro dialect and some of which my readers have spoken of very kindly. The old-fashion before-the-Civil-War negroes have nearly all faded away, and with them goes the old-time negro dialect. The modern negro has lost it—he uses better language, and comes very much nearer to the correct pronunciation. The Northern writers, in trying to imitate the negro dialect, make him use words he never used and could not mispronounce very well if he did use them. Joel Chandler Harris was perfect in his Georgia negro dialect, and the late Thomas Nelson Page was equally as clever in his old Virginia negro stories. There has always been a tender feeling, on my part, for the good old-fashion negroes. I love to hear them talk and in their own unique manner give accounts of their various experiences.

WM. C. GARNETT.

DUNNSVILLE, VA., March, 1927.

I

ESSEX COUNTY

GEOGRAPHICAL *and* AGRICULTURAL

In a historical address which is published in this book there is scarcely another line that may be written on the early history of the county, so accurate is it in data, and so very interesting in detail. So, for my part, I shall confine my writing more to the situation of the county, and its agricultural features, than to its history, save in some very local stories which appear later in this volume.

Essex county is about forty miles long and about twelve miles wide, on an average. These measurements, giving it about four hundred and eighty square miles, an acreage of about three hundred and seven thousand, about twenty persons to the square mile, taking the population at nine thousand.

Essex lies its whole length along the broad and beautiful Rappahannock River, a noble and a historical stream, affording food fish of the most choice quality, and bathing shores for the pleasure-seeker, as well as width and depth for navigation. This stream forms the northern boundary of Essex. The good old County of King and Queen lies next to Essex on the south, and is separated from it for a considerable distance by the Dragon Swamp, the headwaters of the Piankatank River. Caroline County bounds it on the West, and Middlesex County on the east. Along the river there is a low plain extending about two miles up from the river before reaching a line of hills running the length of the county, but broken by the Piscataway Creek, Hoskins Creek, and Mount Landing Creek, all estuaries of the Rappahannock River. From this range of hills on towards the Dragon Swamp the land is broken, but there are a few plateaus, and these gradually become less until in the lower portion of the eastern section of the county the land is nearly level. The above refers to Rappahannock, and central districts, as in Occupacia District the general contour of the land after leaving the range of hills continues as an irregular plateau until reaching the King and Queen line on the south and Caroline on the west. This much in brief for the situation of the county.

The alluvial soil of the river flats is deep and rich, and here and there a deposit of lime is found, making the growing of alfalfa and other lime-requiring crops profitable. Wheat and corn are the basic crops, but oats and rye and other cereal crops may be grown successfully. Beginning about thirty-five or forty years ago, watermelons were cultivated as a market crop and frequently with much profit. Green peas also form a ready-money crop in the lower portion of the county. Irish potatoes do well in the light soil, and some of the farmers cultivate large fields of them. German clover has been very beneficial, both for early grazing and as a soiling crop. All fruit trees do well in this county when properly worked and, in late years, sprayed against the ravages of the San Jose scale and other insectivorous pests. The fish and oyster industry is an important item in the product of this section. The Bowler's Rock oysters have a wonderful and well-deserved reputation in Washington and other cities. The run of shad and herring has not been nearly so large in late years as formerly, yet some of each variety visit these waters in the early spring. The sport-fishing in the Rappahannock is much enjoyed by visitors from the cities, for there is always a good run of rock, trout, and spot. Years ago the sturgeon was abundant here, and even as high up the river as Fredericksburg some weighing as much as two hundred pounds were taken, but this fish, as well as the drum and sheepshead, is extremely rare here now, owing, it is claimed, to the long fish-traps at the mouth of the river preventing their coming up any higher.

From Tappahannock down there are always a plenty of crabs during the summer. The creeks flowing into the Rappahannock furnish royal sport for chub fishing, and the marshes for sora shooting in September when this mysterious bird appears in large numbers, remaining until frost and then disappears to where no man knoweth. Trapping in the marshes is another profitable employment, though the muskrats are not as numerous as formerly. Essex used to be very heavily timbered with oak and pine and other forest trees indigenous to this section of the State, but while the young growth is coming on, the virgin trees have nearly all been felled and sawed into lumber. The excelsior mills have claimed much of the young growth of poplar, pine, and gum. Still, there seems no end to the forest growth, and one sawmill is scarcely out of the woods before another follows, certainly in a few years.

What Essex needs is the establishing of manufacturers that will bring more people here and give a pay roll for their support. And with proper encouragement, these people will settle here, and thus build up our county. There is room and to spare for more settlers, and it is more probable that the Rappahannock Valley Association, with the excellent men as its promoters, may lead to this end. The sawmills and the canning factories are at present the only means of circulating money excepting the daily wage of a few hands. There is room in Essex for a population of 25,000, whereas we have less than 9,000 at this writing. There must be something to attract our young people and give them profitable employment at home, or they will continue to leave and seek employment in the cities.

I will now let appear the history of this county as so masterfully given by Mr. Garnett, as previously mentioned, and then introduce some more local history by following the Tidewater Trail, and by letters which I have written from various sections of the county. These are very local, but contain some bits of history which, I think, will be appreciated.

> The educational is a most important item in the history of any county, and it may be said that Essex in this respect is yet in the formative state—with high schools on the accredited list, but not fully equipped as yet. The need of funds is the principal reason given. This refers to the public schools. It takes a long time to establish and conduct the schools of a State so as to coördinate with the colleges and universities. The aim and object of the educational is to place Essex firmly in that condition so that the graduates from our high schools will feel no embarrassment when entering higher institutions. This will come as our teaching force is stronger and the equipment of the schools is more nearly complete. Even as the schools now are, the students from Essex have done remarkably well.
>
> The St. Margaret's School in Tappahannock is a popular and a growing institution, and evidently will prove a strong educational force.
>
> The Ozeana Colored Academy is well managed and is doing much good among its patrons. This is an agricultural as well as a school for general education. So Essex is not lacking in educational nor other advantages. We want more people and we want those people to stay with us and work with us. The opportunity is here; let's make the best of it.

Bring more people here and issue that honored pay roll Saturday evenings, for this is what builds up a town and makes the working man return to his home, meeting a contented wife and happy children. Instead of about nine thousand, there should be at least twenty-five thousand people in Essex County. We want men with enterprise and some capital, who will take hold of farm work as they now do in the Northern States, with the "come on" spirit, rather than the "let John do it" spirit, for hired help is a problem of difficult solution. It is to be devoutly hoped that the Rappahannock Valley Association, through the efforts of its progressive promoters and members, may bring before the public at large the excellent features which this section presents, and encourage more settlers to come and be welcomed by us, to work with us, to instruct us, and by a hearty coöperation bring the waste places to a bountiful harvest as once they were. The highway from Richmond to Tappahannock, the newly completed Downing Bridge across the river, and the Tidewater Trail, that national highway leading from Washington to Fort Monroe, all have contributed to bring this section to the notice of many who scarcely knew us before. Progress, improvement, thrift, and the spirit of loyalty is what we want, and with these Essex will take the place she once had in the front rank of the State. May it be so.

I will later present that excellent historical address, previously mentioned, which is both valuable and interesting, and then follow with a trip from the lower portion of the county up along the Tidewater Trail to the western limit of the county, briefly mentioning what may be seen from the road as we pass, and with such pertinent comments as may seem of interest.

II

*ESSEX *from* 1608 *to* 1876

I TRUST it will not be by you deemed amiss or inappropriate in me, who am not a native or resident of Essex, to have chosen for the theme of my discourse the history of your county. I say I trust it will not be deemed amiss or inappropriate for, though not a resident among you, I am certainly no stranger, and by descent can claim an equal interest in this history on which today I address you, for my fathers shared with yours the common hardships and attained the common glories, and hence I come today as their descendant to speak to you upon this subject. Lord Bacon has written that histories make men wise; he might have added that the knowledge of that of their native country makes them patriotic. When Demosthenes desired to incite his countrymen to resist the encroachments of Philip upon the liberties of Greece he reminded them of the virtues of their ancestors who fought for those liberties at Marathon.

It is well, then, fellow-countrymen, in this centennial of our country's history to look back to the times of our ancestors and by this retrospect learn gratitude for the benefits which we enjoy from their labors, admiration for their wisdom, and emulation from their virtue.

I have, therefore, chosen for my theme today the history of your native county. That of our common country is so

*This address, delivered by Henry Wise Garnett, of Washington, D. C., at Occupacia, Essex County, Va., on the 4th of July, 1876, is here published not only on account of its excellent and rare history of Essex County in particular, but because it intertwines in this *local* history much of the *general* history of this section of Virginia. In fact, it would require months of unceasing care and toil to find the fragementary bits of history here interwoven into a most beautiful and interesting whole. The author of this address has gone to join his fathers—those who helped much in war and in peace to make the old county what it has been, and what it is today, and what by their example and by their zeal, it is destined to be in the near future. And the history of one county in Eastern Virginia, is largely the history of the entire State. The early settlers were interdependent. There were the strongest ties of blood and of mutual interest. Their love for the old Commonwealth was as natural as their love for mother and wife and children. She was indeed their mother—their soil-mother, and the growth of this mother which was best and rarest and most to be prized, was the offspring who had to themselves and to their mother been true in peace and in war.

short as to be almost within the memory of living men, but withal that short period has been so full of strange events that it has been told by a multitude of voices and recorded by many pens. Not only is this true of our country as a nation, but our grand old Commonwealth has had her numerous historians and in her archives preserves the material to supply the demands of more in the future. Our county's history, however, has never as yet been collected, but remains scattered fragments stored in various depositories, some of which are covered with the dust of more than two hundred years. Be it my task and pleasure to present to you today, not a finished history—for I have not at my command the materials to compile one; nor if these had been vouchsafed me, could I within the limit of this address present to you a complete and thorough historical narration of the events relating to Essex County. I have, however, by delving in the rich soil of antiquity, obtained some facts which I am confident will interest you to hear, as they certainly afforded me much pleasure to collect. To a portion of you some of these may be twice-told tales. If so, they are not of a nature to lose their interest by repetition, and you may well bear to hear again the deeds of your forefathers. Let us then look back to the year of our Lord 1608—a long space of time. Aye, two hundred and sixty-eight years ago; truly a number of years. James I had been King of England only three years. Gustavus Adolphus was not yet on the throne of Sweden; nor had Richelieu arisen to direct the destinies of France. At this early period in the history of the Old World commences that of Virginia. A year previous, 1607, the settlement of Jamestown had been made, and in June, 1608, Captain John Smith, as he tells us in his history, undertook in an open boat with some dozen companions his first voyage to explore the Chesapeake Bay. And it was while returning down the west coast of this bay that he discovered and started to explore the River Rappahannock, or, as he tells us, some then called it

Tappahannock. At this time commenced the known history of the beautiful river which forms one of your county's boundaries, and from its other name—Tappahannock—is derived the name of your county seat. Owing to an accident and the want of provisions, Captain John Smith did not then make his proposed visit to the Rappahannock, but deferred it until the following month of July, when he first encountered the tribe of savages from whom the river had derived its name.

It is an interesting scene, his description of the first meeting of the native lords of these lands and their future conquerors. He writes of how at his approach to the shore he sees some twelve or thirteen Indians on the beach, who with signs of friendship motion him to carry his boat into a little creek; but they are dealing with an experienced soldier, and he wisely refuses to obey their directions and requests an exchange of hostages, to which request a ready acquiescence is given, and Amas Todkill is set ashore by Smith as hostage and was the first Englishman who stood upon what is now the soil of Essex County (for, according to Smith's map, this interview must have occurred in the neighborhood of what is now Tappahannock).

Todkill, on endeavoring to move from the beach, is prevented by the Indians, but soon discovers an ambuscade; he shouted to his comrades; immediately the Indian hostage in the boat leaps overboard, but is killed by his keeper, and the Indians, seeing that their stratagem is discovered, rush forward to the attack. Todkill, seeing that it is impossible for him to escape to the boat, falls flat on the beach and is protected by the fire from his friends, which speedily drives off the Indians, but not before they had shot as many as a thousand arrows, which, however, effected no injury, the boat being protected by shields which were fastened to the prow. Todkill is rescued unhurt from his unpleasant location and the canoes of the Indians are seized and carried away, as a retaliation, and thus ends the first meeting between Europeans and that tribe who have now left only a name to the stream which washes the land which once was theirs. Although defeated in this encounter, the Rappahannocks were not cowed, for the following day when Captain Smith resumed his voyage up the river, and had passed, as he writes, several Indian towns situated on high white clay banks on the northern side, the opposite shore being composed of marshes, as his boat came to a place where the river was narrow, a friendly Indian with their party shouted "Rappahannocks!" and they heard the arrows of these warlike people striking against the protecting shields. In the words of Captain John Smith, "Some thirty or fourty of them had so accommodated themselves with branches that we took them for little bushes growing among the sedge, and when we were half a mile from them they showed themselves dancing and singing very merrily." From this it seems that our Indian predecessors were well pleased at their performance, and this is certainly the first record of a dancing party in Essex. There were, of course, no invitations, for, as we see, it was entirely a surprise party.

On his return down the river, Captain Smith, through the mediation of some friendly Indians, makes peace with the Rappahannocks and receives the bow and arrows of their king in token of submission. The places where the second attack and the friendly interview took place I have not been able to locate.

We hear nothing further of the Rappahannocks for many years. The year following this voyage, in 1609, Captain Smith, who might well be termed the "guardian angel of the infant colony," sailed for England, and with him for a long time departed its prosperity. Attacked by the Indians, who immediately became hostile, thus confined to Jamestown, and scourged by famine and disease, in six months the colonists were reduced to sixty persons in number and had taken ship to abandon their unhappy abode, when the arrival of a fleet from England with recruits and supplies caused them to decide to further test their fortunes in Virginia. Yet, still so badly were they governed that on the arrival of Sir Thomas Dale as Governor, in 1611, he found it necessary to proclaim and enforce martial law, which existed as the common law of the land until the arrival of Sir George Yeardley as Governor, in 1619. He the same year called the first General Assembly ever held in the colony, and, as the counties were not yet established, the Burgesses were elected by townships and boroughs. Under the same Governor in 1622 inferior courts were established to sit in convenient places, thus enabling suitors to have their causes heard without the trouble and expense of a visit to Jamestown, for the colonists were now in a prosperous condition and new settlements were founded upon the James, the York, and the Potomac, and it was becoming burdensome to conduct all lawsuits at Jamestown. From these inferior courts have sprung the system of county courts in this State.

In the year 1622 occurred the general massacre of the colonists by the Indians, by which within one hour's time there fell 347 persons, and by the war which followed the settlements were reduced from eighty to eight, and the growth of the colony materially checked. Therefore, it is not until 1646 that we find the settlements in this region of the colony have grown to sufficient importance to be noticed in history. And doubtless the inhabitants of the plantation, as it was called, would willingly have dispensed with the notice that was taken, for in October, 1646, the inhabitants of the plantation of Chickann, or Chickawane, on the land between the Potomac and Rappahannock Rivers, are ordered to pay taxes under pain of being called off from the plantation. Apparently, however, their being called to meet the inevitable and omnipresent tax-gatherer did not repress the rising prosperity of the plantation, for two years afterward, in 1648, the inhabitants of the plantation of Chickawane, situated on the neck of land between the Potomac and Rappahannock Rivers, are formed into the County of

Northumberland. And four years later, in 1652, we find the name of Lancaster; in 1653 Westmoreland is created. This rapid multiplication of counties and increase of whites was viewed with disfavor by the original possessors of the soil, or perhaps, as is more likely the case, they did not abandon their possessions with sufficient rapidity to please their new neighbors. Be that as it may, at any rate, in November, 1654, the Assembly of Virginia passed an act reciting that the inhabitants of Lancaster, Westmoreland, and Northumberland have made complaint of divers injuries and insolencies by the Rappahannock Indians, and there is danger of war, and therefore ordering that a body of troops shall be raised, whereof Lancaster is to raise one hundred—likewise Northumberland forty, and Westmoreland thirty, all to be provided with boats and necessaries to make a voyage to the Rappahannock towns. The troops are to assemble on the first Wednesday of February next in Rappahannock River, and from thence Major John Carter, their commander, is to march to the Indian towns and demand satisfaction, and he is to act only on the defensive except when assaulted and to report to the Governor and Council, who will determine on peace or war.

There is no mention in the old acts of Assembly of the results of this expedition, but it is a fair inference that it resulted as many an expedition to confer with the Indians has since—that is, in an extension of the territory of the whites—for soon afterward we find that Lancaster County has become so large as to be troublesome to its citizens; and in December, 1656, on a petition of the inhabitants of the lower part of Lancaster County, presented to the Assembly by Captain Moore Fauntleroy, on account of the distance from the county seat, the county is divided; all north of Moratticick Creek is named Rappahannock County. In March, 1675, we find the colony engaged in a general Indian war and an act of Assembly ordering 500 men to be raised, but it does not appear how many troops Rappahannock County is to furnish in this levy.

The year 1676 is memorable in the history of Virginia as being the year in which occurred what is known as Bacon's Rebellion. It is not necessary to enter into the character and object of this uprising of the people headed by Nathaniel Bacon, but this I do say: that no one can read the laws passed during his sway without being struck with the fact that the people were then suffering from the endeavoring to rid themselves of many of the oppressions of the mother country which subsequently led to the War of the Revolution, and it is a curious historical fact that this revolt occurred just one hundred years before the colonies threw off the yoke of Great Britain.

On the 15th of June, just one century to the day, before the resolution passed instructing the delegates in Congress from Virginia to declare the colonies free and independent is passed an act for carrying on war against the barbarous Indians, by which a levy is to be made and Rappahannock County is to levy sixty-three men.

The same year a fort in Rappahannock County, which has been built and was commanded by Major Lawrence Smith with certain privilege, is ordered to be abandoned and the men distributed along the frontier plantations for their protection. Rappahannock County must have been a strong supporter of the revolt, for when the Royal Governor again obtains possession of the colony and proceeds to punish his late adversaries, we find in an act of pardon that John Bagwell and William Potts do upon their bended knees with ropes around their necks acknowledge in the Court of Rappahannock County their treasons and rebellions and be committed to prison until they give security for their future good behaviour. It would seem that there were others ordered to make a like confession and that the offenders received favors at the hands of the court; for in September, 1677, in the proceedings of the Assembly, an act recites that whereas Thos. Gordon and John Bagwell were adjudged to appear at Rappahannock County Court with halters about their necks, appeared with small tape instead—which was accepted—the Assembly take it as a contempt upon them and order their clerk to enquire into it. It is plain that the Assembly of that date would allow no trifling with its orders, and if it decreed that halters were to be used, nothing but halters would be accepted. In 1680 was established the present County Town, for in June of that year a town was ordered to be laid out at Hobbe's Hole and fifty acres of land purchased for that purpose; by the same act all imported goods and tobacco were to be carried into the County Towns for sale, and various privileges were to be given to the settlers therein. Rappahannock County, increasing in population, its inhabitants petition for its division; and, as by this division Essex County was created, I shall give the act in full.

In April, 1692, was passed the following:

An Act for Dividing Rappahannock County.

Whereas sundry inconveniences attend the inhabitants of Rappahannock County and all others who have occasion to prosecute law suits there, by reason of the difficulty in passing the river—

Be it therefore enacted by their Majesty's Lieut. Gov., Councell and Burgesses of this present Gen. Assembly and the authority thereof, and it is hereby enacted, that the aforesaid county of Rappahannock be divided into two distinct counties, soe that Rappahannock River divide the same; and that part which is now on the North side thereof be called and known by the name of Richmond County, and that part which is now on the South side thereof be called and known by the name of Essex County.

Be it enacted by the authority aforesaid, and it is here enacted, that the Court of the said county of Richmond be constantly held by the justices thereof on the first Wednesday of the month in such manner as by the laws of this county is provided and shall be by their commission directed.

And the Court for the said county of Essex be constantly held by the justices thereof on the tenth day of the month in such manner as by the laws of this county is provided and shall be by their commission directed.

Be it enacted by the authority aforesaid, and it is hereby enacted: That whereas the Town land lying at Hobbe's Hole on the South side of said County was purchased by the entire County as now it is, the charge thereof being equally defrayed by the whole number of tytheables of said county; that the moyety of the tobacco arising from the sales thereof to the several takersup of the aforesaid lands be paid unto the inhabitants of the North side thereof, upon the taking up of the said land at the town aforesaid, and that the records belonging to the County Courts of Rappahannock before this division be kept in Essex County, that belonging wholly to their Majesties and the other to the Proprietors of the Northern Neck.

The history of a county is a difficult one to tell in an attractive manner; it is, for most part, so absorbed in that of the state of which it forms a portion that one cannot be narrated without the other, and if I were to confine myself exclusively to facts relating to this county alone, I should be compelled to the recital of the establishment of ferries and public warehouses, with little beside. If, therefore, I appear at intervals in my remarks to treat of the history of the State, rather than that of Essex County, it is because the history of Virginia in itself contains the history of Essex, and to understand the history of a portion of the body politic we must make some reference to the whole body.

The office of Justice of the Peace at this period was looked upon as a position of much honor, and it is interesting to know the first Justices of the then new County of Essex. I therefore give the names of those who held the office from 1695 to 1700: Capt. John Caslett, Capt. Wm. Mosely, Robt. Broky, John Taliafero, Thos. Edmundson, Francis Taliafero, Capt. John Battaill, Bernard Gaines, James Boughan, Francis Gouldman, Rich. Covington; Clerk of Court, Wm. Colson. The Church of England was the Established Church of this Colony, and accordingly the County of Essex was on its creation divided into two parishes, which were named, respectively, St. Anne's and South Farnham, the Parish of North Farnham being in the County of Richmond. The name Farnham is the name of a town in Surry, Eng., situated on the River Wye.

The first minister of the Parish of South Farnham was the Rev. Lewis Latané, a Huguenot gentleman, who settled in the parish and took charge of it in 1700. The two churches were Upper and Lower Piscataway (now Texas and Marigold). In 1702, in the list of ferries established in the colony, there are two in Essex over the Rappahannock.

Three years later an act is passed for establishing ports and towns by which it is enacted that the unpoetical name of Hobbe's Hole be changed to that of Tappahannock, and the town is created a free burg, to have Tuesdays and Saturdays in each week for market days, and an annual fair on the 5th of October and for four days following, except Sunday. Elections are to be held in the town to elect eight of the principal inhabitants, who are to be called benchers, and who are to elect one of their own number, to be called director, these to constitute a court of civil and criminal jurisdiction, and the town is to be made a Port of Entry. The principle of self-control and independence exhibited itself early in the church government of this county, for in 1716 there is on record a controversy between Mr. Latané and his flock. The only complaint made against the Reverend Gentleman is rather a peculiar one when we remember that at this time he had been in charge of the parish for sixteen years. It was that the congregation was unable to understand his sermons because of his foreign pronunciation, and to such a height did they carry their opposition that the vestry actually closed the church doors, and it required a letter from Governor Spotswood—the Royal Governor—to compel them to submit.

Controversies between pastors and congregations were not confined to South Farnham alone, for in 1718 Governor Spotswood had to write a letter to the Parish of St. Anne's to compel them to receive the minister he has determined they shall have. In this letter he informs them that the King is the patron of all churches in Virginia, and not the vestries, and if they doubt this fact they can, when they are so disposed, bring their action of "quare impedit" and test the question at law.

Tobacco was in that period of the colony not only the chief article of export, but also formed the principal currency of the colony, and frequently in the pages of the old statutes we find acts for the establishment of public warehouses for the inspection of tobacco. The earliest, established in Essex in 1730, were at Hobbe's Hole, upon John Griffon's land; at Bowler's Ferry, upon Adam's land, and at Laytons. In 1742 the number of these warehouses was increased, and, in addition to those already mentioned, one is established on Piscataway Creek and one on Occupacia Creek, on the land of James Garnett, where Robert Jones formerly dwelt. This was near the very place where we stand today—one hundred and thirty-four years after the date of this act. These warehouses were for the inspection of tobacco and none could be exported from the colony unless inspected at one of them. The inspectors were to deliver to the owners of the tobacco notes under their hands and seals, setting out the quantity and quality of the tobacco deposited by them, and these notes were to be used in all tobacco payments and allowed to circulate in the neighboring counties not divided by some great river. There were frequent changes and amendments in these acts in reference to tobacco and the regulation of the customs thereon; the forgery of tobacco notes was made a felony.

The free burg of Tappahannock was becoming a place of importance in this region, and was rapidly assuming the pretensions of a city; the streets had become the object of legislative care, as the following act in 1744 will testify:

Sept., 1744: An Act to prevent the inhabitants of Tappahannock from raising hogs at large in said town.

Prior to this date, in 1731, had been built Vauter's Church. The history of the parishes of St. Anne's and South Farnham exhibit the fact that the need of clergy in Virginia was not confined to the present age, but was a need that existed in a greater degree in the days of our fathers and has come down to us as a heritage from them. For long periods there were no ministers to take charge of the parishes, and sometimes we find one conducting both. Indeed, so careless did the people become in respect to public worship, I have the authority of Bishop Meade that after the Revolution the two churches of South Farnham, one of them among the most venerable houses of God in the Commonwealth, were destroyed for the building materials contained in them, and Vauter's itself was only preserved by a threat of the law against any violation of the sanctuary.

Settlements increased rapidly on the Rappahannock, and in 1748 we find twenty public ferries across this river. The same year an act is passed for increasing the limits of Tappahannock by the annexation of certain land, and also one for allowing the trustees of Leedstown to make a causeway through the marsh opposite their town to the high land of Mrs. Sarah Brooks, in Essex County, and establishing a public ferry to connect the town and causeway. In 1755 an act recited that as the County of Essex, among others, is suitable for raising sheep, and it is necessary to preserve them against the ravages of dogs, no slave shall be allowed to carry a dog under penalty of ten lashes, nor shall more than two dogs be kept at any negro quarters in the county. But our ancestors were sportsmen, and it is especially provided that servants shall not be hindered by the act from carrying hounds and other dogs for sport from place to place for their master's diversion. At this time, in Bowen's Geography, Essex County, or Rappahannock County, is described as overrun with briars, thorns and wild beasts.

The year 1755 witnessed the great calamity to the colony: of Braddock's defeat, by which Virginia was laid open to incursions of the French and Indians. The spirit of the Assembly arose with the occasion, and an act was passed in 1756 increasing the Virginia regiment to fifteen hundred men and appointing George Washington its colonel. Still the horrors of an Indian war were sorely felt by the colonists, and to such an extent were the inroads made that the most western counties began to be deserted by their inhabitants. In 1758 the forces were augmented to two thousand men, and in 1760 an additional land tax on each one hundred acres of land and an additional poll tax of one shilling for every titheable is laid by the Assembly for a series of years to meet the expenses of the war, and drafts were made upon the militia of the counties. In 1758 the schedule of indebtedness to the troops, under the head of Essex County, appears the following:

"To Capt. Forest Upshaw for his pay and the pay of the guards conducting the drafted soldiers to Fredericksburg—9 pounds.

"To James Emerson, maintaining drafted soldiers in prison—6 pounds."

From this time to 1762 the history of the colony consists of little else than Indian massacres and increased taxation to support the expense of additional troops. In 1762 the treaty of Fountainbleau gave a short peace to the exhausted colonists, who were almost immediately disquieted by the aggressions of Great Britain, for in 1765 the Stamp Act was passed, and the same year Patrick Henry moved and passed in the House of Burgesses his famous resolution claiming the exclusive right of self-taxation for the colony. Affairs were fast ripening for the struggle of the Revolution. Essex County kept pace with her sisters, but of Essex alone there is little record until 1774. In 1769 a portion of the Parish of South Farnham was added to that of St.

Anne's, and in the same year an act was passed for laying out at Layton's a town to be named Beaufort, and prohibiting the use of wooden chimneys in Tappahannock.

The discontent of the colony, being aggravated by the British ministry, passed gradually into armed resistance. Almost ten years had elapsed after the resolution of Patrick Henry had been passed before the colonists could be forced to realize that the mother country of whom they were so proud and to which they looked with the affection of children for a parent—that this parent was fully fixed in her intention to override their rights. It took them long to realize this fact, but when the truth burst upon them, immediately through the length and breadth of the land ran the cry, "We demand that our rights shall be held inviolate, for we are your children and not your slaves." Nor was Essex behind-hand in this general cry, as the following will testify:

At a meeting of the freeholders and other inhabitants of Essex County, Virginia, at the courthouse thereof, on Saturday, the 4th of July, 1774, seriously to consider the present dangers which threaten ruin to American liberty, Mr. John Upshaw being chosen moderator, the following resolves were proposed and unanimously agreed to:

First. Resolved, That we will at all times and upon all occasions bear true and faithful allegiance to his Majesty, King George the Third, and as free men we have always been and ever shall be willing constitutionally to give and grant liberally our property for the support of his crown and dignity and the preservation of our parent state, but that we can never consent to part with it on any other terms.

Second. Resolved, That the Legislature of this Colony, for the purpose of internal taxation, is distinct from that of Britain, founded upon the principles of the British constitution and equal in all respects to the purposes of legislation and taxation within this Colony.

Third. Resolved, That the people of this Colony in particular and of America in general have a clear and absolute right to dispose of their property by their own consent expressed by themselves, or by their representatives in Assembly; and any attempt to tax or take their money from them in any other manner and all other acts tending to enforce submission to them is an exertion of power contrary to natural justice, subversive to the English constitution, destructive of our charters, and oppressive.

Fourth. Resolved, That the town of Boston, in our sister Colony of Massachusetts Bay, is now suffering in the common cause of North America for the just opposition to such acts, and it is indispensably necessary that all the colonies should unite firmly in defense of our common rights.

Fifth. Resolved, That it is the opinion of this meeting that an agreement to stop all exports to and all imports from Great Britain and the West Indies, firmly entered into and religiously complied with, will at all times prove a safe and infallible means of securing us against the evils of any unconstitutional and tyrannical acts of Parliament, and may be adopted upon the principles of self-preservation—the great law of nature.

Sixth. Resolved, That the inhabitants of this county will firmly join with the other counties of this Colony and the other colonies on this continent, or a majority of them, to stop all exports to and imports from Great Britain and the West Indies and all other ports of the world, except the colonies of North America, if such a measure shall be deemed expedient by the deputies at the General Congress; and whatever agreement the Congress shall come to for the advancing of the common cause of North America, relating to exports, imports or otherwise, ought to be considered as binding as any act of the Legislature, and that we will use our utmost endeavor to support and maintain such general agreement, at the expense of our lives and fortunes.

Seventh. Resolved, That it is the opinion of this meeting that the several courts in this colony ought not to proceed to the forwarding or trial of civil causes until our exports are opened.

Eighth. Resolved, That it is the opinion of this meeting that the East Indian Company, having a desire to monopolize a great part of the American trade, to the injury of the other merchants of Britain trading to North America, and knowing well the fatal consequences that must have resulted from their fixing a precedent for future taxes, by importing tea into the colonies, became the willing instrument of the ministry to destroy American liberty, and deserve the loss they have sustained.

Ninth. Resolved, That we do most heartily concur with our late Representatives in their resolve for the disuse of tea, and that we will not hereafter purchase any East India commodities whatsoever.

Upper—"FONT HILL," THE HOME OF THE LATE R. M. T. HUNTER
Lower—THE HOME OF MR. AND MRS. JOHN CURLETTE ON THE RAPPAHANNOCK
One of the Oldest Houses in the County

Tenth. Resolved, That the spirited conduct of the town of Boston hath been serviceable to the cause of freedom (all other methods having failed), and that no reparation ought to be made to the East India Company or other assistants for any injury they have sustained, unless it be the express condition on which all our grievances shall be removed.

Eleventh. Resolved, That it is the opinion of this meeting that any general censure upon the conduct of the town of Boston respecting the tea, without allowing to them the motives of resistance upon the principles of public virtue and necessity, is inimical to American liberty, and we are persuaded that none but ministerial hirelings and professed enemies of American freedom will adopt a language so impolitic which manifestly tends to create a disunion of sentiment at this time fatal to America.

Twelfth. Resolved, That the Parliament have no right to pass an act to remove our persons to Great Britain, or any other place whatsoever, to be tried for any offense, and that we are determined not to submit thereto.

Thirteenth. Resolved, That it is the opinion of this meeting that no merchant in this or any other colony on this continent shall advance the goods now on hand higher than they are at present or have been for some time, and that the merchants in the several counties sign an agreement to that effect.

Fourteenth. Resolved, That a subscription be set on foot for raising provisions for the poor of Boston, who now suffer by the blockading up of their port, and that Robert Beverly, John Lee and Muscoe Garnett, in St. Anne's Parish, and Archibald Ritchie and John Upshaw, in the upper part of South Farnham Parish, and Meriwether Smith and James Edmondson, in the lower part thereof, take in subscriptions for that purpose, who are to consign what may be raised to some proper person to be distributed; and the before-mentioned gentlemen are empowered to charter a vessel and send it to Boston.

Fifteenth. Resolved, That this meeting have the deepest sense of the injuries in which the merchants and manufacturers of Great Britain must necessarily be involved by a non-importation resolution, they having placed an almost unlimited confidence in us for a series of years, and by that means have the greatest part of their fortunes lodged in our hands, and that nothing but the desire of preserving our liberties could induce us to adopt a measure big with such melancholy consequences.

Sixteenth. Resolved, That James Edmondson and William Roane, Esquires, the late Representatives of this county, be, as they are hereby appointed, deputies to represent us at the general meeting of deputies for the several counties of this colony, on the first day of August, in Williamsburg; and we desire that they will exert their best abilities for the security of our constitutional rights and liberties, and to appoint deputies to meet at the General Congress the deputies of the other colonies on this continent.

Seventeenth. Resolved, That the clerk transmit the foregoing proceedings to the printers to be published in their Gazette.

WM. YOUNG,
Clerk of the Meeting.

These resolutions speak with no uncertain sound. The time for indecision had passed; the struggle had commenced; the first Congress, which met on the 5th of September, 1774, at Philadelphia, adopted a course of passive resistance, and by a strict enforcement of non-importation hoped to convince the British government of the difficulty with which they would be met, in the attempt to enforce their tax laws. Few understood whither they were drifting, and, as we have just seen, their resolutions were generally prefaced with expressions of loyalty. To carry out the measures of resistance, committees were elected in the several counties, and the following is that of Essex:

At a meeting of the free-holders of the County of Essex at the courthouse in Tappahannock on Tuesday, the sixth day of December, 1774, for the purpose of choosing a committee to see that the association is duly kept agreeable to the resolutions of the General Continental Congress, John Upshaw, gentleman, was unanimously elected chairman, and Wm. Young clerk; after which the following gentlemen were elected: Wm. Roane, James Edmondson, John Upshaw, Thos. Boulware, John Lee, Meriweather Smith, Thos. Roane, Robt. Beverly, Muscoe Garnett, Wm. Young, John Henshaw, Wm. Smith, Augustine Moore, John Beal, Henry Garnett, Robt. Reynolds, John Brockenbrough, Thos. Sthreshly, Thos. Waring, and Archibald Ritchie.

WILLIAM YOUNG, *Clerk.*

This committee was no idle form in the County of Essex, as frequent investigations of suspected persons and orders concerning them will testify. In the spring of 1775 the clash of arms warned all to prepare for war.

In July of this year the Assembly of Virginia divided the colony into districts and ordered a battalion of five hundred men to be raised in each district, the age of military service being from sixteen to fifty; these minute men, as they were called, were to be kept and trained under an adjutant for twenty consecutive days, and, beside such battalion duty, the companies should in their respective counties meet and exercise for four successive days in each month, except December, January and February, at times and places appointed by captains; in addition, the battalion was to meet twice each year and train for twelve successive days at places appointed by each committee of deputies. Gloucester, Middlesex, Essex, King and Queen, and King William Counties were made one district, and the time for the meeting of the battalion fixed for the 4th of May and 28th of October. All free male persons, hired servants and apprentices above sixteen and under fifty, with a few exceptions, were liable for militia duty. Owing to its exposed condition, in the distribution of troops, in 1775, a regiment is assigned for the protection of the peninsula between the Rappahannock and York.

It is interesting to read the oath prescribed for the troops of Virginia in December, 1775:

"I do swear that I will be faithful and true to the Colony and Dominion of Virginia; that I will serve the same to the utmost of my power in defense of the just rights of America against all enemies whatsoever; that I will to the utmost of my abilities obey the lawful commands of my superior officers, agreeable to the ordinances of the convention, and the articles of war to which I have subscribed, and lay down my arms peaceably when required to do so, either by the Gen. Convention or Gen. Assembly of Virginia. So help me God."

It would take too long a time to enumerate the various events concerning Essex County with the War of the Revolution. Her sons represented her on all its hard-fought fields. In the person of William Dangerfield, Esq., she furnished colonel for the Seventh Continental Regiment, and in Meriwether Smith, Esq., she supplied one of the counsellors who, in Congress, guided the newly launched ship of state safely through the tempest which raged around her. In all the counties whose sons are to step forward to repel the invader, and bravely did they respond. It is impossible to tell the counties from which the troops of Virginia came, but on looking over the list of officers of both the Continental and State service there appear many names still familiar in this county.

The theme of the Revolution is one on which it is natural, this day at least, to dwell with pride; the lapse of a hundred years has made it a tale of long ago, and yet not so old a story but that its history is still fresh in the minds of the descendants of its brave veterans, and we can with a feeling of just and honest pride whenever its glories are repeated exclaim, "And in all these Essex County has gained a part."

Peace at length achieved the independence of the Commonwealth of Virginia, and a wise judgment and foresight caused the formation of our country, the United States of America; to this happy consummation our grand old Commonwealth effectually contributed by the cession of the Northwestern Territory, thus generously quelling the animosities of faction. In all these acts the people of Essex by their representatives bore a part. Although there was a nominal peace between these States and England, an almost open war was waged against their borders by British agents who dwelt in strongholds unjustly retained from the United States, and another war had to be fought to compel that peace which was so earnestly desired: it was inevitable, and it came. In 1812 again were our fathers called upon to take arms in defense of their homes, and now the war was brought to their doors. A British blockading squadron, consisting of four 74-gun men-of-war and several frigates and sloops of war, commanded by Admiral Warren and Rear-Admiral Cockburn, was stationed in the Chesapeake; their tenders and barges penetrated not only all the rivers, but every creek, and no home situated near the beautiful streams of this section was safe from their licentious depredations; and weekly, aye, daily, accounts of their outrages shocked the public ear. The following extract from a paper of the times narrates how near our fathers' firesides bayed the dogs of war:

TAPPAHANNOCK, ESSEX Co., April 5, 1813.

The militia of Essex are now under arms; the British are now in the Rappahannoc and six of their barges were sent on Saturday last above Urbanna to take two privateers said to belong to Baltimore, and two letters of marque; they had a very severe engagement, and, being a calm, succeeded in taking the privateers, etc. Some fought bravely and would not strike their colors; the British officer went on board and hauled the colors down himself. Many lives were lost, but we have not the particulars. There is no doubt of the engagement, and the Colonel of Middlesex County has called on the Colonel of this county and King and Queen for men.

Colonel John Dangerfield, the commander of the Essex troops, responded without delay to the call, but the enemy fell down the river. The ravages on the shores of the Chesapeake, with the burning of towns, long made the name of Cockburn odious to Virginia ears. The Treaty of Ghent, in 1814, at last gave a permanent peace to our country. From this date to 1861 few events mark the history of Essex. The history of Virginia is its history. Consisting chiefly of large plantations, its population from 1790 has increased but slowly. In that year the first census in the United States was taken, and Essex returned a total population of 9,122, of which 5,440 were slaves. Although small in number of its citizens, Essex has been prominent in her representatives, for within the sixty-one years from the beginning of this century to the late war she has supplied four Representatives and a Senator to the National Congress, and for twenty-eight years in the Hall of Representatives and fourteen years in the Senate Chamber her sons have assisted in directing the destinies of the nation.

Of the last war I shall say nothing. Our memories still retain its history, the hearts of many of us are yet bleeding from its wounds, and its desolation yet blackens many of the broad fields of our State. Yet, while we think on it with sorrow, there is no shame mingled with our regrets, for there was no disgrace in our defeat. The unequal fight was bravely fought, so bravely that success often appeared within our grasp, and although our last flag went down, it did so in a halo of glory from the privations and hardships endured; the victories won the bravery and endurance of its defenders, among whom were the sons of Essex.

Like our forefathers, we have been looking and longing for peace since that bitter struggle. Let us hope and believe that on this centennial of our common country a new era of good feeling is to commence, nay, has already commenced—for the breeze which sweeps from the North, and which in 1775 bore to our fathers' ears the clash of arms, has in 1876 borne to our ears the shouts of welcome uttered by Massachusetts to her late antagonists, as, marching under the flag of our common forefathers, they come to commemorate a victory in our common history. I trust the time is not far distant when heroism of both North and South will be regarded as the common glory of the United States of America. What the next century will bring forth we cannot know: we stand, as it were, on an eminence from which we can view all things past, but beyond us lies the unknown future.

You inherit the fields whose soil your fathers reclaimed from the forests, and whose possession they conquered from savages and defended against Europeans. Young men of Essex, your lot is the same as that of your fathers—the common lot of all men—in the sweat of your brow to eat bread. Work is, and always has been, the secret of success. To you is confided the task of building up the old Commonwealth, weakened as she has been by war and stripped of her territory. She should be an object of honored trust to you, and her soil watered by the blood of your ancestors and your companions is indeed sacred, too sacred to be deserted for the wilderness and rocks of the West, where it seems there is some still fancied Eldorado.

Let, then, this country be your home, and may you by honest labor make it to blossom like the rose. Let your days be passed in the land of your fathers, that when another generation shall take your place your graves may be found, not in a strange land, but among those of your sires.

III

A TRIP *on the* TIDEWATER TRAIL

WITH tires pumped up tight, with a tank full of gas, and a driver safe, good-humored, and ready to answer all questions as far as his information goes, we may tell B. F. Hall, merchant and member of the County School Board, "Good morning," as we leave Laneview, soon to meet Abrams & Kerr, merchants at Montagues. Across the way, to the left, may be seen, where old Kalamazoo stood, the home of Thomas B. Garnett, the father of the late Judge Taylor Garnett, of Mathews County, and the grandfather of the Garnett brothers of Washington, prominent attorneys, one of whom was Assistant Attorney-General of the United States during the World War. Jeane Ingelow puts it this way when referring to an old home, once beautiful and inviting, but then like a ragged beggar sunning:

"Were it mine, I'd close the shutters,
Like lids when the life has fled,
And the funeral fires should wind it,
This corpse of a home that is dead."

Old Kalamazoo, once a place of hearty welcome and abundance, yielded years ago to the flames. Better so, perhaps. Yonder is where the late Dr. Jack Hundley lived, and now the property of Hamilton Seward, of Newport News. Dr. Tom Hundley, the grandfather of Dr. Anderson, lived not far from this place. He was the grandfather of Dr. John Fretzall Anderson, distinguished physician. This residence seems to be preserved from the ravages of time and tenants. On the right is the home of Judge H. L. Newbill, a gentleman of the old line.

But we must pass on, for there is much ahead. St. Luke's Episcopal Church is on the right. This recalls the memory of Rev. Dr. Hervy Hundley, so long the rector. Center Cross, the most prominent village in the county, is right up the road, and suggests much comment which will appear in a sketch bearing on its history.

Time is precious when you are burning gas, but we must detour and run down to Bowler's to shake hands, if no more, with "Live Wire" Sam Neale and hear him tell about Bowler's Rock oysters and the canning business. More of Bowler's appears in this book also, for one cannot write very much when your car shakes you and, maybe, your pen goes dry. Back on the Trail and on to Ozeana. Here is where Crawford Taylor, that prince of traveling men, lived, and in that grove over there he sleeps his last sleep.

Mrs. Muse, on the one side, and Mr. Smith on the other, stand ready to wait on their trade. These merchants in the country are a great help, for they buy all farm and poultry products, giving you either cash or merchandise in exchange. Where Rob Rice built and lived for years, Mr. Smith, the merchant, now lives, while Rob lives in Richmond.

Angel's Visit (Colored) Church is in Ozeana. This church has a large membership and is a potent factor among the colored people. A little higher up the Trail, and without much eye-strain you have Ozeana Colored Academy, with Professor Robinson at the head of it. He is an effectual trainer.

Now comes "Ben Lomond," the grand old "four-square" dwelling overlooking the Rappahannock in far-reaching prospect from its high observatory, the home of the late Judge Muscoe Garnett. The Garnett tablet in the courthouse at Tappahannock tells the story that needs no repeating here. But as we pass it comes back to me in playful memory an incident in the judge's history that may not seem inappropriate here. Judge Garnett was a large landowner, with many slaves, and wielded a force in his county and beyond. He was an excellent example of the old Virginia gentleman, and lived like a prince. He was kind and affable on general principles, but—and here is where this incident comes in—being accustomed to having his way both at home and abroad, he was severe when crossed. Living adjoining to his property was Major Cauthorne, a bachelor, but a beau to the day of his death. The major was in every sense an unique character, tall, raw-boned, red-haired and red-faced. Like the judge, the major was accustomed to having his way about matters in general. From his house to a mill it seemed to him convenient to have a new road opened through a portion of the judge's land, but not adjacent to his home tract. Well, without a word of warning to the judge, the old major petitioned the old majesterial court, under the old *regime,* to open the road, and this they agreed to do. When the judge found out all about the proceedings, hostile to him in every respect, chiefly, perhaps, because he had not been consulted, he was simply furious. The next day he met the major, and this brief but potent colloquy followed: "Major Cauthorne," said the judge, "I hear that you are going to have a road cut through my property, and not a word have you said to me about it. Now, sir, it will be more convenient for me to have a road right from my barn leading right by your house to the main road, and, sir, I shall have it done." The old major bristled up, and with his hat in hand, in order that his stiff red hair might have room to rise, simply said with all the emphasis at his command: "I, God, sir, I want you to understand that you ain't *king!"* This was all, but it ended right there.

On the opposite hill and near the Eubank Garage and Lumpkin's Store, is Strawberry Hill, where the late Orville Jeffries lived and flourished, now the home of the pastor in charge of Angel's Visit Church. Mr. Jeffries was full of fun. His son, the late Dr. William George, of Tappahannock, inherited much of his father's disposition. Mr. Jeffries and the judge were close friends; they exchanged hands at busy times and lived as neighbors should. Well, Mr. Jeffries had among his other fruits some large tartarian cherries. He picked a bucket for the judge, and called up Lucindy, as black as the cherries she was to take. So, to prevent any pilfering, Mr. Jeffries wrote these lines, after taking a piece of chalk and making a line all around Lucindy's mouth:

"To keep the cherries safe and sound,
I chalk Lucindy's mouth around."

It was effective. Mr. Jeffries had a negro named Anderson. He was a good hand, but in hot weather a nap in the shade under an old walnut tree near the ditch bank was inviting, and not objectionable to the mule he was plowing. One day Mr. Jeffries saw the mule standing near the walnut tree, but no Anderson was in sight. He walked along quietly and found the negro fast asleep in the cool of the shade. He then crept up close to him and lay down by him as close as possible without disturbing his repose. After a while he took a little switch and tickled Anderson on the face. Anderson struck, spasmodically, half-asleep, as he still was, at the imaginary fly. He turned his head, and there close to him, at full length, was his master, apparently fast asleep. With every precaution Anderson got on his feet and then to his mule, and old Sampson had never gone down a corn row so fast in all of his plowing days. Mr. Jeffries never alluded to the incident to Anderson. The punishment had been administered in full.

Opposite this place was once the home of the gallant Captain Oliver, who gave his life to the "Lost Cause." A few turns of the wheel brings us to Maury Hundley's home. Maury Hundley was an educator and full of public spirit. And here is Ephesus Baptist Church. We must stop and read the names on the slabs in that "home of the dead" right back of the church. Rev. A. F. Scott, so long the pastor; William Campbell, a power for good, and Wilton

Phillips, the leader of the singing for years and years, and whose voice in that sweet old hymn, "Sweet Hour of Prayer," was inspiring, and so many, many who have crossed over, dear friends of the writer, men and women who bore their burdens nobly and did their duties well.

And now we approach Dunnsville, the history of which village may be read in this book further on. Approaching is the home of the Hon. Deane Hundley, the Treasurer of Essex County. With a well-kept yard and a house in full repair, there is a reason to think there is prosperity there. On the opposite side is the cement dwelling of A. Ransone, surrounded by fertile fields, and near a very commodious barn, reminding you of the barns you find in the western portion of Virginia. E. M. Ware, Jr., & Co., with a large stock and many customers, do a considerable business. And there is the Tidewater Inn, with Ryan Ransone to furnish food for the hungry and to repair your car at his garage. Across is W. O. Atkins, a successful and highly respected merchant. If you drive as far as the parsonage, you will have a view of the home of H. W. Dunn on one hill and the home of George B. Kriete on another, both having lovely views of the river off in the distance. A short run in detour brings you to Ware's Wharf, on the Rappahannock. Here H. H. Ware operated a ferry for several years, but the Downing Bridge at Tappahannock relieved this very convenient means for crossing before the bridge was built. There are summer homes along the river here, and higher up there are more. R. L. Ware, member of the Board of Supervisors, lives here, and his brother, John Ware—a mere colony. The father, Robert L., Sr., built Ware's Wharf. He was a man of sterling qualities, and his children do follow him. It would be pleasant to go up the river bank and see W. L. Waring, whose home is near where old Fort Lowery was constructed during the Civil War, but soon destroyed by the Confederates for some purpose, ineffectiveness, it might have been. And Robert

Daniel, a first cousin to ex-Governor A. J. Montague, is right near. He would meet us with a smile and a good joke had we time to go there. Old Bathurst, a colonial home, built by Lady Bathurst of England, in 1692, with its wonderful, both social and tragic, history, is tempting to the writer, but not now. Later, perhaps. The home of W. R. Lumpkin is ideal for a view of the Piscataway, and his farm shows that industry is not lacking.

Further up on the creek we might visit Clyde Side, the home of Monroe Hayes, but once the home of Andrew Hundley, the grandfather of our present Treasurer, and before Mr. Hundley possessed the property it was owned by the Tompkins family.

No, we can't go to these places just now, and must trust to memory. The road leading to them is not yet improved. Just outside of the village of Dunnsville is the home of E. M. Ware, substantial in appearance, and with no lack of flowers. Opposite is where his brother Catesby Ware lives, and with the alfalfa field in front of his large dwelling, it indicates a desire to grow along with present-day progress. "Hoskins Hill"—but Willard is not there, nor his wife, for they sleep side by side nearby, having been buried the same day. The Rappahannock Church is perhaps one of the largest church buildings in the country, and has a very large and influential membership. On special occasions immense crowds come from various sections of the county. From this church some very prominent ministers have gone, among them Rev. James A. Dunn, of Richmond, Mo.; Rev. John S. Trible, president of Bethany College at the time of his death; Dr. Peter Ainslie, of the Christian Temple, Baltimore; Rev. Dr. John T. T. Hundley, president of Lynchburg College; Rev. Dr. Ritchie Ware,, of Beckley, W. Va., and Rev. Francis H. Scott, of Roanoke. This church was organized way years before the Civil War, and the organization followed the preaching of

Alexander Campbell, whose oratory and arguments were invincible.

But we must not miss the Dunnsville Grammar School, the building having been intended for a high school and conducted as such for some years. The older pupils were taken to Center Cross High School, and this lowered the grade of the present school. Miss Manie Leroy Garnett, with Miss Garnett Ellis to assist, sees that the young idea shoots in the right direction. And near here is where the old Tanyard Storehouse stood, where the late R. C. Phillips, of Tappahannock, began his mercantile career. Not a brick nor a block left to tell where the building once was. Oh! the ravages of time, and changes it makes. Up on the hill there is where Dr. Peter Ainslie was reared. His brother Charlie's widow owns and occupies the old home place.

And now to the right I see a place that is very dear to me, for it is home, and while flowers bloom in so many places elsewhere, there are none sweeter than those that grow right there, and hallowed memories cluster around every foot of the old spring path and the ivy-clad hills nearby. "Cottage Park," named by Mrs. Ella Jeffries, who was Miss Ella Fisher before her marriage with the late Dr. Wm. George Jeffries, of Tappahannock. It is now the home of Miss Laura Fleet Garnett, and the sloping lawn gives an inviting approach to the pretty yard trees around the house.

And next is where Miss J. L. C. Garnett, the authoress and philanthropist, lives. In the quiet of her home she devotes her time to literature. Right opposite is dear old Woodland, now unoccupied and for sale by the heirs of Charlie Bray. He and his wife sleep not far off in the garden, where once they delighted to till. Where the flowers grew the ragweed and the wild honeysuckle grow undisturbed.

Way up on a commanding hill lives Tom Sadler, a bachelor and a modern-day Samaritan. May he live long and prosper. Down a steep hill, a little turning, and here is the Piscataway Creek, the playground for the Richmond sportsmen throwing their lure to the wary chub and shooting the king of edible birds, the sora. Old Jim Parker, the keeper of the bridge, a typical Chinkapinite both in appearance and in dialect. Jim keeps the bridge and is ever ready to do you a good turn. When Stephen Bundy, a carpenter, living in Tappahannock, speeding to his work early one morning last fall, failing to see the red flag and piece of timber that Jim had placed to warn all drivers that the draw was open, plunged into the creek and was drowned, Jim, though not at fault, was distressed beyond comforting. He told his friends that he was going to drown himself. So urgent was he to have some one witness his plunge, and so much did he talk about his mental suffering, it was thought he had gone crazy. So one of his friends said, "Jim, if you really are going to drown yourself, I will go out there on the bridge and see you jump off. Come right along now." Of course this was but a test, for his friend was fully able to prevent the threatened suicide. When they had reached about the middle of the bridge, over where the water was deepest, his friend said, "Now, Jim, jump right off here, and be over with it. I am tired of all your talk about drowning yourself. Go ahead and jump right off here." Jim said, "Oh!! wait a minute," and sat down and began to tug at his heavy gum boots to get them off. "What are you about, Jim—what are you pulling off your boots for?" Jim replied, "Man, dese here gum boots is heavy, and I can't swim a stroke; you know I'd be drowned sho' 'nough if I jumped into dat ar creek right here, case de water is fifteen feet deep." Jim might have been temporarily crazy, but he wasn't any fool.

Over the bridge and on up the Trail. Off to the right is where the late Dr. Henry Gresham lived, and still the property of his children. Dr. Gresham was a graduate of the School of Medicine of Paris, France, and the second Superintendent of Public Education for Essex County. He was a man of high culture and sought to instill his love of literature into the minds of his teachers, and his visits to the schools always left a deep impression for good. A little further, up on a high hill, to the left, is Poplar Spring, the home of the late Mace Clemens, an uncle of the late Hon. Thomas Croxton, of Tappahannock. Mr. Clemens was a bachelor. There is not one of the name left in this county, so far as I know.

And next, "Berry Hill," the property of Mr. Jeffries. The view from this home, as from so many others along the ridge, is commanding and beautiful. And yonder, like a great red monument left to mark the past, but with no present for it save its history, is Mount Clement. The blood stains on the floor tell of a tragedy, but who knows?

Now, here is where the Richmond Highway meets the Trail. It would be very pleasant and equally as interesting to follow the highway for a ten-mile run and see Brays, with Mr. Hudgins in charge of a mercantile business, and Joe Blanton in his garage or his store. Then Bob Lou Pendleton, justice of peace, and member of the County School Board, lives on this road, and Trinity Methodist Church, where the camp meetings are held, is on the highway. And it would not take long to reach Millers Tavern, and see Dr. Ferry, a member of the Board of Supervisors of Essex. St. Paul's Episcopal Church is near, and its history is tempting to the writer. From this point we could easily reach Minor, just on the line between King and Queen and Essex. Mr. John Haile lives not far from this place, and to visit him is always a delight to the author of this book of fragmentary history. And there are others of which I could say much the same in expression of my friendship who live near Minor and Millers. And it would be equally as pleasant to visit the home of Mr. George T. Brooks, and to meet and talk with Mr. Walter Dix, bright as a new dollar, and so many others in Dunbrooke. But we must run along on the Trail.

Herbert Mitchell lives over there to the right—farmer and progressive in his farming endeavors. "Noels" is the name of his home. This was once the property of the late Hon. Thomas Croxton. On we go by asparagus fields and neat dwellings, and the road that leads to Richmond Beach, the pleasure shore for the pleasure-seekers in summer.

Here is a flour mill, and right by it the bridge over Hoskins Creek. And from this bridge you may see the mouth of the creek and the Rappahannock River. And do you know that right at the mouth of this creek, where the marsh grass is high, the first white man to place a foot on the soil of Essex landed in July, 1608, as a hostage to the Indians there assembled and who proved treacherous? Amas Todkill was this brave Englishman's name, and but for his crawling on his hands and feet to let Smith's men shoot at the Indians over him, he would never have reached the ship again. It does seem altogether appropriate that a slab to the memory of this brave soldier, offering himself as a hostage to these savages, should be placed in the courtroom of Essex, along with so many others there on those walls, to commemorate our noted dead. Hon. Wm. A. Wright, following the spirit of his distinguished father, may take this matter to heart. I hope so.

Just a short mile, and we must slow down, for here is Tappahannock, the county seat of Essex, as old as Philadelphia, and while of slow growth and leg the city of brotherly love surpass her, she is now awake from her slumbers and speeding ahead.

The first building to attract notice is the Town Hall. This building was for many years a house of worship, and was the first church building in the town, the land on which it stands having been deeded to trustees to be held for the express purpose of building a church on it for the general use of Christian worship. And for many years the building was so used, but later abandoned and was going fast into decay. Rather than see it like this, the town took it over and remodeled it and turned it into a hall for entertainment and such other uses as town halls generally have. So now where once was heard the voice of the inspired clergyman and the saintly hymns of "ye olden tymes" may be heard the sound of flute and viol and gayest laughter. But the honored dead, marked by the slabs nearby, sleep undisturbed. Why not this rather than complete decay? It is difficult to locate where some of the old churches were in this county, so thoroughly have time and neglect done their silent but sure work.

Potential and solid in appearance stands the hall of justice, the most thoroughly equipped court building in Tidewater Virginia, with fireproof vaults for its records, and its courtroom adorned by portraits and tablets, resembling a veritable hall of fame. This beautiful conception for preserving the history of Essex was the exponent of the loyalty and love of country held by the late Judge T. R. B. Wright. Not only in this courtroom, but in the courtrooms all through his circuit, did he leave his impress for honoring the worthy. And Essex, to be sure, had many a man who well might bear the name of worthy citizen, both in peace and in war. The Confederate monument in front of the courthouse bears record true of many of them. There on the left in passing down the street is the old Ritchie place, now the home of Mr. Willie Passagaluppi. Ritchie and Roane Brockenborrough were called the political triumvirate of this section, yielding a powerful influence, not only in county and State affairs, but in the affairs of the nation as well.

So Tappahannock must have had intellectual giants in those days. Later this house was owned and occupied by the Mathews family, and there the late James Muscoe Mathews was reared; lawyer, and author of Mathews' "Digest of Criminal Law," and "A Guide to Commissioners in Chancery." But it is not my intention to write a biographical history of Tappahannock, certainly at this time. So much has been said and written of the town of late, since the coming of good roads and the building of the Downing Bridge across the Rappahannock, that what I may say is simply in threads and patches as we pass along. Yet almost a volume comes back to me in memory thoroughly intertwined with pleasure and with sadness, for many of those whom I knew so well walk the streets no more, but to think of them brings back pleasures and past-times. Now others have taken their places, and among them we count many a one whom we may call friend.

Let's see who is out and hustling today. Ah, there is Hon. William A. Wright, our Representative in the Legislature. Just a word with him to urge him to start a movement for placing a tablet in the courtroom to the memory of Amas Todkill, as previously mentioned. And right across I see Hon. James M. Lewis, the Commonwealth's Attorney, so full of smiles since the opening of the bridge that all the world goes well. And there is Mayor H. C. de Shields, walking so fast we can scarcely overtake him. He takes the loss of his ferry by the building of the bridge very philosophically, for he would not throw a stone in the way of progress though it be to his loss. And Allan Latané, editor, and booster, with his hands full of mail, is in a hurry to get back to his office. Coming out of the clerk's office is H. C. Southworth, worthy successor to his faithful and efficient father, who kept the records safe for so many years. And there is Len Henley, ready to sell you drugs and to talk on any subject that comes to mind. George Dangerfield with a new insurance proposition he wants to tell you about, and Charlie Shearwood, standing near him, his partner in the investment for old-age savings. But Charlie had rather talk race horses and setter dogs.

Charlie Sale is out of town today, for he must see that only good fertilizer is sold in this county. Dr. Charlie Warner is busy in his dental office as usual; we can't see him and hear him discourse on any topic that comes up. George Derieux is too busy to talk today, for his customers are first. George Anderton steps as lively as he did so many years ago when first he came to Tappahannock, and just as anxious to sell goods. But the driver warns me to hurry up a little if we are going as far up the Trail as planned. Still, so much comes to me that I must steal a little more time. I just cannot help mentioning some items that have laid away so long in my memory, perhaps unknown to some of the present residents of the town. I may not pass this way again, and these items with me may pass.

As is known by the readers of local but ancient history of Virginia, Essex County was formed in the year of grace, 1686, and the town of Tappahannock was laid out as the county town for holding courts. The first courthouse is now the Beale Memorial Baptist Church—from a hall of justice to a house of worship. In the act which established the county seat the place designated was at "Hobb's Hold," certainly not Hobb's *Hole,* as some historians have written it. Land *holden* under some grant. Hence Hold. But who was Hobb? I know of no such family name. This is mentioned simply as to the name of the place before the town was built.

But did you know that this was an Indian town when Captain Smith came up the river in 1608? Some age to Tappahannock! And the name is really the same as the name of the river. Did you ever talk with Indians? Their words are very guttural, and the name of this tribe as taken by Smith and others in his party sounded different, and was so written. Some wrote *Topponocks* and some *Topponecks.* Later Rappahannock was accepted as the correct name of the tribe and the river, and simply by beginning with a T instead of an R we have the present name of the town. But this is ancient history.

Writing from early childhood memory, Zebulan Skinner Farland was the leading merchant of Tappahannock. His business was immense—great shipments of wheat and corn bought from the farmers the country around and goods of nearly every variety furnished. His first wife was Miss Croxton, a sister of Hon. Thomas Croxton; his second wife was Miss Ella Garnett, daughter of Judge Muscoe Garnett; his third wife was Miss Jane Gordon, daughter of Dr. Gordon, of Tappahannock, and his fourth wife a sister of the last-named. She survived him, the Rev. Z. S. Farland, of Richmond, being a son, and Mrs. Maggie Hall, wife of Professor Hall, of William and Mary, a daughter. Joe Farland, whose mother was Miss Croxton before marriage, went to West Virginia to reside. Yes, Mr. Farland was a merchant king in those days. Later there was Hipkins, and he it was who built the brick store which was destroyed by fire not so long ago. This house was called "Hipkins Folly." Whether because it was too large for the town or that he made a failure I cannot say. Later, again, was Howard Cook. What a business he did! And R. T. Cauthorne, another landmark among the merchants. Then Jack Williamson, who seemed to hold the business of the county in control. There were others, of course. R. C. Phillips, coming from Dunnsville, did a prosperous business where his nephew, Sydnor Phillips, of the firm of Phillips & Powers, is now.

When I look at the courthouse I think of Mr. James Roy Micou, the almost lifelong clerk of the court. Mr. Micou was most efficient in his clerical work, as the records show today. All of his writing was with a pen and much of it with the old goose-quill. His handwriting was truly *sui generis* and difficult to read until you had become fully acquainted with it. He made nearly all of his penstrokes downward, and the letters were separated as if they had been printed. While copying a document he would repeat the lines over and over again as he wrote, but always taking time to mumble, "Oh, Lord, I wish I was in Heaven." He would say these words over and over and grunt as he said them. Yet, while he longed for his celestial abode, he was not anxious to be sent there by being struck by lightning, for he was dreadfully afraid of this potential means of removal.

The late George Croxton was Mr. Micou's deputy for some time, when he (George) was quite a youth and full of fun and youthful pranks. He called the venerable clerk Cousin Jimmie. George was fond of bathing and fishing, and the summer evenings were more suggestive of sport than copying court records. He knew his Cousin Jimmie's dread of a thunder-cloud. So to have holiday occasionally he took an old cannon-ball up to the jury-room and would roll it across the floor and then go down into the office below and see the effect. "George," Mr. Micou would say, "didn't you hear it thundering a while ago." George would tell him that he might have heard it, as there was some signs of rain over in the west. George would then slip back up to the jury-room and roll the old cannon-ball across the floor in a manner to sound like the near approach of a thunderstorm. "George, I heard it thundering just now. Ellen is all alone at home. You better lock up, for I am going home." Down to the river George would go, as happy as a lark.

Mr. Micou by curling his upper lip and letting it meet the tip of his Roman nose could hold a pen instead of holding it behind his ear as most clerks hold pens when not writing with them. This was always amusing to one not accustomed to Mr. Micou's ways. During the Civil War, when the clerk's office was for a time located out in the country, for the safe protection of the records, Mr. Micou was one day called out of the house by a man who lived way up in the forest somewhere to ask for his marriage license. Mr.

Micou came on out with his pen held between his upper lip and the tip of his nose as usual. The man had his prospective wife's name and age and parents' consent and the money to pay the fee. The old clerk went on back towards the house, telling the man that he would be back in a short time. Soon he returned and handed the paper to the expectant groom. He had come there in an ox-cart and was standing by his team when the clerk approached him. "Well," said Mr. Micou, "is there anything else you are waiting for?" "No, sir," replied the man, "I's jest waiting for de license." "Why," said Mr. Micou, "you have the license in your pocket." "Is dis de license? Lord, man, I thought dey was a great big thing like a piano and brought my ox-cuart to put 'em in."

Looking at the courthouse again reminds me of one day when the Board of Supervisors had adjourned and they and some others were standing out in the courtyard near the street. It was a beautiful day. The street seemed absolutely free of traffic. While they were standing there they heard yelping and rattling from the lower portion of the street. Suddenly a dog appeared dragging a tin can attached to his tail. As he passed at full speed an old fellow from out in the forest remarked, "He's done finished his shopping and is guine home." The crowd roared with laughter.

One more incident, unique and hard to believe. Harking back very far, yes, very far indeed, way up in the forest, there lived a man, named Silas Bush, we will say. He was uneducated, but had common sense enough to till his little place and make the best of his lot. He dreaded the very thought of ever being called to court for any purpose whatsoever, and had never attended a court trial in his life. He was in no sense a public man, but stayed strictly at home. He paid his taxes and was accredited as being honest. There was nothing against him.

Well, one day the sheriff rode up to his house and summoned him to appear at court to serve on the petit jury, a murder case being on the docket. Silas hated this. Oh! he just dreaded it. He was present; he was examined and accepted as a proper juror. I pass over preliminaries and particulars. The Commonwealth's Attorney had to assist him a prominent attorney, and the defense was strongly represented. One of these attorneys for the defense was a tall man and remarkably long of arms, and these arms were used in furious gestures. He had a way of leaning over the bar as far as possible and pointing his long arm in the direction of the jury, almost reaching them. Now, Silas occupied a seat in the panel nearest to this vigorous lawyer.

In his closing speech he made an appeal for mercy, for the evidence for conviction was strong, and he feared the halter would be his fate. As he reached his highest pitch of oratory, accompanied by his loudest tones, he reached over and pointed his long finger right towards Silas, and said, "Remember, gentlemen of the jury, it is better for ninety-nine guilty to escape than that one innocent should perish. Oh, gentlemen! and if this man is innocent and you should convict him and take him from his poor wife and little children, and take his life on the gallows, and it should appear later that you had caused the death of an innocent man, and then at the final day, when all secrets will be made known, all faults appear, and this man should come before you and shake his bloody locks at you, and say, 'You did it, you did it!' what will you have to say—what will you have to say?" He was pointing that long finger right at Silas, who seemed the picture of misery. The argument closed.

The jury was sent to their room for consideration. In a short time there was a knock on their door and the sheriff went up and brought them down. "Have you agreed upon a verdict, gentlemen?" said the old judge. The foreman handed a paper to the clerk, and this is what he read aloud: "We, the jury, agree, and hang Silas Bush." This was enough. Silas grabbed his hat, cleared the bar, stepped on a sleeping dog in the aisle, and in full tilt reached the street, and bareheaded he went up that street like a quarter-horse. It does not appear of record that he was ever brought back for contempt of court, but it is quite certain that the sheriff would have had a hard time bringing him.

Mr. Joan Passagaluppi, an Italian, who was a valiant soldier during the Civil War, and after it was over settled in Tappahannock, was quick to reply, and it was risky to say anything to him that was offensive. He was a strong Democrat. On an election day when Cleveland was the successful presidential candidate, Mr. Joan (for we all called him by his first name rather than run the gamut of his last) was coming up the street hollowing "Hurah for Cleve! Hurah for Cleve!" He approached two colored men standing on the corner, who were red-hot Republicans, and very offensive to the white people. "Hurah for Cleve!" shouted Mr. Joan and slapped one of them on the shoulder. This was all bitter to the man. He turned and said in a surly manner, "Whur was you born, anyway, Mr. Joan?" "In Italy, near the France border. Hurah for Cleve!" he shouted, for he was in gala mood. The man who seemed disgusted then said, "You are too far away from home to be hollowing 'Hurah for Cleveland'." This was enough. Mr. Joan had his temper up in true Italian style, and turned on him with cutting satire in these words, potential, effective and absolutely silencing: "No far nor way from home nor you, you d—— babboo from Af."

So many things both interesting and amusing come back to me, for Tappahannock was a place of great delight to me even in my earliest childhood, going with my father to court and hearing him and the rest of the lawyers speak and buying horsecakes large enough to feed a family for a quarter, and later in the educational work there for four years forming most pleasant friendship among my students and making stronger those ties of friendship begun in youth with the older people.

I will say this with assurance, that Tappahannock has always had a strong collective personality and never lacking in that self-respect which every town and every community should have. It would be pleasant to go to the Riverside Hotel and see the fine equipment for the coming tourists, and pleasant indeed to go over to the Monument Hotel and meet the Misses Gresham, who preside over it. These ladies are daughters of Dr. Henry Gresham, previously mentioned. Is that Ernest Wright way up the street? Delightful to talk with him. And now, too late to meet him, is Mr. Willard Gresham. And A. A. Cralle, cashier of the Southside Bank, on his way to dinner. Mr. Jones, cashier of the Bank of Essex, is busy, so we may see him later. There is Mr. Crosby, farm demonstrator, and he, too, is busy with his fair plans, for he expects to have the best fair this fall that Essex ever had. Hurrah for Crosby!

It comes to me impressively as we leave that some one of the bar should write a history of the Essex Bar, running back to the time when the two Wrights were powers before the jury, and then Robert L. Montague, the "Red Fox" of Middlesex, was in his prime, and Colonel Wm. R. Aylett, and Harry Dangerfield, and Muscoe Garnett, later judge, and his son, Lewis Henry Garnett, and Thomas Croxton, and Thomas Evans Blakey, later judge, and E. M. Ware, later judge also, and so many others. Who will do this? A valuable acquisition to our county's history.

Just beyond the limit of Main Street was the home of the late John Waller Faulconer, lifelong friend of mine, and just as we turn to leave the town we pass the home of the late Judge E. M. Ware, another cherished friend. Now we are passing the high school and hear the merry laughter of large and small, as I have heard them so many times before when I had the honor to be principal of the school. Pretty farms on the right and on the left. Here is the sharp turn on the Trail not far in detour is Croxton's Mill, where the late George T. Croxton lived in a beautifully situated cottage, not by the sea, but by the mill-pond.

Climbing a little hill, we then make a straight shoot for Mount Landing. There is poor Waller Parker's residence. Treasurer of Essex for years, and a pillar in Mount Zion Baptist Church. Sadly missed by his church and county. They tell me that the first courthouse in Essex was somewhere in this vicinity, but I can find no trace of it. This, of course, was before the act establishing the courthouse at Tappahannock. If Ben Rennolds, of Rexburg, were here, he might give some information, for he is, perhaps, the best informed historian on local matters in the county. I have just heard that it was at Caret, and not Mount Landing, that the first courthouse stood. An old tree marks the spot. Crutchfield's Store and a sharp turn to the right. What a dread was Waring's Mill hill until the State Highway Department put it in good condition. And here is Caret. This makes me think of Phil Taliaferro, prominent farmer and successful huntsman, but he does not live on the Trail. There are, indeed, others who live some distance from our route today, whom it would be a pleasure to see, and from whom to gather information interesting and helpful to me. Mr. Robert Beverly, of Blandfield, whose residence is, perhaps, the largest and handsomest in all of this section, could, I am sure, assist me in many ways, for I do not claim to know it all. We have driven fast, and here is Champlain; Mr. Ashby Gresham is the merchant here. Way behind us now is old Lloyds, a relic of the long ago, when Pitts flourished there and trained so many young men for mercantile business. Whence came the name Lloyds? Who knows?

And still behind, on the left, is where the late B. J. Saunders, educator and county surveyor, lived. Another devoted friend of mine, tried in his friendship both at home and abroad, for we were years together in the educational work in Louisiana. Right near Lloyds is where the Hon. R. M. T. Hunter lived. "Font Hill" is the name of the old mansion. A man of State and of national fame. The old home, though not as well cared for as formerly, still brings the thought of the high culture of the distinguished statesman.

Hunter's Mill is where they used to hold political gatherings and have a fish-fry. Those were days, and those were men who gathered there. Were we to leave the Trail at this point and take the road on the left, leading towards Hustle, we would pass the home of William Taliaferro, a gentleman of great industry and most deserving. Where he lives was once the home of the Bentley family, among whom was the late Professor Robert Ryland Bentley, a teacher of wonderful attainments and force, having a reputation both in Louisiana and in Virginia as a prominent educator. Elmwood was the home of the Hon. Muscoe Russell Garnett, nephew of the Hon. R. M. T. Hunter, whom we have mentioned. There was once a girls' school at Elmwood, presided over by the mother of Muscoe Russell Garnett, and there, too, his father, Hon. James M. Garnett, delivered those highly prized lectures, a copy of which being in the State Library, to his wife's students. As Elmwood is to the upper-county Garnetts, so is Ben Lomond to the lower-county members of this family.

Higher up on the Hustle Road lives Captain Edward R. Baird. Captain Baird was for years Superintendent of Schools of Essex County. There in a beautiful grove is the home of this old Confederate soldier, and the house and its surroundings mark the influence of refinement, while the large library tells that culture is a part of that household. The large farms on the river flats, rich in lime deposits, with the beautiful homes high up on the ridge, overlooking the river and beyond, would be interesting and instructive for historical research—the Baylors, the Sales, the Warings, and the Brookes, and others.

Loretto sounds like Spanish. Is this correct? A very old settlement and surcharged with interesting history, for here the gentlemen from down on the large river estates would come and meet those who lived up on the hills, and there discourse on the topics of the day.

Now we are abreast of Vawters Episcopal Church, ivy-covered, and high-pewed, telling that it was erected way back in the Colonial days. It is said that at one time the congregation of Vawters represented more wealth than any other church in the country—Lord William Boulware with coach-and-four and out-riders, driving from Newtown, and scores of others of wealth and influence. Services are held in this church yet, and not long since some repairs were made. The present membership may not be large, but it is forceful and bears the stamp of the influence of the past when old Vawters was stronger in membership. Right at the top of the hill is Iraville, Mr. Williams being the merchant in charge. And this is the end of our trip on the Trail.

Port Royal is so near I wish we could go there, for it was in that old town I first saw the light, and it was where my mother, Miss Fanny Care, was reared, and where I spent many a joyous day when visiting my grandmother, Mrs. Care, and my aunt, Mrs. Louisa Urquhart. Port Royal, it is said, was laid out the same year as Philadelphia, and while the latter soon surpassed it in size and population, yet for the size and population of Port Royal, there was no town in all the country with more refinement and culture, with more beautiful flowers, or with more beautiful ladies. Mr. Fitzhough, the law writer; Mr. William B. Lightfoot, the exponent of the old-line Virginia gentleman; the Catlets, the Peytons, the Gravatts, the Robbs, the Pratts, the Thorntons, and others well worthy of mention—such were Port Royal folk just before the Civil War, and surely the impress and influence of such people is still there.

Port Conway, it is said, lacked but one vote in Congress to select it for the site of the National Capital. Be this as it may, still Port Conway has passed on down into history on account of Booth, the actor, and slayer of President Lincoln, having crossed over the Rappahannock from this point to Port Royal in his flight from Washington. And Garrett's barn, not very far from Port Royal, is where he and his companions hid, and resisted arrest by the military authorities who had trailed him, and was shot to death. Dr. Charles Urquhart, that grand old Scot, the village doctor, was sent for to see Booth, hoping to save his life for a while, but his wounds were mortal. He was laid out in Dr. Urquhart's yard, awaiting burial preparations, and then carried back the route he had come to Washington. Did you know that the silk-worm industry was attempted in Port Royal years ago, when the mulberry trees were set out in large numbers as food for the worms? Why abandoned I do not know.

And that was the time that the game of "nine pins" was a craze, so great a craze that it is said that a special act was passed against playing the game. But this was circumvented by adding one more *pin,* giving the game of ten pins as it now is. Bowling Green was the rendezvous for the players, and its *green* the favorite place for the alleys, where the players *bowled* the balls, and thus, it is said, came the present name of the town, Bowling Green. Quite apart from the history of Essex, but I could not well help it. So back on the Trail we go, and fast, too, for the sun is getting low, and we would not risk meeting the hundreds of tourists that pass over the Trail at night.

There are many other points in Essex interesting to me, among them Howertons, in which church parish James Greenwood, a relative of T. T. Durham, a merchant, died while at prayer, and the services were completed by Captain Lewis Booker, great-grandfather to the author, as it has been handed down to me. And a parson of this church was arrested for preaching the doctrine of the Baptists, before the separation of church and State and freedom of religious belief was granted to all. There is so much more to tell, for when you think of the history of a county covering 319 years you know that but a brief may be given in a small volume.

I have taken the liberty to add some special stories written from certain community centers in the county, which I trust may be read with interest. And after these some stories in negro dialect, and others—all of which in some measure bear on the history of this county. So now, hoping what I have given may be of interest, and to some degree of pleasure and amusement, and by reading the sketches from the various centers of the county interesting and pleasant memories will be revived for the old and items of local history given to the young which will be new to them. The dialect stories and other sketches I hope may be appreciated.

NOTE: Knowing that a history of the part the men from Essex took in the last war has been written, I considered that it was needless to repeat that history here. The men of Essex have never been lacking in true heroism, whether fighting in that sad and fratricidal struggle when the sons of the North and the sons of the South grappled in deadly combat, or when the need to arrest and suppress a would-be world-conquering foreign foe arose. The bugle-call and the drum-tap has always been music sweet to the ears of Essex when might opposed right, and when the test for loyalty was made she promptly answered "Here" and fought for the right.

IV

EDUCATIONAL

For any one interested in the establishment and growth of the public free schools of Virginia, I know of no other single work that will give as much historical data as that excellent contribution to the Columbia University Library, entitled "The Free School Idea in Virginia Before the Civil War" (numbered 93), by Dr. William Arthur Maddox, onetime assistant professor of education in Columbia University, and now President of Rumford College, Illinois. The research necessary to obtain all of the very valuable information contained in this work was voluminous and the patient search perplexing. There is probably not another word to be added to cover the full educational history of that period. And though Essex, being somewhat remote from the earlier settled counties, was late in settlement, yet the history of one section of East Virginia is in large measure the history of all of them. It is well to remember that there was a leaning towards educating the poor even before the establishing of the Benjamin Syms School in Hampton, 1642, by an act approved by the royal Governor of Virginia, Sir William Berkeley. But the idea was to educate along the study of mechanics, in order to benefit the students for trades rather than for professions which called for more than the three R's, for the Royal Governor was timid of higher education, seeming to fear that free schools, *i. e.,* such as they then had in England, giving higher education, might lead to such dangerous activities as the patriot party in England had set forth in the reign of James I, which strongly savored of latter-day democracy. So he reported to the "Commissioners of Trade and Plantations" in England his pleasure that there were no free schools in the colonies. "Thank God, there are no free schools," he said in his report. This

Upper—"BEN LOMOND," THE HOME OF THE LATE JUDGE MUSCOE GARNETT
Lower—THE HOME OF WM. G. RENNOLDS, SUPERINTENDENT OF SCHOOLS

was in 1671, yet it appears that he had sanctioned the Syms School in 1642. It is evident then that the Governor was in favor of limited education among the poor, but opposed to their receiving too much for fear they would do their own thinking, just as they did do in 1776, even though the poorer classes had but little opportunity for education of any kind.

The desire for public free schools was very strong in the Colonial days, and after the Revolution this desire became stronger; for freedom of thought, freedom of the press, freedom of religious belief and religious worship all slanted towards cultivating the intellect of all, both male and female. Still, as late as 1841, ninety-nine years after the Royal Governor, Berkeley, had signed the charter for the Syms School in Hampton, a measure was before the Virginia House of Delegates for the purpose of improving the educational system of the State, but was practically defeated.

"Father Ritchie," formerly of Tappahannock, but then editor of the *Richmond Enquirer,* which journal he established and ably edited for so long and so effectively, seems heartily in favor of improving the system of public education, but is of the opinion that the tax should come direct from the patrons. He was opposed to the $140,000 that had to go to the sheriffs for collecting and $9,500 to the treasurers for handling the funds. He was in favor of abolishing both of these officials and letting the teachers collect their salaries direct from the taxpayers. This would put the so-called free schools right in the class of private schools, unless the taxpayers were forced to pay the teachers. So it is quite evident that there was much discussion about the educational problem as far back as 1841, and may be educational rings as now, when a prominent speaker recently pronounced the educational of Virginia to be the strongest political ring in the State. If this be true, then the pity of it when we think of the thousands of little children deprived of their rights for the sake of the few heartless politicians who profit by this unjust sacrifice. But such is the game of politics.

I find that in 1841 the State comprised 64,000 square miles, and it was proposed in this very important convention of that year to have a school for every block, five and a half miles square. This would have given 2,133 districts, leaving out those in the cities. This plan was to place each child within not more than, say, two and a half or three miles from the school. The report of the committee passed favorably the House, but was defeated in the Senate. We are late in having our budget system, for as early as 1841 there was a complete budget of school expenses rendered by the committee in their report. I see there were to be employed 2,300 teachers at $300 each. Think of that, now! And this proposed plan gave them $50 more than they were receiving under the "old-field school" plan. And these "old-field" buildings were no better, it was reported at the convention held in 1842 for formulating plans for improvement, than the houses built for cattle. And I find at this time there were 58,000 illiterates in Virginia, to be, as a writer of that day expressed it, "hewers of wood and drawers of water." There was evidently a fervent desire for improving the public schools at that time, and it seemed to grow stronger, causing more agitation for school improvement. Yet, at that time the State paid $950,000 for public education, with 22,000 poor children and an indefinite number of those who were not poor not attending school at all. This was reported authoritatively by the committee when trying to show the need for another and a better plan. It is evident that at that time public education was at a very low ebb.

From time to time further efforts were made which did improve the situation, up to the Civil War period, when all activities were hampered. During the war a few male teachers were exempt from military service in order that they might teach. This enabled a few schools to continue, but under such strenuous general conditions, the schools, in many places, were a mere make-shift, being interrupted by fear of raids from the enemy, and by many of the boys having to remain at home to work the fields while their fathers were in the army. So it may safely be said that from the earliest settlement, 1607, to several years after the Civil War, public education suffered materially. Those whose parents could afford a private teacher to prepare them for some academy and from there to college had a decided advantage over the poor children for education, and from those private teachers and the academies and the finish given at William and Mary, a wonderful product came, the great scholars and statesmen in Virginia at that period. With a governess in the family to teach the girls not only the three R's *thoroughly,* but also music, and French, and drawing, it was better for the girls.

From the governess many of the girls entered a female seminary for higher instruction, perhaps, than was given them at their homes. Occasionally a lady teacher would have a private school for the girls, or, maybe, for the girls of all ages and a few little boys. These private teachers must have been wonderful, for the result of their work shows in this county, even at this late day. We cannot say that the pupils of that day were well rounded in mental training. Some of the less important subjects that are now required were not taught at all. But it is a fact that whatever was studied was understood and seemed to have an effective lasting feature about it. While now, be it said, it seems to be a matter of learning quickly and as quickly forgotten. It is not what one once knew that counts; it is what he knows now and can use. Learning is a storehouse with many shelves. It is well to place each daily lesson learned on the proper shelf—you may need it when you least expect it and will know where and what.

The schools of Essex were about on an average with those in the eastern portion of the State. Some gentleman would engage a teacher and his neighbors who were able would help to pay the salary of the teacher. Then, a few who could not afford to pay might let their children attend free of charge. Others might pay just a nominal sum. In this way, for preparatory work, and Fleetwood Academy, in King and Queen County, for higher preparation leading towards college, and with Miss Gray's school in Tappahannock for the girls, Essex had an unusually good opportunity offered to those whose parents could meet the expense. Many of them did meet all demands made, and the intellectual of Essex before the Civil War compared favorably with any other county in the State.

After the Civil War, that wrecker and ruiner of homes and of property, there were the reconstruction days, days when men who had lived like nabobs were turned suddenly into paupers, and it required both brains and nerve to come forth from the wreckage and start anew. But the men of Essex, as the men all over the State, proved themselves as great in peace as they were brave in war. The educational was not the least of problems before them. But it was not neglected. There came a Renaissance, a new intellectual birth indeed, and from this spirit of giving to each child in the State the present system had its foundation, with William H. Ruffner, appointed by a Republican Legislature, recommended by General Robert E. Lee, and a most ardent worker for public education, as State Superintendent of Schools, and there never was a more thorough one, nor one with quite as difficult task to work on. In Essex he had an able co-worker in Dr. Henry Gresham, the second Superintendent of Essex. But he did all that was possible in that formative condition of affairs that could be done. From his efforts the present system had its foundation. It is but fair to state here that the improvements have been wonderful, and it is quite true that some very effective good has resulted.

Before and directly after the Civil War there was some prejudice against the public schools on the part of those who had been accustomed to private teachers. Maybe it was that old feeling of patricianism against plebeianism as in the early days of Rome, but the plebeians slowly climbed up until they were fully recognized socially and politically. Does it not look as if the high schools, in reach of all who really desire to attend, have in large measure brought about almost the same changes, even here in our old county, where once social lines were made of adamant. The children of the best families have found that the children of those who at one time might not have been recognized by the wealthy were *human,* with as bright minds, with as strong a grasp, with as high ambitions as the best in the land. Why not, why not, indeed?

The mission of the best is to raise to their level those below them, not to shove them lower. At this writing there is much hope for more improvement in the schools of Essex —a strong central high school with a business course, with practical agriculture taught, with manual training given and the present high schools to be feeders for such a school, giving in them perhaps two years of high-school work, seems to the writer to be the best plan, a plan which will equip our boys for work upon graduating from such a school.

Among the schools for the girls in Essex there was not one better than that at "Elmwood" conducted by Mrs. Garnett, wife of Hon. James M. Garnett, and mother of Hon. Muscoe Russell Garnett, one-time speaker of the House when his distinguished uncle, R. M. T. Hunter, was prominent in the Senate. There is no other instance on record where the uncle and nephew occupied so high positions at the same time. This was in ante-bellum days, and these men were the products largely of home-teaching. Speaking of Hon. James M. Garnett, his lectures to the students attending his wife's school are very highly prized, and a copy is in the State Library. Mr. Garnett was nothing short of a finished scholar. I have never read any other book in which there was so well preserved that clear and dignified style of the Victorian classical writers. With such a lecturer, with such a teacher as Mrs. Garnett, there is no wonder that the product was typical of the best of the day, and has there ever been a better day?

I take occasion to mention that way back before the Civil War Richard Cauthorne, of Essex, wrote an arithmetic. A copy is under a glass case in the State Library. Much praise to him. I wish we could erect a monument to him. In latter years Essex has not lost her intellectual strength. It has only been sleeping. It will come forth after a while with the strength of a youthful giant. I predict it. Watch for it.

Hasten it with your encouraging words, if no more. In one issue of the *North American Review,* a magazine ranking as the best, there were but twelve articles. But, think of it!—two of those articles were written by citizens of Essex County. "The Secret Causes That Led to the Civil War" was one, and that was by the late Colonel John A. Parker, of Tappahannock, one-time minister to Honolulu. The other was contributed by the late Mr. Willie Baird, brother of Captain Edward R. Baird, for years Superintendent of Schools of Essex, entitled "A Review of Judge Black's Novels." A very unusual instance. Let's wake up, men of Essex, and do what our fathers have done—sounded out the fame of their county. There is a lady author whose contributions in prose as well as in poetry deserve recognition and appreciation. We will wait and hope for the best educational system that the State can give, and then, as a matter of right, Essex will have her share. May it come soon!

V

UPRIGHT

FROM time to time, through our local paper, *The Rappahannock Times*, published and edited by my good friend, Allan Douglas Latané, I have published some sketches bearing on the very local history of certain centers of the county. A few of these were preserved and herein republished, but others were lost, or sent away to friends out of the county. Among those I should be pleased to incorporate in this work is "Upright," and I now, in a very brief account, give such items as may be of interest to those who may read this in years to come.

As to how this name was selected I do not know, whether from the perpendicular weather-boarding of the first store-house or from the uprightness of the neighborhood—maybe from both, and this would seem appropriate, for the planks on the first building were upright, and there is no reason to question the moral standing of the place and vicinity. "Upright" is rather a new center for Chapel Grove, not so far away on the road leading from Upright to Howertons, which was the business center for years, with Winburne Mitchell as the proprietor of a thriving mercantile business. For it was there that warrant trials were frequently held, and warrant trials were numerous soon after the Civil War. There Dr. William Jeffries Newbill lived and began his successful professional career. Dr. Newbill, though now past the fourscore landmark, is active and vigorous, and enjoys a horseback ride as much as he did in the halcyon days when he followed old "Rock," his favorite hound, and the rest of his pack over the hills and down in the hollows around Chapel Grove.

The doctor has been living in Irvington for years, where he is prominent and popular. And here was the Methodist parsonage, with Rev. Mr. Evans as resident pastor. Mr. Evans and the late Dr. Christopher F. Newbill were brothers-in-law, their wives having been Misses Beckwiths, of Maryland. When all of these good people were at Chapel Grove it was indeed a pleasant place to visit—Mr. Mitchell's family, the parsonage, Dr. Newbill, and those nearby—but time has done its work. Not the Goths and Vandals, but fire and decay, for there is nothing there now, "not even a rose on its stem, to mark where the garden had been," and scattered to the four winds or dead are many of those who gathered around that old store fireside and told stories of love and war, and discussed politics and religion.

So, as Chapel Grove went down Upright built up and became the center of the community. But Lebanon Methodist Church is now, as for years and years, a pillar of strength, and its walls are sainted, and near them the cemetery holding the sacred remains of those who walked and talked with us and worked faithfully for the good of mankind. Those who have followed them carry on the work and are faithful representatives of their fathers.

With two stores and a grist mill, Upright seems to be prosperous. Mr. John Ferdinand Sadler is interested both in his store and in his poultry-yard. He seems to be successful in both lines. Upright is not far from what is called The Little Dragon Swamp, an estuary of the larger Dragon, which is the boundary of Essex on the south and divides this county from King and Queen County. The Dragon flats are very fertile, and before the Civil War, when labor was plentiful and efficient, were under a high state of cultivation, and perhaps the most productive wheat lands in the county.

The farms along the Dragon, in many cases, were neglected on account of the scarcity of labor, but now, it is pleasant to record, there is a disposition to reclaim the abandoned lands and to improve the farms lying adjacent to the flats. The farm once owned by the late William F. Smith is now the property of his son, Benjamin Stewart, who has repaired and improved this property with the management of his nephew, Benjamin Smith, Jr. At one time Mr. William

F. Smith's was a home of beautiful old Virginia hospitality, and on Sunday afternoons the yard was fairly filled with horses and buggies—a rendezvous for the young people. The hospitality is there now, but many of those who welcomed the guests years ago have gone "the ways of all the earth," or moved away to distant sections of the country.

Passing from Upright in the direction of the Tidewater Trail, you pass Merigold, the home of Mr. Noel Lewis. There once lived at this place a man named Billy Garnett, who was a good citizen and a good neighbor, but having peculiarities along strange lines, if what they have passed down about this gentleman be true. He was very fond of company, and if his neighbors failed to come to see him frequently he thought strange of it. One time when no one had called for several weeks he advertised the sale of his property. When the day for the sale came he had an immense dinner prepared, but no steps were taken towards having his household effects or stock or anything else displayed as if for a sale. The crowd gathered, as might have been expected, but no one could understand why the old gentleman should sell his property. He welcomed them all and talked about almost everything else except the sale. Among the crowd were some fox hunters, and they, of course, had their dogs with them. Long tables were spread in the yard, great quantities of food were brought and the waiters ready for service. When all was ready for the feast the old gentleman told them that they wouldn't come to see him, but he knew a sale would "fetch 'em." It certainly had, for there was a crowd. When the men had all been filled with this free and abundant display of strange hospitality, he told the huntsmen to call up their dogs and let them "finish the scraps." There was nothing sold, there was nothing bought, but old man Billy had surely had company that day, and the company were doubtless satisfied.

In those days the "marster" always carried his barn key, generally an immense piece of iron as compared with our little keys of this day. One morning old man Billy had just returned from his barn, where he had overlooked the feeding of his stock as usual. When he got to the house he heard his faithful old eight-day clock striking away at a furious rate. This old timepiece had been a guide for all the other clocks in the neighborhood, and now going wrong. He stood by the fire and his wife near him, both in absolute astonishment. The old clock sounded out, with all of the rattling and clattering of the old clocks of its time. Old man Billy counted fifty strokes. And then on to seventy-five and still striking. He counted on up to ninety, then ninety-one, ninety-two, ninety-three, ninety-four, ninety-five, ninety-six, ninety-seven, ninety-eight, and at that he said, "Dolly, if she hits a hundred I'm guine to smash her." And just as the faithful old timepiece struck ninety-nine he pulled out that immense old barn key, drew back ready for the "smashing," and as the one hundredth note was sounded he let drive with all force right into the face of the clock, and with many a jingle and rattle and clatter she struck her last, for she was indeed smashed to the very edge of total destruction. A queer one was old man Billy.

After the days of Billy Garnett, General Muse owned and occupied old Merigold. General Muse was very prominent and one of the old-time politicians. His three sons, William (Buck, as they called him), Lallie, and Hunter, were men of unusual strength, perhaps the strongest men ever reared in Essex County. Hunter is living, and I trust well and prosperous, but Buck and Lallie passed away some years ago. There was another son, Jim, who was an unusually small man, but said to be as strong as his large brothers. Jim was small in size, but he was immense in appetite, as his visits to protracted meetings could testify. Jim believed in filling the spiritual portion of a man and then in equal degree filling the physical. There is much more I might say of Upright and around, but this must suffice for the present.

VI

FRAGMENTS *of* HISTORY CONCERNING DUNNSVILLE

IN my writings I have been to Dunbrook, and Restland, and Upright, and Center Cross, and now, very much in brief, I have come to Dunnsville. And I must be very careful, very guarded, even as guarded as if I were walking over a carpet in a dark room where a paper of tacks had been spilled, and I shoeless. But of a truth I would say nothing in any sense unkind, nor would I drag from the dark closets any gruesome stories, if indeed any such there be, as so often it may have been the case with old, very old, communities where the same families have dwelt there for years and years, and frequently intermarried.

I have found it true of many of the old settlements that old feuds occasioned by somebody's great-grandfather killing somebody's great-uncle's cat, or a matter as trivial, that the bad feeling had been handed on down to the present generation, and maybe it will go on and on until it wears itself out by contact with the onrush of progress and the present-day breaking down of established precedents as well as a departure from the old social standards.

So much for all this, which I might have put in a line meaning that I hold nothing against my own community. Mark you well that I say I hold nothing against it—no spite, no desire to see misfortune come, no envy for its prosperity, if such there be. Being of a forgiving disposition, I would banish all from the book of memory that seemed unkind to me, and have written on that book only the many kind acts of those I have claimed as friends, and thanks to that One who metes out to all even more than they deserve, I have my full share of friends, true and tried.

But this is not the history of Dunnsville. Let's see about it. As far as my information goes, Mr. Dunn, the grandfather of Mr. H. W. Dunn, of Norfolk, was the pioneer in business at this center. He built a storehouse near where the Tidewater Inn now is, and there conducted business.

At that store, as at all of the country stores, whisky was sold. There lived in the neighborhood a man who was counted a toper. One day Mr. Edward Macon Ware, father of the late Judge Ware, chanced to be at the store when this man came in and bought his supply of whisky as he often did. Mr. Ware talked with him about his habit and urged him to reform. He took the lecture kindly. And right there poured out his quart and promised to reform. He turned to Mr. Dunn and offered him the money for the liquor. Mr. Dunn, with that kindness of heart that has been handed down to his grandson, refused to take a cent. The lecture and the kindness so impressed the gentleman that he kept his word and not another drop did he touch to the day of his death, and became a faithful member of the church, and the many of his name who have followed him are worthy citizens. The first dwelling was constructed by the late Dr. William L. Waring, uncle to Mr. Lowery Waring, of Ware's Wharf.

This house is now owned by the Hon. Deane Hundley, Treasurer of Essex. Various owners and occupants have followed since Dr. Waring's tragic death in front of the present Town Hall in Tappahannock. There is quite a story about this, but we will leave that until we get to Tappahannock. This Dr. Waring also built the present store occupied by E. M. Ware, Jr., & Co. The old house was strictly up to form of stores in those days: a cellar bricked up above the level of the ground, then the storeroom, and counting-room, and a room above for sleeping quarters for the clerks. This house has been added to considerably and holds a well-selected stock of goods suited to the usual country trade. It is not exaggeration to say that enough whisky has been stored in and dispensed from that cellar to float a yawl boat. And on rainy days there would gather a crowd to while away the time with quaffing pure liquor and swapping innocent jokes. How many stories have come to me from what happened there in those days, whether better days than these some might not agree. But one comes to me worth repeating, and I must make it snappy. It was one of those rainy days. There was gathered the usual crowd. Two of the men were at "lagger-heads," spatting at each other all day. After a while some of the young men, full of fun as the young men are right now, proposed that these two sore-heads would fight a duel. It was agreed, seconds chosen, pepper-box pistols produced and turned over to the seconds for loading. Well—and here is where the fun begins—these seconds, chock full of mischief, loaded one of the six-shooters with powder to the very muzzle, and put on the caps. Now, the other pistol they loaded with sand to the muzzle, and, likewise, put on the caps. They took one of the expected deadly contestants into their confidence and told him that there was no harm in either of the weapons, and so arranged it that this one should draw the powder-loaded pistol. The other fellow had but caps and sand to fight his antagonist with. The ground was marked off. The command was at the count of three and drop of the hat to fire. If neither fell, then to advance three paces and fire again, and thus continue until one or both fell, or their guns were empty. "One, two, three, fire!" and there was a loud explosion from one pistol, and from the other *Snap*. . "Advance and fire again," the seconds shouted Another loud report, and, horrors! another snap. Further advance and more explosions followed by a *snap* as before. When the poor fellow with the sand-loaded gun had snapped it five times, and the other man was right upon him, he dropped his gun and started in full retreat. Then, as so many times since, there was a lot of cedar brush on the hillside below the church. Running at full speed, and turning to see how near his death-dealing enemy was to him, he hung his foot in some of this brush, and a somersault followed. The other fellow was right upon him. "I surrender, sar, I surrender!" 'Twas over, but the boys who got it up had departed, without leaving their addresses.

Well, just another. The farm now owned by Mr. A. Ransone was called Byron Park. The owner and occupant in those days was, as some now are, opposed to hunting on his farm and stuck up notices to keep off intruders. This was new to the huntsmen, and the young crowd were highly incensed. To somewhat get even with the old fellow, they wrote the following poem and posted it by one of his signs. Let's see, now, how it ran:

"Huntsman, huntsman, warning take!
I pray you no depredations make
Upon my farm called Byron Park,
Not half so large as Noah's Ark.
The birds are mine and so are the hares;
I therefore warn you from setting snares."

So ashamed was he after reading this that he tore down every sign and it does not appear that he objected to hunting ever afterwards.

By the way, another man of peculiar tendencies, since this was the time before very strict grazing regulations, lived at that old home. To see a horse not his own on his grass was the immediate cause for high temper and verbal explosions. A neighbor had a white horse, which was turned out every night to nip along the roadside and be better prepared for the morning's work. But the roadside was not enough for the under-fed animal. Red clover in full blossom just over the fence was better suited to his appetite. Fortunately for him, he was a jumper. The rest may be supposed. The old gentleman who owned the clover field had gotten the horse out on several occasions at dead of night. Drastic means seemed necessary. So he gave notice that the next time that horse was found in his clover lot he was "a 'guine" to shoot him. Well, some of the same crowd of full-of-mischief young men learned of this threat. They told the owner of the horse to keep him stopped up a certain night. Then, armed with a bucket of thick whitewash and a brush, they stole quietly to the stable where the old gentleman's pet mare, as black as a coal, was, and whitewashed her until she was as white as the trespassing horse belonging to the neighbor.

They turned the quiet old mare out and let her into the clover field. Then these prankish fellows made noise enough by hammering on the stable door to arouse the old gentleman. Out he came in *nightly* array. There in his best clover was the neighbor's horse as before. He had threatened, and now he was going to put it to action. In he went and out he came with his old single-barrel gun loaded with No. 10's. He was mad, and he got close. He drew back and let fly a broadside, raking his own horse from head to tail. With a powerful snort she sprang off and went like mad round and round the field, and after a while jumped the fence and retreated into her own stall for protection. The old fellow followed her, and when he found that it was his own horse he stood amazed. He went back into the house, called to his wife, and said, "Liza, fore de Lord, I's gone and shot Thisby." And he certainly had. Queer folk in Dunnsville then. Are they all gone?

It is probable that the same Mr. Dunn who built the first storehouse in the village built the first dwelling which may be the same house now owned and occupied by his direct descendants, Mr. H. W. Dunn and family. The Rappahannock Church was built in 1860. The first building was of wood. It was saved from fire once by the heroic efforts of the late Dr. David States Garnett. The ladies of the church presented him a Bible as a token of their appreciation. Your correspondent owns that Bible and values it highly. I mentioned that the church was built in 1860. On a slab high up is written, "Anno Domini, 1860." A man stood gazing one day as if his mind was fully centered on some very surprising discovery. "Hi," he said, "I had always thought this church was named Rappahannock. When did they change it to that Domini and all that." On one occasion, when there was on foot to raise money for purchasing a chandelier for the church, a young gentleman soberly remarked that he did not see any use in buying one of the things, for there wasn't a soul who knew how to play on it. Maybe there wasn't.

This village now has two stores, a hotel, a garage, and a blacksmith shop, besides the church, which is a large brick structure and in excellent repair. The acoustics of this church are wonderful. Just how it came about, whether by accident or by excellent forethought of the architect, I do not know, but from the furthest part of the gallery, when the auditorium as well as the gallery is packed, you can hear every word of a clear-voiced speaker. There are some very nicely "kept-up" dwellings in and around the village, and, all told, it makes not a bad impression upon the passer-through. The one item which is probably most worthy of mention is the water supply—this coming from a spring on the farm of Mr. Ransone, and the same spring from which that rare character who shot his own horse used to drink from.

The graded school is nearby, and is, of course, a factor of importance to the neighborhood. The Essex Grist Mill is about two miles away, and this gives excellent flour. Dunnsville is in a very thickly settled section, and while there is no wealth, as wealth is counted now, the people seem right "well to do" and reasonably comfortable. The bathing on the Rappahannock and the fishing in the Piscataway have attracted quite a number of people from Richmond, and some have bought lots and built summer homes along the river. All this makes a country neighborhood a little more up to the times.

And yet it is all quite different from what I wanted to give—something of real history that my boys and your boys might have to file away. This much may be said: I have not written a word of harshness, not one. And let's think that there was not one to write. You know it is said that good neighbors make good neighbors. And, of course, the converse must be true. I much prefer being the good article. And maybe I am. There are many other chapters, but we will hold them for a cooler day.

VII

BESTLAND *and the* ROAD *to* ESSEX MILL

When one writes of his own county, that section which should be ever dear to him and calling for his loyalty, there seems no limit to just how much he should write, for there is so much that comes to his memory which seems of interest, and instinctively he wishes to write it all. This, however, is not practicable in a work of this size. Still, Bestland, way over there on the very crest of the hills overlooking the Dragon flats, and carrying in its history the good old days before the Civil War, when money was plentiful, credit unlimited, and the negroes as happy as good food, good quarters and regular work could make them. The old storehouse at Bestland, as I remember it, was typical in structure of many of the country storehouses of that day; in fact, many of them seemed to have been cast in the same mold—a cellar for the molasses, and vinegar, and salt fish, and the barrels of whisky. For a few feet above the cellar the brick work extended, and on this the frame building was erected—the store proper—and back of it the counting-room with its big fireplace. And did you ever think of what might have gone on in one of those old counting-rooms a cold day, when the snow was on the ground deep, and no need of one staying at home? How many wheat crops of thousands of bushels were sold prospectively to close big store accounts; how many gallons of old brandy were drank; how many times a "nigger" was bet on a game of poker, and, again, perhaps with another assembly, how many candidates were nominated and elected *in futuro* right there by the blazing fire, with the air charged with tobacco smoke and all hands talking at once? The royal jokes that were told and the hearty laughter that followed—pity it is that there were not dictagraphs in those days.

The first merchant whom I have any knowledge of at Bestland was the late David Scott, and he was very prominent in business affairs, and successful. Mr. Scott was a small man, but had almost superhuman physical strength. It is said that he could lift a full barrel of whisky from the floor and drink out of the bung, and that he could take a sack of salt weighing over two hundred pounds under each arm and walk up the granary stairs. He was a man of great energy and did not seem to know when it was time for him to stop and rest.

Mr. Bunny Scott, of Tappahannock, so well known, and so useful, is a nephew of Mr. David Scott. With the coming on of the Civil War and the freeing of the slaves, the Dragon flats became waste places, where bountiful crops of wheat and corn had been produced. Then the merchants would buy the wheat crops of many of their customers and load the wheat on vessels bound for Philadelphia or Baltimore. Mr. Scott owned the farm called Bohannans, now the property of Mr. Fred P. Bray, and used his own wharf on the Piscataway Creek. Very much of the produce in the vicinity of Bestland was shipped from Bohannans Wharf. *En passant,* it may be mentioned that Bohannans is still a shipping point, but mostly for cord wood and lumber by lighters; large schooners scarcely ever come up beyond the Ferry Bridge. Bestland, as a mercantile center, is not what it was in the days of David Scott, yet there is a store not so far away from old Bestland, and Oak Grove (Colored) Baptist Church is a neat and attractive structure. The colored people throughout this county deserve credit for the energy and the co-operation they have manifested in establishing their places of worship.

Right at Oak Grove is where the road from Upright meets the road from Bestland, which leads to Howertons, and on towards the Tidewater Trail. The Howertons

High School building tells a sad story, the story of patrons struggling to have a high school, and when their efforts had been successful and they felt safe for educating their children conveniently, by a strange turn of public-school officials the high-school pupils were taken away and hauled for miles to another school, leaving this school a grammar school of two rooms, but the building remains as a monument to the splendid efforts of the citizens of Howertons to educate their children. This building of high schools, as in Dunnsville, and as in Dunbrooke as well as in Howertons, and then breaking up the entire plan, is both strange and pathetic. Professor Maury Hundley is in charge of this school now, and was principal of it when ranking as a high school.

And here lives Grigg Davis, expert wheelwright, and an honest man if there ever was one on this earth. Poor John Ritchie Owen, cut off by that dread disease, consumption, in the very flower of his usefulness, lived where his brother, Morton, now lives, where Mr. John Owen, his father, also lived. It was John Owen who built up the mercantile business at Howertons. Later, his son, John Ritchie, conducted the business to his death. Then Mr. Willie Frank Durham succeeded in the line of business at this point. But he, too, when all seemed well and his business prosperous, was taken away. His brother, T. T. Durham, is in business at Howertons at this time, and is regarded as a successful business man and an excellent citizen. Just beyond Howertons, on the Millers Road, is the residence of Mrs. Fogg, widow of Elza Fogg. Both of these people were kind to the author of this sketch when he was in the educational service at Howertons.

"Lombardy Grove" was the home of the late Captain Covington, and now the home of Mrs. Willie Frank Durham. The old house was destroyed by fire years ago, but Mr. Durham built an attractive and convenient house where old Lombardy Grove once stood. Captain Covington was a man of much influence in his neighborhood and in his county. His wife was a Miss Trible, sister of the late Dr. John S. Trible, the father of Rev. John Meredith Trible, who was president of Bethany College at the time of his death. And here stands Howertons Church, a landmark of faithful service of its members since way back in the days when one of its parsons was arrested for preaching the Baptist doctrine, and its members now are as stalwart in their faith as their fathers were before religious liberty was granted to all in this country. The first building was where the cemetery now is, a frame building. In that church, while Parson Greenwood was praying, he had a stroke of paralysis and died. No better attitude is it possible to conceive than to pass on to that Being to whom your petitions are made when in the very act of addressing Him. A most solemn time at old Howertons that day, I am sure.

Going from the solemn to the light and frivolous, there was a colored man named Page who drove his master's carriage to Howertons. It was said that under the high seat of that big carriage Page used to store a bottle or two of whisky, and on the sly during the recess at a big protracted meeting Page would sell what he had stored by the drink to those who were a-thirst. This violation of the law on the part of Page had been suspicioned more than once, and Page had become uneasy and more careful. One Sunday when a protracted service was going on Page not only sold his goods, but took an unusual quantity for his own stomach's sake. He ate a big dinner and then repaired to the gallery, where the colored people always sat in the white people's churches. Rev. Howard Montague, powerful in voice, powerful in persuasive eloquence, was conducting the meeting. Mr. Montague was known far and wide, and the church was filled. Now, Page loved religious services, and was inclined to listen, but soon the big dinner and what he had taken before overcame him, and he went into a profound sleep. Now, be it remembered that Page was fearing trouble, for he knew that he was under suspicion. The sermon went on, and the congregation was, as usual, held in rapt attention and interest. In those days, when a negro violated the law in not very serious degree he was punished by having laid on him nine and thirty lashes. Now, the word *sing* and the word *fling* may sound alike sometimes. The sermon closed, Mr. Montague stepped down from the pulpit with hymnbook in hand. Page was partly awake. Then it was that Mr. Montague shouted, "We will now sing on page nine and thirty." To Page's ears it was *fling on page nine and thirty*. This was enough. The congregation was decreased by one, and somebody else had to drive that carriage back home that day.

Yes, Howertons is a landmark for the faithful; those who somewhat back from the thoroughfares of the county, without unnecessary display or notoriety, have labored on to uphold the cause of righteousness. What a story old Howertons could tell, and how interesting would it be to have the full history of that church from its building to the present! And this is true of all of the churches—a history of them would be a history of the entire county. Years ago Muscoe Dunn had a store very near the church. It is probable that he sold intoxicating liquors, as most country merchants did in the olden time. I can find no trace of that storehouse—gone, like its master, years ago.

Near the road is Jimmie Davis' home. I cannot pass there without a word of praise, for he deserves it—a man who has the respect and confidence of all his acquaintances, a case of the simple annals of the poor, but, be it said, honest, every inch of him, and a man who has fought bravely against misfortunes. May Jimmie live for many years and his strength be renewed like the eagle's. Going down a steep hill, we have before us the Essex Mill Pond, a beautiful land-locked and forest-lined lake, where the Richmond sportsmen come and chase the wary chub and then repair to their clubhouse for refreshment and rest. Right where the flood-gates now are there was once a cotton gin, and from there large brigs were loaded with cotton and tobacco for either foreign or distant domestic ports, going right down the mill creek into the Piscataway, and thence to the broad Rappahannock. Yet now one can scarcely paddle a sora skiff up that creek to the mill. What has become of the water, and what the tobacco growing, and the cotton growing in Essex? Hon. Deane Hundley, now the Treasurer of this county, owns the Essex mill, and, with Francis Johnson, a very reliable and efficient colored man as miller, the product of this mill is excellent. We will climb the hill and see Dick Dabney's truck garden from the road. Dick is one of the most successful colored men we have. He deserves credit. Now we are at the Trail again.

VIII

CENTER CROSS

IT does not appear of record as far as I can find how this village derived its name. It may be because the road leading from the King and Queen line towards the Rappahannock River crosses the Tidewater Trail. At this point is the source of the *Cross* portion of the name, and, maybe again, the village is considered somewhat the center for Rappahannock District, and thus complete the name. An elderly citizen informs me that at one time the place was called Hermitage. This was news to me. At any rate, Center Cross it is called, and, I suppose, all being considered, is the most prominent village in the county, Tappahannock now being a town, and soon to be a city, if it continues to grow as it has done in the last few years.

Here we find the Rappahannock District High School, a flourishing accredited public institution. Here is the home of Mr. William Gregory Rennolds, the Division Superintendent of Schools for King and Queen and Essex. Here we find the home of Mr. Charles E. Newbill, Judge of the Juvenile Court for Essex County. Here the home of Mr. Henry Bareford, the Deputy Commissioner of the Revenue. Dr. John Newton de Shazo is a citizen of Center Cross, and not so far away is Dr. Peyton Hundley, and in another direction Dr. Frank Stiff.

So, officially and professionally, this center seems well equipped. Then we find Mr. I. G. Carlton ready to take your order for a supply of lumber, and Mr. D. Croxton, an experienced shoe repairer, and Mr. James Rice, fully equipped for auto repairs and supplies. We find the mercantile business well representd by Mr. Willie Bareford, and a little way down the Trail by Mr. Will Rice, and nearer the old part-brick store with a colored man in charge. Then you can find cool drinks and ice cream at Garnett's Ice Cream Parlor. If wishing to talk schools and schoolbooks, Professor Walter Acree, another resident, is ready and willing. But that pioneer of convenient and rapid travel, Mr. J. Harvey Dillard, a very potential factor in the progress of Essex County, lives in Center Cross. He took the plunge, and all unite in wishing him success, and the same is true for Mr. Rice and Mr. Evans. 'Twas a big jump in the dark that these men took. The assistance that they have rendered to this county alone can scarcely be estimated, for there are some things you cannot well measure in paltry dollars, you know. Convenience when you need it is one of these. So with school, and church, and doctors, and a judge, and stores, and garage, and shoe shop, and bus terminal, and so on and so on—it does seem that this is a right potential center.

As it comes to me, the first house in or very near this village was Bob Douglass' Shop—blacksmith, wheelwright, undertaker, etc., ready to meet most any demand. He was quick of speech and of ready reply. One morning a man came along while Bob was busy fitting up a coffin. The man said, "Who you making that coffin for, Mr. Douglass?" "For poor old man Griffin, who lived across the Dragon yonder," was the quick reply. "Hi! is he dead?" the man asked. "What in the devil do you 'spose I'm making his coffin for if he ain't dead? You 'spose we going to bury him alive?" Silence followed. The first store, as far as I can remember, was conducted by the Dillard brothers, William and Harvey, in the old storehouse now the place of business of a colored man. This is a typical pattern of the old storehouses of that day—Lloyds, Bestland, one at Newtown, and the present house occupied by E. M. Ware, Jr., & Co., at Dunnsville. The cellar seemed a very potential feature of these old buildings. Salt fish, molasses, and—well, you may guess the rest, but I did not mean vinegar alone.

There is so much in this running rapidly style I could tell of this old neighborhood, but I must not be too long. Maybe some don't like to read as much as I like to write. But Mr. Tom Boughton comes back to me. Mr. Boughton held the record for not permitting any one to outbrag him. Of course, it was all done in fun, and understood. One day a man was telling about having a flock of guineas which had white spots on them. Mr. Boughton told him that was nothing, as he, Mr. B., had a large flock of *snow-white guineas*. Such a thing as a white guinea was unknown here then, though now there are some nearly white.

At another time he was in company with a lot of fox hunters, and, as usual, each one was bragging on the speed of his dogs. Mr. Boughton let them go along with their boosting for a while without any comment. When he had a silence, he said, "Gentlemen, you don't know a fast dog when you see him. Now, my old Nina is what I call a little fast. The other day when she led the pack across Oakhill flats I saw her head in the woods on the other side of the field by the time her tail was out of the woods on this side. She is right fast, I say. But I had to stop hunting old Venus. Why, gentlemen, on the last chase, when she ran across Bob Cauthorne's lower field, she set the broomsedge a-fire, and the whole set of us had to stop hunting and tote water from Brown's old mill swamp to put the fire out. No, gentlemen, I am afraid to risk her again, unless it is raining." There was not another grunt. How could there have been? I have often felt when the braggarts come around if I had Mr. Boughton's gift for closing their exaggerations I would use it. Still, this might not be fair, for the poor fellow who brags enjoys it, and why take any joy out of his life?

You heard what that distinguished criminal lawyer from Richmond, Mr. Harry Smith, had to say about the probability of Tappahannock becoming a suburb of Richmond before so very long. This is possible. And I go further in casting the prophetic eye and say that in the years to come this Tidewater Trail will be but a series of villages, as we now find the roads in New Jersey, and the banks of the Rappahannock dotted, not with summer cottages alone, but with costly and potential mansions, as there are along the Hudson now, as on the islands in the St. Lawrence now. It is bound to come. Not immediately, but in due course of time.

Once this section was equal to any in the State, save, perhaps, Westmoreland County, and at old Vertis Church there was more wealth represented by that congregation than by any other congregation in the State. Nations go down, and then come again. We were potential here in days gone by, and no fault of ours, but the fault of a fratricidal struggle, we went down. But, thanks to Providence first and then to those progressive citizens who have been willing to risk much and strike out in the ranks of those who have faith in our future and are willing to back their faith with their works, we are surely climbing the hill again, and when we reach the top, Center Cross, we feel certain, will be in the front line. May it all be so.

IX

DUNBROOKE

THE HON. G. G. CANNON, editor, politician, and farmer, christened this village in honor of the Dunn family and the Brookes family living in and around this place. Mount Zion Baptist Church stands here, a solid brick structure, and a power for good. The late Rev. Howard Montague was the pastor of this church for many years. His home was in sight of the village. Mr. Montague was powerful as a pulpit orator, and as a revivalist he was known far and wide, and his efforts were wonderfully successful. His son, Professor Andrew Montague, now of a college in the South, inherited much of his father's gift of oratory. His portrait hangs among the many of the prominent men of Essex on the courtroom wall. For some time after the Civil War the church was the only building where the village now is, the property being owned by large land-holders, but when the land was for sale it was eagerly sought and purchased. The store now owned and operated by Walter A. Dix, postmaster and successful merchant, was for years the business of Mr. Dunn, for whom the place was partly named. Near is a business conducted by Mr. Johnson, and not so far, but in another direction, is Mr. Courtney's, and in another direction, again, is Mrs. Sisson's, all well supplied with the country's needs. So Dunbrooke is not lacking in stores.

When the building of high schools' spirit permeated the county some years ago, when there was a cry for a high school at every cross-roads, over-reaching both the real needs as well as the means for conducting these schools, Dunbrooke was not behind in this most commendable spirit prompted by the love for and interest in the children. There was no limit to the efforts put forth by the good people of Dunbrooke to have a high school. A building suitable for this purpose was constructed and the school established and successfully maintained for several years, but just as all seemed well the building was destroyed by fire. Nothing daunted, a temporary building was constructed by the strenuous efforts of the entire neighborhood, so that the work might not be interrupted.

Then followed the building now there, large, well constructed, and meeting with the modern-day requirements, and for some years conducted as a four-year high school, with an over-plus of high-school pupils as required. This was the very pride of Dunbrooke, and well the brave patrons deserved to be proud. But—and here is the sad part of it—by some strange manipulation of county-school affairs, this school was reduced to a grammar school and all of the high-school students and some of the advanced grammar department hauled to Tappahannock, a distance of about ten miles. The why and the wherefore of this strange proceeding is a mystery, but it left Dunbrooke sick and sore and lamenting. The time will come, and may it come soon, when there will be but one high school in the county, and that with a business course and a practical manual-training course and agriculture taught by practical application of the methods presented in the textbook. Dunbrooke, the highest point in Essex County, with spacious grounds and more land convenient for extensive farming, seems to be an ideal spot for such a school. Then the present high-school buildings may be used for grammar schools as feeders for the one well-equipped, well-managed, fully-patronized high school.

Mr. E. E. Baughan lives in Dunbrooke. He has reared a large family. Mrs. Marion Brookes, wife of Professor Irving Brookes, a successful educator, is the only daughter of Mr. Baughan. And just on the outskirts live Mr. and Mrs. George T. Brookes. These excellent people, like so many others around Dunbrooke, are the soul of hospitality, and, like the rest, did very much towards building and maintaining the high school there.

Passing along towards Tappahannock, there is Howard Bareford, a wide-awake merchant and successful farmer. Right opposite his home is the Whitlocke estate. Mr. Robert Whitlocke was the last of his line in this county, his three maiden sisters, wonderful teachers, all of them, having died before him, and there is not one of the name either in this county or in the adjoining counties, so far as is known to me.

Further on you pass Desha. Near here it is said that there was an Episcopal church, way back in the Colonial days, and I hear that the colored Baptist church at this place, or near it, stands on the ground where the Episcopal church once stood. Going on further, we are at Croxton's Mill, with its beautiful pond and fish in it to tempt the sportsman, and a lovely little cottage on the bank nearby. George Thomas Croxton, the eldest son of the Hon. Thomas Croxton, judge, Congressman and orator, conducted this mill for years as owner and operator. He inherited his distinguished father's conversational powers, and it was a delight to be in his company, for while the old water mill chugged along and the meal came pouring into the trough he would entertain you with his wit and his humour and interesting stories bearing on local history. All along the route from Dunbrooke to Tappahannock there is much to prompt one to write, for this is Essex, and Essex is dear to me.

X

PAUL'S CROSS ROADS

FROM what source this center derived its name I am unable to find out. There might have been a family in this section bearing the surname of Paul, or it might have been named Paul for the great apostle. The cross-roads portion of the name is easy, for this is where the road leading from Howertons Church crosses the Richmond-Tappahannock Highway. With Mr. Hudgins on one side and Mr. Blanton on the other, the mercantile business is well represented. Then, too, Mr. Blanton enjoys the well-deserved reputation of being an excellent mechanic, and his garage is ready to serve his customers. Robert Louis Pendleton, justice of peace, member of the County School Board, and extensive farmer, lives near this center. Mr. Pendleton is a grandson of Mrs. Kitty Micou and lives at the old home. The trees and the flowers and the quaint old building all tell the story of long ago when there was a servant for every class of work, both in the house and on the large estate. Cousin Kitty was as intelligent as she was large, and she belonged to the heavyweights, and as kind of heart as she was intelligent. So we have from this a well-rounded old Virginia lady. Mr. Edgar Micou, her son, lived at this old home for years—in fact, until his death, about fifteen years ago. Cousin Edgar was an excellent type of the Virginia gentleman, the soul of hospitality and kindness, and a loyal friend.

Near Paul's Cross Roads is Gordon's Mill Swamp, the upper waters of the Piscataway Creek. Until the building of the Richmond highway, the hill on each side of this swamp was dreaded, being both steep and muddy. Now a cement bridge spans the swamp and both hills have been graded so as to make the passing convenient. The name Gordon, as given to this swamp, is doubtful of origin. Mr.

Sam Smith, of near Millers Tavern, tells me that it has been handed down that a man named Gordon was thrown from his horse at that swamp and killed. The swamp was named for him. But it comes to me from some other source that there was a mill just above this bridge owned by a man named Gordon. Was he any relation to that Bowler Gordon who made the trip from Richmond on foot and when asked how he came, promptly replied, "I came by main strength and awkwardness, that's how I came." And from this it has been handed down to express a long walk when there was no other mode of travel, "I came like Bowler Gordon came from Richmond, 'by main strength and awkwardness.' "

The road leading from Paul's Cross Roads towards the road from Howertons to the Essex Mill passes over Mussel Shell Hill, a hill to be remembered by all so unfortunate as to have driven over it at night. If in a buggy, and you are coming from Paul's Cross Roads, if fortunately your horse is gentle, with good vision, mighty to hold back, and your harness strong, then give him the reins at the top of the hill, speak very kindly to him and urge him to be careful, say your prayers and hold your breath, and if by the best of fate you are not hurled down a deep gully to your right, amid stumps and stones clean to "kingdom come" or some other place you are not then looking for, *be devoutly thankful.* If a car chanced to be your mode of passage, when you approach the hill shut off your gas, press heavily on your brake, shut your eyes; you will go somewhere, and that quickly, and if, perchance it be the foot of the hill, you, car and all, with no doctor needed for you and only a half-a-day repairs for the car—well, profit by your experience, that's all.

At the foot of this hill, with pebbles and shells on its bed, flows merrily along a limpid stream, offering cool refreshment to man and beast. This is Mussel Shell Swamp. At its head they say there was once a grist mill, not very

Upper—"HUNDLEY HALL," THE HOME OF HON. DEANE HUNDLEY
Lower—"WAITING FOR THE TIDE"
Jim Parker, who is mentioned more than once in this book, may be seen at the right

far from where the late Colonel Evan Rice lived, and where his grandson, Webb Baughan, now lives, but no trace of the old mill can be found. And in its onward passage this stream used to turn the wheel of another mill before reaching the Piscataway Creek. And yet no trace of that can be found. The stream flows on, offering as free as the air its power; this is nature; man has failed to continue to use the power.

On goes the stream, growing a little wider, a little stronger, and soon reaches where there was once a bake-house to bake bread by the wholesale in the long ago, now a few handfuls of bricks remaining to mark the spot, but giving to what is Mussel Shell Swamp, above this spot, the name of Bake-House Creek, short, and soon to reach the Piscataway; but what a memory store for the sora hunter, for its marsh is the home of the wild oat and the happy feeding ground for this bird, reckoned the most tempting morsel that man may eat. Personal history is frequently interwoven with more general occurrences, and it may not be amiss to relate that on a lovely little island at the mouth of this creek the author's wife, when a bride, sat and watched the author kill about forty of these birds, at single shots, of course, for the sora is not gregarious, as Charles Minter, Esq., now prominent attorney of Logan, W. Va., kindly and skilfully shoved the canoe through the marsh. This is mentioned, not for the number of birds killed, for a hundred and sometimes two hundred were killed during a single heavy flood-tide, but because, so far as the author knows, his wife is the only lady who ever saw sora shooting on the Piscataway, or anywhere else. And this brings Mussel Shell Swamp to the Piscataway, there to mingle its waters from way up beyond Paul's Cross Roads with the Piscataway and help to feed with its food brought down from the hills the gay and wary bass and make them fat for the anxious sportsmen, who in their canoes do from early morn until dewy eve trouble the waters and cast the tempting lure.

Did you ever go chub (bass) fishing with a stammering man to paddle your boat, one who continuously tries to talk when you want perfect silence, for the chub is quick to hear, and yet takes about two full-grown minutes to answer a question when the answer is needed? No? Well, some calm day in August when the ebb-tide is nearly over, ask Henry Akers, the splendid fellow that he is, to take you chub fishing. Just try this. No harm intended at all, for who can stop stammering, and who, if he be a stammerer, can cut short a speech that has come bubbling up from somewhere and must have utterance or burst the very roof of the mouth, coming as it does with all of the facial contractions and distractions closely allied to the face of a child when his father has held him by the nape of his neck with one hand and the hair of his head with the other and his mother poked a full tablespoonful of castor oil down his throat? You wonder what he is trying to say and why in the devil he does not say it and be through with his agony, and your agony as well. I said try this, but I will add be sure to have concentrated within you all of the patience of Job and the richest sense of humour, as you will need both, and I am unable to say which will be needed most.

Don't complain, for immediately will come a protracted explanation that may take the rest of the tide to be fully launched into articulate speech. And, as for your humour, don't laugh, for patience sake, for if Henry sees you laughing he will take fully two minutes to ask what you are laughing about, and away goes the tide. I suggest gestures, and pray that gestures may come in response, not words, no indeed! for one gesture may require frowns and gulps and beating of the breast and stamping of the foot, and by the time all of this scenic display is over the chub that you felt sure was lolling around Sadler's landing right at you almost, and you were so anxious to "cast at," has moved to some other part of the creek. The better way is to hold your peace and your patience absolutely, and trust to Henry, for who knows the creek better than he, and you may have a day of royal sport. The author has learned all this by intensive and pathetic experience. He knows now just what to do. If any questions are to be asked, ask them a quarter of an hour before you start. If any special directions are to be given, give them on the shore. Henry is quick, smart, reliable, but Heaven knows if ever he has used the method found effective by Demosthenes—it is slow in its action.

When writing of the Piscataway, it recalls that a sail vessel is scarcely ever seen above Bohannans, which is about a mile above the Ferry Bridge, while some years ago they went as far as Sand Landing, the highest landing for vessels, and then Deep Landing, and lower down Bohannans. The creek traffic is nearly altogether by motor-boats now, and the depth of the creek is becoming less, marshes growing where the boats once passed.

I must not fail to mention that very near the top of Mussel Shell Hill lives Uncle Carter Braxton, now over one hundred years of age, and yet robust enough and energetic enough to cut timber for excelsior wood and doing other work as younger men by fifty years or more generally do. This is written in the year of grace, 1927, and something for those who may read it in years to come to know that Essex was not lacking in longevity more than the mountain sections of the State. Nor does Essex lack opportunity—she lacks means and energy and for our young men to remain here and help to develop the natural features. That's the need.

XI

The COURTROOM *in* TAPPAHANNOCK, VIRGINIA

WHEN Cicero stood in the Senate Chamber of the Roman Forum among his toga-clad brethren, filled with invective against Cataline, treacherous and plotting the ruin of the empire, doubtless the great orator was inspired by these distinguished Senators, as well as by memories of the eloquence and the renown of those who had stood years ago in that grand and spacious hall, when he hurled his philippics in scathing tones at Cataline, and he himself said that that hall was a most pleasant place to speak in. Surely it was. I believe very much in environment and in personal influence for the speaker, that which, though unseen, is felt to nerve and to encourage. Daniel W. Vorhees, the tall sycamore of the Wabash, said, when delivering that beautiful and patriotic address, "The American Citizen," at the University of Virginia in 1860, that the ground upon which they then stood was holy ground, and, to me, with a feeling of love and respect and cherished memories, I feel that as we stand in this courtroom, whose walls are hung with the portraits and tablets to memorialize the worthy men of Essex, that we are standing on holy ground and should be inspired to do our best in every effort, for indeed it is like the Roman Forum, a most pleasant place to speak. And does not the man who addresses His Honor and the jury with a serious theme for his argument feel stimulated when he casts his eye around and beholds as if looking down upon him the portraits of these noted jurists and bar orators of Essex? Does not one in political harangue or in patriotic address feel inspired when he sees the shades of the distinguished statesmen and the valiant soldiers who made Essex worthy to be counted among the best of her sisters, both in peace and in war? And it seems to me that the best within one is demanded in this hall, for the best alone will be accepted—her past is too sacred, her standard high. Do you not feel their presence? Look around and see Hon. Meriweather Smith, the first to represent this congressional district. Look again and see Hon. George W. Smith, born and reared at old Bathurst on the Piscataway, Governor of Virginia, and, losing his life in that saddest of disasters, the burning of the Richmond theater; his sacred ashes were not preserved, but a slab in a cemetery near Dunnsville bears his epitaph. Look again and see R. M. T. Hunter, statesman, Senator and far-famed, and near him his nephew, Hon. Muscoe Russell Garnett, gifted orator, Speaker of the House in Congress, while that distinguished uncle was in the Senate, an unusual, if not the only, instance of the kind in our history. Brockenborough, Roane, and Ritchie—do you see them, the Tappahannock junta wielding a force in both State and national affairs?

And there is General Robert S. Garnett, in the Union Army when the South made her call, and hastening to her, but losing his life at Craig's Ford early in that sad and fratricidal strife. And right near is General Richard Brooke Garnett, falling in that heroic charge at Gettysburg, when, maybe, somebody had blundered, and lying in an unmarked grave where he fell. There is Colonel Evan Rice, brave as a lion, and without reproach. Captain Alfred Rennolds, scholar as well as soldier, for he was there when General Jackson was mortally wounded by his own men that sad night at Chancellorsville.

And right over there is Professor Andrew Montague, prominent educator in the South, the son of that great revivalist, Rev. Howard Montague. Austin Trible, gifted orator, but dying as his fame was spreading. Look again, if you will, and see Judge Muscoe Garnett, of Ben Lomond—the tablet to him and to his seven sons tells its story—and near is his son, Lewis Henry Garnett, attorney for the Commonwealth and gifted in speech, and, indeed, love and honor prompt me to say more of him, but delicacy of feeling forbids. Do you see that handsome face over there, the one with the kindly smile and piercing black eye? That's Hon. Thomas Croxton, Congressman, lawyer, and unequaled, in my memory, before a jury with that grand voice and searching argument.

Don't you older men recognize that handsome face just over there, the one that prompts a smile, for he is smiling, and that tells the story of his jovial nature? That's Captain Lawrence B. Roane, as brave a man in battle as ever drew a sword, as gentle in peace as a lady. Judge Harry Dangerfield, distinguished in family history as he was genial and kind, and learned in the law—you see him there, don't you? There he is among his fellows.

There they are, many of them to prompt your very best. Judge Thomas Evans Blakey, fluent, genial, but powerful in debate, and cutting to the quick when necessity compelled him. Judge Edward Macon Ware, a deep reasoner, and learned in the law. Oh! they are here, these men of Essex, to prompt you to your best. Harrison Southworth, courtly gentleman, and both faithful and efficient in his clerical work, and knowing court procedure as well as the attorneys whom he served in the clerk's office.

There are so many we are proud of, so many that we might take as proper examples, and so many to whom praise is due, but of them all there was not one more loyal to his county, to his State, than Thomas R. B. Wright, circuit judge, and the one who conceived and in large measure executed this memorializing the men of Essex by placing their portraits or their tablets in this hall; and of all the men I have ever known, there is not one who seemed to love his county so much, and who was more anxious to see the young men come forward and follow the splendid examples set them. He was, indeed, an inspiration to those who would accept his teachings and profit by them.

Indeed, this is almost holy ground, and you have found it so as you have studied these men of ours—ours to remember with pride—and there are others you have not scanned closely, and there are others in this county who deserve respect and honor and are guides for the youth of our land.

Passing into the clerk's office and making a study of the records, there you will find rich and rare history of "ye olden tyme," the seventeenth century and on; wills that are as unique as they are amusing; court orders for celebrating marriages with rum and sugar to sweeten the same, and so many pounds of tobacco to meet the cost of the festival, land grants and various and sundry other documents interesting to him who feels an interest in the past and is a student thereof. With the standard equipment for preserving the records, and the convenience for executing business, with that congenial clerk, H. C. Southworth, who has worn so faithfully, and is yet wearing, his father's mantel so gracefully, so willing to guide you in your royal search, you may well spend your time with pleasure as well as with profit.

There is much praise and high appreciation due to Mr. Alfred du Pont for his liberal donation for repairing and improving the courthouse. This assistance stands as a very high mark for the liberality of this gentleman; nor did he stop here for improvement, as evidenced by the gymnasium for St. Margaret's School.

So with the portraits and the tablets and, I may add, the fine acoustics of the hall, one may well say with that Roman orator, that it is indeed a most pleasant place to speak in.

XII

ST. MARGARET'S

The EPISCOPAL SCHOOL *in* TAPPAHANNOCK, VA.

It was a most fortunate selection for location that the former home of the late Judge T. R. B. Wright was available for establishing a school for the education of young ladies, in not only the fundamental branches, but in liberal arts and sciences, in the old and much-storied town of Tappahannock.

I am a strong believer in environment, both social and material, and I believe that splendid impulses are given by the effect of beautiful scenery and the memories of the deeds of those who have gone before us, as emphasized by paintings and portraits and buildings and flowers and works of art, so when these advantages are ours, and if ours be the minds to appreciate, we feel ourselves gradually growing stronger and better and longing to be the best that our capacities will permit. So I believe that a school building should be a house of very much beauty within, and surrounded by handsome trees, with flowered walks approaching, and the interior the suggestion of culture, with its portraits and paintings and its antiques—these things all go to form some aspiration for the young who daily see them, and a school is the garden for culture with impressions formed that last. St. Margaret's has all of these features to commend it; and for the training, for the suggestive, for the control, it has a worthy faculty, not only to interpret for the students the lessons which teach the vital truths that go to form strong character, but by example lead them along the better and the higher way.

It seems to me that this institution has so much to commend it, so many opportunities to offer. Apart from the stiff and steady course of the daily assignments, a stroll along the banks of the Rappahannock, when in thoughtful attitude, and when looking in the direction of Hoskins Creek, it may come to you as a fact worthy to be remembered that at the mouth of that creek, 319 years ago, Amas Todkill, brave spirit that he was, offered himself as a hostage in exchange for one of the Indian warriors standing on the shore and offering one of their braves in exchange, and that through the treachery of the Indians this brave fellow came near losing his life, but did succeed to escape the arrows flying over his head as he crawled to the shore and then plunged in and swam back to the ship, as Captain Smith's fusillade from his blunderbusses drove off the Indians. And this same Amas Todkill was the first white man to place a foot on the soil of Essex County. You will remember this, and as you grow older, young ladies, you will consider it a fact worthy to remember. And there is much more to impress upon you that your school is on very historic ground. Did you know that Tappahannock was an Indian village for years and years before it was settled by the white people? That is what is said. It is reasonable when we may find arrowheads, tomahawks, chalk pipes and other indications on this ground and for miles up and down the river being the habitat and the hunting-ground of the Rappahannocks by whom the river was named. Yes, very historic ground it is. And then as you stroll along through the town and talk with your teachers when in historical mood, you will remember that it was in 1681 that the town was laid out and a courthouse ordered to be built. This is local history, but it must be interesting to you. But do not think that the present large and substantial building was the first that was built. The Beale Memorial Baptist Church was then the courthouse. And don't you think it a beautiful conception to turn a hall of justice into a house of prayer? Yes, the old courthouse was abandoned when the present one was completed.

You can remember these things, young ladies of St. Margaret's, for I find myself lapsing into my second-nature attitude of lecturing, and writing as if you were before me. But before you get to the courthouse you will see the old Ritchie house, the oldest of the buildings in the town. Your instructors will tell you something about this prominent citizen of the town where your school is located, and they will tell you that Ritchie, and Roane, and Brockenbrough, the Tappahannock junta, powerful in State and national affairs, were all of Tappahannock. You are very close to the Brockenbrough home, you know, and when you walk in the direction of the mill and will look way up to a very high hill you will see where Pigeon Mill stood, the home of the Roanes—so you have them all allotted, Ritchie, Roane, and Brockenbrough.

But should you stroll as far as the Town Hall, there you may even yet see tombstones, and maybe sunken graves, indicating that this was once a church, and it may be told you that it was the first house of worship to be erected in the town. It was better to restore it and improve it as a hall than to let it go to decay. And when in the Monument Hotel have the ladies there to tell you how Tappahannock was shelled during the War of 1812; they have heard the story, and will tell you that there was a hole in the old building on the hotel lot, which was pulled down not so long ago, made by a solid shot from a British ship as the town was shelled. Ask them what became of that plank having the hole in it. Maybe it is preserved as an 1812 war relic.

Then these ladies may tell you that what is now their inviting house of public entertainment was once the home of a flourishing and widely patronized boarding school for young ladies. They may tell you that their mother was one of the students, and it looks a little strange that now her daughters should be the owners of the house where she attended school. So many of the ladies of that time received their excellent instruction at Mrs. Gray's Boarding School, it was noted.

And you will probably read in this book a sketch entitled "Old Rouzie Gray," which I think you will enjoy. I met this poor old negro way down in Southern Louisiana, near the Gulf of Mexico. He was reared in and around Tappahannock, but sold to the Mississippi planters to work in the sugar cane and grapple with fever and hardship, just as you read about it in the songs and story-books which tell the history of these old negroes who were taken from their homes in old Virginia and sold far away from home. It may be that you will be pleased with the sketch. I invite you to read it, because it has to do with the town where you are now being educated.

Now, some pretty day when your instructors will accompany you, and Mr. Southworth, the genial clerk, is not too busy, you may see some of the old records pertaining to this county. Some of the old wills may make you laugh, when you read that so much money was left to buy liquid refreshments when they sat up at the *wake* at the testator's demise. And to see how very careful those old folks were in the distribution of their property—a spinning-wheel, a quilt, and maybe a clock. Those were the days of the formative period, the days when the men and the women who have made Virginia so prominent in peace and in war were reared and labored. Their earthly rewards did follow them in their noble offspring. Yes, it will be of interest to you to read these records, for they are authentic history.

There is much more that you could learn of the town, for those who lived way back in the seventeenth century were not the only ones deserving of your study. The courtroom will prompt you to inquire and, it may be, to be interested in many others. So, it seems to me, that this is a most suitable location for a school, and as it has grown and prospered, it will continue to grow and to prosper as it is known and its advantages considered.

You are particularly fortunate in having the worthy support of the rector, Rev. H. S. Osborne, and I may add that you are equally as fortunate in having among your worthy board of visitors Professor Elmer J. Carruthers, bursar of the University of Virginia, a gentleman whom I had the pleasure to instruct for three years, and know his worth, and value his friendship.

A school such as yours, young ladies, is a power for culture, not only for you yourselves, but through you as you pass along and give it to others.

With your grounds, your tennis court, your basketball court, and the large and beautiful gymnasium, the noble donation of Mrs. Alfred du Pont, with scenes inviting without and ancestral halls within, it does seem that you have much to inspire you to follow the best and purest lines of thought when prosecuting your work in the classics and in art.

And if, for pensive attitude, you desire, sit on the beautiful lawn near the river's bank and let your imagination take flight way back to the days when the red man held sway and see his light bark canoe go skimming over the waters of the silvered Rappahannock, or see along the shore some tall and handsome young brave walking beside his dusky beauty, telling her love tales as they have been told along that shore so many, many times since.

Or, think of a dance given to the successful huntsmen bringing in their deer, their wild turkeys, and maybe a bear, for the feast. Think of the Indian girls, untutored, but bright, sitting around the camp fire as they listened to tales of dash and danger, and the young Indian boys taking lessons from what their sires told them. It would be easy, very easy indeed, to draw all of these pictures. And maybe some of you may write a story laid here, and it is quite certain that with what you have read, with what you have heard and what your well-trained intellect may do to form the imagery, a beautiful story you may write of the days when your school-ground was the camping-ground of the Rappahannock Indians.

So I repeat that it was a most fortunate selection, where your institution is located, and as the old town has taken on new life and seems to be rising from its long slumbers, ready to join the onward march of improvement, and truly St. Margaret's will keep in line.

XIII

The RISE *of* CHINKAPIN

In some of the counties in the Old Dominion there are certain sections seemingly set apart by common consent, independent of geographical limits and magisterial appointments.

In one county there is Terrapin Forest, having derived its name, perhaps, from the number of these slow-crawling animals having been abundant there at one time.

In another county there is Guinea, the dwellers therein being water-farers, and in the long-ago were of the rough-and-ready kind.

And in another there is a section bearing the dismal name of Hell Bottom, with deep gullies and high hills covered with scrub growth of oak and pine. If not suggestive of the regions its name would make, it is dismal and uninviting, to be sure.

And in still another there is a section known as Chinkapin, well known for the growth of chinquepin bushes, and from this, doubtless, it derived its name.

No one knows just where Chinkapin begins or where it ends. A stranger on his way to this section was told that Chinkapin was about three miles ahead of him. But when he had covered this distance, and more, another informant told him that the place that he was trying to reach was three or four miles behind him.

While the dwellers of Chinkapin were spoken of as poor folks, this unsavory appellation was more to distinguish them from the wealthy landowners, with their many slaves, than as a term of disgrace and poverty, for the Chinkapinites were not paupers at all, but did not own any slaves. They did own their little farms, however, and were thrifty as far as their condition allowed, without education, without roads, save the roughest kind, and burdened with hereditary tenets and superstition. They cultivated their small fields with oxen for pulling the plow, and with hoes for close culture. The log cabin was their home, but with the large log chimneys with broad fireplaces, and with wood convenient, they had comfort.

The Chinkapinite had a dialect all his own. Not the negro dialect. No, not that exactly, but somewhat like it. Having no public schools then, and the old-field private schools being too remote and too expensive for the Chinkapinite's purse, there was almost total illiteracy, but the Chinkapinite had a full measure of old-fashion commonsense and knew how to use it to the best advantage. They were expert fishermen and trappers. The broad marshes along the winding creek were the home of the muskrat and otter and feeding-ground for the wild ducks; while in the fall schools of alewives were trapped in nets or weirs and salted up for the winter's use, making a rather poor substitute for the herring, but helpful to the food supply of the Chinkapinite. They raised their own cotton, but bought their wool. With their looms handy, they were supplied with comfortable home-spun clothing. They raised their own hogs and had good gardens and nice orchards. All told, the Chinkapinite did not suffer for food or clothing. Most of these people were connected with some church and attended the regular services occasionally, but when the protracted meeting season in August began the Chinkapinite was always on hand to enjoy the spiritual feast in the forenoon from the enthusiastic revivalist and then to repair to the free spread on the long tables in the grove, and then to listen to another sermon in the afternoon, or, maybe, so filled both physically and spiritually, to sleep through it.

The Chinkapinite was not a politician, but the men were always at the polls, whether county, State or national elections were coming off. He cared not a penny who was elected, but he did care very much who had the most "quater-dollars" to dispense, and who had the best "likker" to give for his favorite candidate.

As a rule, there was good order throughout Chinkapin. Apple brandy was distilled on many a farm, and sold for about a dollar a gallon, and while the Chinkapinite generally had a little for "sickness" on hand, but few abused the privilege granted to all in those days before the Civil War. He attended court regularly once a month, and then some might take a little too much, have a fight or two just to keep in practice, for the Chinkapinite was game, and this not only at home, but on the front during the war.

About the time of the outbreak of the war there was a spirit of unrest brewing—as if asking the question, why can't we do better for ourselves, have schools, have nice homes, wear better clothes. I mentioned that trapping was a means of support for these people. It was indeed a great help, for with their muskrat hides they obtained some ready money to meet their taxes and to purchase what they could not raise at home.

Jim and George were two expert trappers, and to follow these two brothers on one of their daily rounds will give some idea of the Chinkapin dialect, how they spent their time in the marshes, and an expression of that spirit of unrest and dissatisfaction which seemed to be spreading throughout the section among the poorer classes. Jim and George lived with their widowed mother and were her faithful support. She was low of stature and stout. Her wrinkled features showed that hers had been a life of toil, but her genial countenance indicated that she had done her part bravely and willingly. She stood in the doorway watching her boys prepare for the day's work: getting their paddles and their extra traps ready.

The path that led from the cabin to the creek was steep and winding, and all of the stumps had never been removed, though that path had been used for years and years. Jim was ahead. George close behind him. Jim's eyes were fixed on the creek below. He did not watch his feet carefully. But a stump was there and his foot found it, and over he went, head first, down the bank, scattering his traps as he fell. "Wur de marter wid you, Jim?" said George. "Couldn't you see dat stump right in you way? You done passed by it a hunerd times."

"To de debble wid de stump," said Jim, and recovered his traps and went on down the path.

The sun was just above the fringe of pines on the bank, and its early rays silvered the smooth surface of the water. A flock of blackbirds was feeding on the rich wild oats in the marshes, flying from one side of the creek to the other leisurely, in graceful curves, their black wings glittering in the sunlight. Further up the stream a stately-looking crane was wading in the shallows, watching for his morning meal; while high above in the air a flock of ducks was circling as if about to light, and then deciding to visit some other feeding-grounds.

Jim was an expert paddler, but no better than George, so with the combined efforts of the two men, the little sharp-at-both-ends boat glided along rapidly. Neither Jim nor George was large, but of the closely-knit type, active and tough. They were not handsome—their faces browned by the sun and wrinkled by hard and, often, dangerous work in the creek, frequently night and day.

The Chinkapinites were fond of music, and it seemed that every other household had a fiddler, and their old folk-songs, meaningless in sentiment, but suited to the dance, were cherished, and as the fiddlers would play some spirited tune the dancers would sing gaily these old folk-songs, fitting the words to almost any air. The Chinkapinite knew how to put the joy into living—good health, good food, comfortable homes, and but few cares, certainly not as many as the highly educated seem to have—he fared very well.

Jim was feeling well that October morning, and he wanted to sing. So out he poured this lyric (?) on the still air:

"Sallie and Sam went fishing one day,
Way down yonder on the bay:
Sallie caught a shad and Sam caught a whale,
He had hooked his hook in the old whale's tale.
Then get up soon in the morning,
Get up soon in the morning,
Get up soon in the morning,
Just before the break of day."

It was George's time next, so he treated the blackbirds and the crane to this song:

"Jaybird sitting on a hickory limb,
Hickory limb, hickory limb, hickory limb,
Jaybird sitting on a hickory limb,
Hi'o, hi'o, hi'o!
Up with a rock and hit him on the shin,
Hi'o, hi'o, hi'o!"

The blackbirds had all flown away, and the crane, giving three very unmusical squawks, stretched out his wings, poked his long legs behind him, and flew off to some other feeding-ground.

But just at this moment, as George had concluded his song, a single duck flew up from the marsh and started across the creek. Jim picked up his old flint-lock and fired. The bird fell, but was only winged. "Paddle up, George," said Jim, "jess as hards as you kin stave it. Dat ar duck guine to git away from weall 'fore I kin load dis gun."

To load an old-fashion muzzle-loader is a slow process at best. First you would pour three drams of powder from your powder-horn into your hand, guessing at the quantity, and then down the barrel. Next, a wad made, perhaps, from an abandoned hornet's nest. This was rammed in with a wooden ramrod. Then from the leather shot-bag *about* an ounce of shot was also poured into the hand and down the barrel. Another piece of hornet's nest was pressed down very lightly on the shot, carrying out the old hunter's maxim of:

"Ram your powder, slack your lead;
Take good aim, and shoot him dead."

Then the pan had to be looked after, to see if the powder was in it to catch the spark from the steel and flint. When Jim had done all this George had overtaken the wounded duck and finished it with his paddle. The men paddled along in silence for quite a while. They had not yet reached their trapping-grounds.

"George," said Jim, "how much money you reckin we-all got in dat ar bank ober yander in Richmond?"

George did not know, he said, as he had left all of their business to Jim, the elder brother.

"How much, you reckin, Jim?"

"Well, when I went ober dare wid Mr. Tom Brizendine, de time he took we-all's mammy's hens and eggs to sell for her, I took a lot of hides and sold them, and all 'cept I fetched back home, I took 'round dare to dat bank, and I axed dat ar man behind de window in dare how much money we-all had in dare. He went back dare and looked at a big book and den he came back to de window and told me dat we-all had more den a thousand dollars in dare, case we-all had been putting our money in dare for ten years and had not taken any away, and so de in-trust had done built it up some. And we has been sending some ober dare ebber sense. So we got, I 'speck, ober twelve hunnerd dollars in dare by now. George, I is tired ob libbing like we-all has to lib up here in dis part ob de county. Dey call us poor folks, and we is poor, but we's honest, and we can't help it if we don't own no niggers. I don't want 'em, myself, for dey is a torment and take all de farmers make to feed 'em. But dey tell me dat 'fore long nobody will own any ob them. Dat's de way de people is talking. Some kind ob 'sturbance is going on soon, I reckin."

"De great trouble wid all ob Chinkapin is dat we-all hasn't any book-learning; we hain't got no schools. But dey say dare's guine to be a book change and den we-all will hab schools like 'tother folks. When I goes out on de big road and sees the nice houses and sees how 'tother folks dresses and all like dat, it makes me feel mighty bad. So I's guine to take dat money what is mine and build me a house wid a brick chimbly, and glass windows, and blinds, and a porch, and hab dat kivered ober so you kin sit on dare outen de sun. Dat's what I's going to do wid my part, and den I's guine get marred."

George at once offered his part of their savings to help Jim carry out his plans.

"We has done wukked mighty hard, George, and we-all done took good kere ob our mammy. Yes, we has wukked hard, and been in all kinds ob hard wedder. You 'members de night down yander in Peter Taylor's creek, when we had dat live otter in de boat, kotched by one ob his forelegs in one trap and by one hind leg in another. Well, sar, it was dark as pitch, and we couldn't see how to do nothing. So thought we-all would wait tell we got home to kill him. You was setting jess whur you is now in de boat dat night. All at once dat otter gin a plunge and scrambled right under your feet, snapping like a mad dog. You rolled out backwards into dat mud and water nearly up to your neck. I kilt de otter wid my paddle, and den you got back in de boat. You looked like a muskrat. And nearly frozen. We-all paddled home quick as we could, and we-all's mammy had a good fire for us, and a good supper, too. I 'members it all mighty well. Yes, George, we-all has wukked hard, and I'm guine to try to live more like 'tother folks, and hab some comforts."

The men visited their traps and had their usual luck. Then for home to skin the muskrats and stretch their hides. When they were approaching the landing Jim continued to express his determination to make an effort for improvement. The odor of frying fish and boiled coffee made the hungry men hasten up the winding path to their cabin.

In a short time lumber and bricks and shingles were hauled to Jim's little plot his mother had assigned him, a spot from which the creek was in full view, and where the breezes from the big river a few miles away seemed to follow the valley of the creek and bring its refreshing comfort in summer. It did not take long to build just as Jim had planned—the upstairs, the covered porch, the blinds, and glass windows and all.

Jim went over to Richmond with a market wagon loaded with such country produce as could be readily sold. When it returned it was loaded with Jim's furniture, a well-selected lot, as Mr. Lightfoot, whom he had taken duck hunting and remembered him, had aided the man in his purchases. So Jim did his best to arrange it all, but in a few months Mrs. Jim appeared on the scene, and she it was who put the finishing touches on, as Mrs. Jims the world over know just how to do. And she planted rose bushes and vines to help the appearance of the porch. Jim's friends came to see and to admire. Some seemed determined to follow his plans, and before long they did. The old log cabins in many places gave way to neat little cottages.

There seemed to be an awakening throughout the whole section, for it had been passed around from house to house the improvement which Jim had made, and others wanted to follow his example. But just about that time that sad and fratricidal war began, and Chinkapin furnished her full share of men for the front, though not a negro did she own. The boys and the mothers were all that were left to till the soil when the draft for men sixty-five years of age was made. The names on the monument in the courthouse town may tell how well they did their duty and how many remained on the fitful fields.

When the war was over, the Chinkapinite, like so many thousands, had to adapt himself to the new conditions. He made the waste places come back to a harvest. He was not distressed at the freeing of the negro. He had never had one to be set free. He had known hard work all of his life. He did not mind it then.

Then came the reconstruction days, with all of the aftermath of civil war. And later new life and improvement set in. The establishing of public free schools came as a bountiful blessing to Chinkapin. From nearly every house the children came to school. And they were anxious to have what their fathers and their mothers for generations past had been deprived of—an education.

Then there was road improvement. The log cabins disappeared and nice homes stood in their places. Better culture of their crops, better clothes were worn, more conveniences around their homes, and signs of improvement on every hand. From the schools have gone out into the busy world teachers and preachers and merchants to take their places among the workers who do things and build up the country.

And it may be said that today there is no section in the county that deserves more credit, and that has shown more marked improvement than the once-benighted Chinkapin.

Jim had a vision, and followed it.

XIV

MAJOR BOB

How well do I remember the Major, and who, pray, does not remember him if ever he knew him? A unique character, indeed, and standing apart from all his fellows in a strong and strange personality all his own.

The Major was a bachelor, but still a gallant to the day of his death. How many love affairs he had I do not know, but the tide of love never seemed to flow smoothly, or certainly not to his desires. He owned a large farm and house enough for a large family. He had servants in plenty before, during and after the Civil War.

So the Major was in position to have comfort and such pleasures as his taste suggested. He enjoyed the blessing of satisfaction as to all that was his—his *estate,* for he never said farm; his horses, his cattle, and every other blessed thing owned by him, was just as he would have it, and there was no one to rob him of this glorious satisfaction, for who would think of offending the Major by telling him he was mistaken in his appraisment sometime?

The Major was tall, raw-boned, long of limb, red-haired, red-faced, and red-handed. Under no conditions would I ever have entered him at a beauty show; he belonged to a different type. But I would not have had the Major any other way—his personality might have been lost, and it was this personality, hard to describe, that was the Major's chief attraction.

At church or on any other public occasion he always wore a suit of French broadcloth. It was a handsome suit, and had the power of endurance, for he wore it for about forty years. 'Twas a pity that it did not fit. The sleeves were too short, and the pants likewise, and both had a way of crawling up, a habit not improving to the Major's general appearance.

The Major had what semeed to me a grand accomplishment—he played the fiddle. His playing was what perhaps gave me my first impulse for studying that king of instruments, fashioned so tenderly of Norway pine and whispering maple. Yes, he played the fiddle, and played the old-fashion tunes in his old-fashion way. I can see him now as he would tune, and tune, and tune, and then rosin, and rosin, and rosin his bow. All being ready and to suit, he would shove the end of his violin somewhat under his vest, throw his head back, make about three unmusical *snorts,* then begin to pat his foot vigorously. Then he would in full force draw down on "Lassie, Art Thou Sleeping?" and "Billy in the Low Grounds," and others of those good old tunes, generally winding up with the "Arkansaw Traveler." As a child, I would sit and be thrilled by his performance, and, as it then seemed to me, all that he had done was the Major's and not to be imitated by any living soul. Oh! had I the wealth of an Eastern nabob, all would have been the Major's could he have passed over to me his power over the fiddle and the bow. I since have made a study of the violin under a master, and learned the classical music so suited to the sighs and sobs, and, yet again, to the merriest, the wildest screams of delight and pleasure, but I have sometimes thought that I would be willing to lay aside the reveries, the concertos, the melody in F, and all the rest of that beautiful but stilted assortment, and saw down in the old Major's way on the old-fashion tunes.

The Major would sometimes give a party, as dances were termed in those days, and then it was that some of his cousins would come and make preparations, which meant not only putting the house in order in general, and the dancing floor in particular, but a supper potential enough to feed scores of guests, for a party in those days without supper was no party at all. On one occasion a crowd was expected. It came. The Major stood in his front porch awaiting and welcoming the arrivals.

Now, be it remembered that sidelights to carriages were just coming into use in the country, and the Major had never seen them on any one's carriage. A gentleman living not far off had purchased a new carriage equipped with these sidelights. When he reached the Major's gate there was some need of stopping to repair the harness, or for some other trivial reason, and the carriage was just inside the gate. The old Major saw these brilliant lights down at his gate, and he was simply bewildered. "Come here, Cambridge, run here quick!" His body servant came a-trotting. "Some dum fool has gone and set both of my gateposts a-fire. Run, Cambridge, run!!" Cambridge ran all right, but met the carriage coming up the driveway, and the mystery was explained.

Soon the dance began—happy folk, they were, and no lack of beauty or of chivalry.

When the dance had gone on for an hour or two it was suggested that they would play some parlor games for the benefit of those who did not dance. Among those games was one called "Dumb Priest"—why I never knew, however. In this game one of the party would go around the room and tell each one something to do which might be amusing: to stand up and crow like a rooster, or to bark like a dog, or to sing a song, or to repeat some poetry, or any other unexpected piece of performance. On this occasion a deep and diabolical scheme was hatched out. Each one was told in whisper to do something with the Major, while his part was to stand in the middle of the room awaiting action.

Some pulled off his old stock, some pulled his hair, some unbuttoned his vest, while a group took him up bodily and laid him on the floor, as others pulled off his boots and tickled him. He cleared himself from those holding him down and arose to his feet in a fury. Great Scots, he was a beauty with his rumpled hair and his face as red as a beet! He stood there in most menacing attitude, shaking his fists and seeming ready to whip out the whole crowd. One of his lady cousins, seeing his anger and dreading what might happen, went up to him, and, trying to place her hand on his shoulder, said, "O, Cousin Robert, don't get angry! It was all just in fun." By God, madam, you stand off, or I'll pick you clean as a bird." She stood off.

Soon 'twas all over, and the dance went on, but those who laughed had to be very guarded about it. No one wanted to raise the ire of the Major again. Then came the supper, and it was a supper to please and appease, with its boiled ham, roast turkey, stewed oysters, and all manner of cakes and pies and other things, for suppers then were princely. Well, while they were at supper the ladies in management had ordered the servants to wax the parlor floor again. When this had been done the floor was as slick as ice. The first set was one in which each lady would go to the right and dance before each gentleman as she approached him, and then turn him. Then the gentlemen would all go to the right as above. The old Major was feeling fine, and, wanting to show his agility, he tried to perform that step known in dancing as cutting the pigeon wing. He did not know the condition of the floor. Both feet slipped from under him at once and he measured his length on the floor. He jumped up at once and hollowed, "I'm as clear-footed as a deer. I never had a fall before in my life. Some dum fool has gone and put soft soap all over this floor." The dance went on, and while there might have been some suppressed giggles, none laughed out. The Major did not enjoy laughter when it was at his expense.

The Major made several trips to the Greenbrier White Sulphur Springs, and but few ever registered at that noted resort who got more pleasure from the association than the Major, and for years after he took great delight in relating his pleasant experience. While on a trip to this section, where many fine blooded horses were raised, he bought several blooded animals and brought them to his home. The stock of those horses was apparent in this county for years, and even today a trace may be found of the blooded horses the old Major brought here years ago.

The Major was a regular attendant at church, coming up the road every Sunday morning, on old Archie, his favorite riding horse, at a slow pace, and the Major's arm extended and keeping time to the gait of his horse. He always tied his horse to the same tree, Sunday after Sunday, and year after year. And he would put his left hand in his pants pocket and go promptly into church, and occupy the same pew every Sunday, and the back of it most suited to resting his head, so that he might enjoy complete repose. He seemed perfectly willing to trust the preacher, for ere the secondly of the sermon was reached the old Major was in the land of dreams, with his mouth open and a pudding-cooling snore proceeding regularly, the harmony of which being broken only when several flies would parade all over his face, and this would bring a gulping, guzzling sound decidedly unharmonious. I loved the Major, and felt solicitous of his health when the flies crawled all over his face. I was afraid he might swallow more flies than he could possibly overcome.

As the choir would sing in loud tones, the old Major would slowly arouse, scratch his head, and stand up for the benediction, shake hands with all whom he passed in the aisle, and then to find old Archie patiently waiting for him, for the Major loved old Archie and old Archie loved the Major. Down the road they would go with the same even pace with which they had come. The Major has long since gone to his rest, but the memory of that strong personality lives on.

XV

ALL *for* FUN

NOT a thousand miles from here, in fact, not nine hundred and ninety-nine miles even, there lives on a commanding hill a bachelor of the new type; for, convenience and comfort and sociability he considers as much his as these things seem rightfully to belong to the happiest benedict in the country. And there is not in all the country-side a man more inclined to charity and general helpfulness than he. But in his love of fun he may sometimes go a little, just a little, too far. Maybe so. Of course, it depends on the viewpoint of the other fellow as to a joke, anyhow. For, indeed, this good fellow would not harm a soul, but he does just love to laugh, and a laugh he must have occasionally.

This gentleman had a friend, also a bachelor, who frequently visited him, and sometimes spent the night. They were cronies. Neither one of them required overpersuasion at the proper time, in an orderly manner, to indulge, not excessively, but with moderation, in something to enliven their spirits and whet their wits.

At a certain time a portion of this gentleman's house was rented to a tenant who had quite a large family. I wish I could describe this tenant, but I am not a Dickens, nor a Mark Twain either. Still, since he figures as one of the principal actors in this little play, I may say, in brief, that he was a type absolutely all to himself, for I am sure I have never seen his counterpart. He was very short, and as small as he was short, but had a voice heavy enough for a 250-pounder—that's a fact. There was nothing strange about his disposition nor his general character. Only his general make-up in appearance. Still, he was not bad-looking; just queer. So much for him, except to mention that he was strictly religious and a regular attendant at church.

There came to the neighborhood from the city a widow to visit her sister and family. Now, this widow, Mrs. Berry, was very much of the Salvation Army style in her religious propensities, and wherever you might meet her, whenever you might meet her, she was then and there ready forthwith and immediately to vouchsafe her religious enthusiasm.

There is another of the *dramatis personae* in this little play that cannot be overlooked. Jim Parker was as strictly of his type, not rare and radiant at all, as that tenant was of his. Jim was not pretty, the good Lord knows, for he was of the rough-and-ready sort, but good-hearted, and his own worse enemy at times. Jim, though not to the "manner born," as the gentleman of the house, would sometimes come to visit him for a pleasant talk and often a hearty laugh, and he was always welcome. Now, on a certain night this tenant had entered into negotiations with Mrs. Berry, the religious enthusiast, to come to his house to hold a prayer-meeting. The crowd had assembled. The two bachelor friends were together in a room apart from the tenants, and not taking special interest in the prayer-meeting; on the other hand, they were having all to themselves a right good time, and ready for any harmless joke that might develop. Now, be it said that neither one of these gentlemen had any too much faith in the afore-mentioned Mrs. Berry. It is proper to tell this. Still, they had no reason to question her sincerity.

The meeting was in full force, and I doubt not, for my part, that all were in earnest. Let's think that way, anyhow. Mrs. Berry was loud and fluent, nor was she lacking in the gestures and poses of a true female religious expounder. About that time there was a knock on the door where these two bachelors were quietly having a right good time. In walked Jim Parker. His black hair was hanging down over his forehead, his garments savored of fish, and his face clearly indicated that he had been celebrating some occasion, and if more was lacking for this proof, his bulging coat pocket with the mouth of a quart bottle peeping out was fully sufficient. He and the bachelors exchanged greetings, and—well, you may guess the rest. After a while the gentleman of the house said, "Jim, you ought to get married. You need somebody to take care of you and look after your home." Jim replied, "I know hit, but dare ain nobody who'll hab me, dat's whur de trouble comes in, you see."

"Oh! yes," said the gentleman, "plenty of them will have you. Plenty of them, if you will only go at it in the right way, and ask them. Plenty of them would be glad to marry you, Jim." Right then and there it could be read between the lines that a diabolical scheme was in the hatching. Jim had been impressed by the advice given with such seriousness. They, all three, then had just a little more, by way of the continued sociability. "I tell you what you do, Jim; go in there and ask Mrs. Berry right now. I believe she will marry you. Try her right now." "I be dog if I don do hit," said Jim, "I be dog if I don." Without knocking, in the prayer-meeting Jim walked, and then right up to Mrs. Berry, right in the midst of her sermon, I suppose you might call it, and said, "Mrs. Berry, I come in here to ax you to hab me. I wan you to marry me right away. Won you do it?" "O, Mr. Parker, this is entirely unexpected, entirely! I could not think of such a thing, Mr. Parker. No, indeed, I could not think of it." "Well," said Jim, "I don give a damn if you won't." This started it. And 'twas a start, too. The tenant jumped up on a chair that he might reach his double-barrel shotgun hanging on the wall, saying as he reached for it, "I'll be durned if I am going to have any cussing at my prayer-meeting."

Mrs. Berry sprang from her pulpit to the floor and, with skirts at half-mast, jumped out of the nearest window, and next hopped a wire fence around the yard, leaving much of her nether garments to mark where she had hopped; but nothing daunted—she sped across the field. Her sister jumped, head first, out of a window, and her brood followed her like brownies in the pictures. Others took the shortest and seemingly safest means of speedy retirement. Jim, in his rapid exit, butt against a window and carried off a sash around his neck. Across the yard at top speed the tenant pursued him, and catching a glimpse of his receding figure going down the hill, let drive at him. The effect was an increase of speed. Another shot followed, with further increase of speed, and the last that was seen of Jim he was rapidly disappearing to some place of safety among the highways and the hedges.

No doxology had been sung, but there was a complete dismissal.

* * *

These same two bachelor friends, when returning home one bitter cold night from a walk over in the forest, saw a cow tied out in the yard near a widow's house, while she and the rest of her family had gone to a dance. These humane fellows were so thoroughly incensed at this wanton cruelty that their sympathy overrode the law, and they drew the staple and turned the poor, shivering animal in the dwelling-house, no other place of shelter being available. The cow, as cows generally do, at once began to ramble, to investigate, and to try to determine what kind of quarters had been assigned her. From room to room she went, bumping against and knocking over nearly every blessed thing that had legs. This rambling must have continued all night, judging from appearances the next morning. Well, when the widow returned after a night of tripping the light fantastic, or watching others in high-spirited pleasure, she was just dumbfounded to find the door still locked and her cow in her house, still rambling, and still upsetting and injuring wherever she rambled.

The widow, after viewing the conditions, bad enough, I am sure, to unnerve a Job, decided to call in some one to view the scene and to give her advice. There lived across the road a merchant named Winder. He was a man of few words, and uttered these few always as if very mature thought had preceded them. He was tall, and rheumatic, and limped as he walked, even with the aid of his big stick. To him the widow, in her distress, appealed. He walked over slowly, and, at the widow's request, went in the house and through the rooms. Not a word did he say. After a while, the widow, to emphasize conditions, said, "Now, Mr. Winder, just look at my sewing machine, and at my cooking stove, and at all of my chairs, and my washstand, and my bed, and all of my clothes scattered on the floor, and the rest of my things. Now, Mr. Winder, what must I do? What do you think the damages are worth?"

Winder walked slowly to the front door, relieved himself of his chew of tobacco, and then slowly walked back into the room where the widow was and the damages were greatest. With the dignity of a supreme court judge, he asked this one, but potent, question: "Are you certain, madam, there wasn't but one cow?" This was all. It was enough.

* * *

There were two other bachelors, devoted brothers, who kept bachelors' hall in the strictest old-fashion way. They were devoted to each other and always called each other *brother* when together, but when out among friends, and apart, they always spoke of each other by the *surname,* which was Rouzie, I will say, and indeed it does not matter if I say for a fact that it was Rouzie. Good-hearted fellows they were, played the violin well, told good jokes, and were most companionable. Still, they had their little family jars, as other brothers may have, which to the outsider is often more amusing than serious. Let's tell of one of these, which, to me, is as small as it was foolish. A good-hearted, humor-loving gentleman by the name of Bob D—— used to

Upper—THE WALNUT TREE AT CARET
This tree stands where another stood from which criminals were hung when the first Court House in Essex County was at this place

Lower—THE OLD RITCHIE HOME, TAPPAHANNOCK
The oldest building in the town

pass near the yard on his way to stores and to mill, using the private road as a short cut over the highway. Well, one morning as Bob was passing by one of the brothers hailed him and asked him to wait a minute, that he had something to tell him. Both of the brothers were deaf, very deaf, indeed, and spoke in that high key common to hard-of-hearing people. Bob stopped his team and waited, and, the truth to tell, he expected there was some fun ahead for him, for he knew these brothers well. As one of the brothers approached, he said, "Bob, that fellow Rouzie is a grand rascal. Yes, sir, he is a grand rascal." "What in the world is the matter, Mr. Rouzie?" "Well, this morning when we were cooking our breakfast I had my piece of meat and bread on one side of the skillet, and Rouzie had his piece on the other side of the skillet. Rouzie asked me to go out to the wood pile and get some more wood. Well, sir, when I came back I found that he had gone and put a chip under my side of the skillet and let every bit of the gravy run down on his side, so his bread could get it all. I call that a durn mean trick. Yes, sir, Rouzie is a grand rascal." Bob tried to console him, and restrained his desire to laugh.

* * *

Another time when Bob D—— was passing near their house, one of the brothers came out and hailed him, as the other had done some time before. "Wait a minute, Bob, I want to see you." Bob waited. "Bob, you were not out to the church meeting last Saturday, were you? I didn't see you there." Bob told him that he was not out there that day; that he was busy, or had to go away, or something of that kind as an excuse for his non-appearance. "Why, what went on, anything important?" asked Bob. "Yes," said Rouzie, "they had the durnest time of it up there at that meeting I ever saw in my life." "What did they do, Mr. Rouzie?" said Bob. "Bob, you know I take a little something to drink once in a while, and Saturday evenings when I go down to the village I generally take a drink or two and bring a little back home with me. But I don't take too much, you know that well enough, Bob, don't you?" Bob told him he never had heard of his being drunk or anything of that kind, but knew he took something to drink occasionally. "Well, sir, I got there a little late Saturday, and you know I am hard of hearing, so I did not know what was before the meeting. Presently they asked all who were in favor of the motion to rise. So I got up with the rest. And I'll be durned if I hadn't voted to turn myself out of the church. That was the durnest trick I ever heard of in my life, Bob." And Bob thought 'twas pretty bad, and, as a matter of fact, it was.

XVI

AGRICULTURE *in the* PUBLIC SCHOOLS

In the sweat of thy face shalt thou eat bread until thou return unto the ground" faces us today as seriously as it faced Adam when the curse was pronounced, for bread we must eat, and it matters not whether it comes by the sweat of the brain or by the sweat of the face, with an honest and a deserved coming there is perplexity and multiplicity enough to make us long for an easier way.

Agriculture is today recognized as the greatest of all sciences and the basis of human prosperity. And yet it has lagged behind as a taught science, and until but recently has it had even a minor place in the curriculum of the public schools. Somehow, we have for centuries gotten far away from "mother earth" and soared to dizzy heights in abstruse liberalism of theories, unsatisfying as well as impracticable. Man gets hungry while you try to square the circle, and he gets cold when he follows you to the North Pole, and he longs for eternal peace and rest while you spread your modern views on that Bible, which in its simplicity he learned at his mother's knee. But a reactionary period has begun to dawn, and we find the great thinkers getting closer to the earth. They are watching the apple fall; they are catching the lightning from the clouds; they are writing sound waves on waxen plates as the ocean writes her heart-throbs on her shore, and they are going down into the soil and asking what it needs to give them a bountiful harvest, in order that the sweat on the toiler's face may have its reward and the cries of his children be hushed.

If Americanism stands for anything besides freedom of thought, it stands for practicability—the easiest and the best way to make a substantial living. From this has grown the results of Yankee ingenuity, fairly flooding the country with time-saving machinery and conveniences innumerable. Mathematics may rest awhile, for it matters not whether some distant star is a spheroid or a sphere. Economics political may test the many propositions already nurtured and fostered without another new one being given for a score of years. Art may put other touches on its highest canvas, and we will *wait* for the unveiling. And we will sing the old, old songs over and over again and feel no need of a new one when we hear the mocking bird from the topmost branch of the loaded cherry tree and the woodpecker's drum way down yonder in the clearing where the pumpkin vine is clambering over the pine stumps, and the plump partridge whistles to his mate.

What we want is to make two blades of grass grow where one grows now, two ears of corn grow where one grows now. And this leads us to consider the subject of "Agriculture in the Public Schools." Of course, the old farmer will laugh when he hears that some teacher who has had to buy corn all of his life, if he ever had any corn or any need of it, is to teach his son how to farm. And so did the farmers laugh when that teacher out West made the boys each bring the best ear of corn he could find, that it might be tested scientifically—tested as to its size, shape, weight, quality, nutriment, power of reproduction, and bulk. But from that little cross-roads school work there sprang the greatest force in the agricultural line that this country has known in its history. That teacher taught how to test seed-corn and how to find the best seed-corn. He reasoned strictly upon "like producing like" and the necessity of the first tender roots having well-prepared and fertile soil to feed from. From his teachings millions of bushels of corn have been added to the corn crops of the West, and glad are the railroads to haul free of charge the private car of this once unknown teacher as he goes through the country lecturing to the farmers. I do not hold that every teacher may even approach this man, but every earnest teacher may do some part in the work, and every teacher may easily find a responsive interest among *some* of his scholars. Ignorance on the subject is no excuse. With "Duggar's Agriculture for the Southern Schools" in hand, and a love of nature at heart, you will soon be in position to help.

It is not my province to tell you just how to teach the subject. But a suggestion may be in order. First of all, get Professor Duggar's book. Next, study it yourself. If you do not wish to use it as a regular everyday study, with stated periods, use it once or twice a week, lecturing on the subject in a conversational manner. Put the pupils to work. Make them bring something to school bearing on the subject. As soon as you become interested you will think of scores of things helpful in your work. "Interest begets interest." They will catch the fever. But you must have it, and your pulse must run very fast, and your temperature must be very high. What is a science, after all, but close observation and test, going from the known to the unknown? Mathematics, that essence of logic, teaches us *how* to think. Grammar teaches us how to tell what we know. But science is the knowing; it is the thing to tell, the thing to reason about. Here is where you need that reasoning force that mathematics has given you; here is where you need the expression force that grammar has given you. It is just as scientific to learn why field peas and red clover belong to the same common family of legumes, bearing nitrogen to the soil, as it is to learn the principles of hydrostatics, or the inverse ratio of Newton's terrestrial attraction. It is just as scientific to study why alfalfa feeds on lime, and asparagus feeds on salt, as it is to study that the final clause in conditional sentences is put in the subjunctive in Latin, or that a noun clause may be the logical subject of a complex sentence in English. I mention these things because some teachers are going to think that it is very unprofessional to suggest pumpkins and potatoes and wheat and corn and hog-feed and buttermilk and bran and oats and ashes and "so forth" to their higher culture and higher tastes and reason. But for patience's sake, teachers, let us leave the theoretical just for awhile and try to teach something that the boy can take back home with him and use. Let him see what a beautiful mystery crop life and propagation is, common though it may seem to him, just because he sees it every day. Point out the beauties of his home to him; beauties lost to his sight because he had not looked at them right.

And tell him how he can, with a little care and a little thought and just a little work, assist nature and make what seemed commonplace beautiful. Did you ever mark how beautiful a bit of holly looks when placed on your parlor mantel? You saw trees of it in the woods, all hanging with blood-red berries, but you did not notice them because they were so common. *Here* you get the idea. Teach the poetry of the wild flowers by the old spring branch, and the geology in that old gully that he had never noticed before, and the geometry in the shape of the leaves, and the shades in the fields and fallows. Show him his home to be a beautiful place, and how he can make it more so. Compare his life on the farm, with all of its liberty, with a slave life in the city. Make him satisfied with his home, make him want to be a farmer and a good one.

Wasn't it Thoreau who said he had rather sit on a pumpkin in his own garden and watch the beans grow during the day and the stars twinkle at night than to ride on a palace car with its stuffy cushions and dust and noise and form? I somehow think that man would have made a good lecturer on agriculture, so happy was he way off there on Walden Pond, all alone, save for his crops, which to him were as companions. No, my friends, this subject of agriculture is no mean subject, and you will find that the best within your equipment of teaching force may work on it now and then and not lose one whit by the acquaintance. You will remember that Diocletian wrote Maximian, who was trying to persuade him to regain his imperial position as Emperor of Rome, that if he, Maximian, could come to Salona and see what vegetables he was raising with his own hands in his little garden, he would never ask him to think of empire again. I can see where he was right.

The scarcity of labor in this section of Virginia makes it necessary for the owner of the farm do his own work. This, or no work will be done. The few that may be hired are, in most cases, poor indeed, and seem to feel that their duty is undone unless they break something, or lose something, or do something absolutely contrary to your instructions. You must do the work yourself, or, at least, lead it. And this naturally suggests small acreage for tillage, and that done in the very best manner, and the soil improved to the maximum fertility within the reach of your means, and this at the least cost, and your entire farming equipment arranged for the greatest convenience and highest use, and for the least expenditure of energy in order that you may secure the necessary results. This, then, in brief, is the object in studying agriculture. You want to combine a science with common sense. If you know what you are buying as a fertilizer, and know the need of the land you wish to use this improver on, you are in position to work scientifically, and, we may say, to work with more pleasure, for you are working intelligently, combining somebody else's experience with your own, and with your own knowledge of your soil.

That works on agriculture are in demand there is no question. I notice in the columns of the *Rural New-Yorker* that a railroad has requested that paper to give the name of a good work on farming, something brief, but comprehensive, strictly scientific, but readable. The railroad men want to distribute this book among the farmers where their road runs. They know that more culture information should bring better crops, and better crops bring more freight. The *Rural New-Yorker* frankly acknowledges that it knows of no book to recommend. Here is a chance for the farmer who thinks he knows his work. Let him put it in print, and fill this bill. But we do not know it, friends, and, worse still, we *think* we do, and that is where the trouble lies. We need doctoring, but we think we know better than the physician, and go on and doctor ourselves. Some say the reason that we have not advanced more rapidly in this section is because we are lazy; others say because we lack the means to improve our lands; others that we try to cultivate too much land, and others still that we ruin our lands and empty our pocketbooks by purchasing cheap or worthless fertilizers. It may be that some or all of these factors enter into the failure product. But we do need light on the subject of farming, and a careful study of good farm papers, and the study of some standard work on farming should help us. We study law and buy books at high prices; we study medicine and stock our shelves, but we are perfectly satisfied to trust to luck and our own experience when it comes to dealing with the greatest of all human problems, bread-raising.

But we will assume that every teacher agrees fully with us, and seconds our plea for the study of agriculture in the public schools. And this leads us to say that we are not here to map out a cut-and-dried course for the teacher to pursue. If he be equipped for other work, he can, with some preparation, equip himself for this, and especially is this true of country teachers. The subject of grafting alone would prove of great interest to the pupils, and it is one that may be taught during the winter. Professor Duggar will tell you how, and to this you may add the full instructions given in the last edition of the *Rural New-Yorker.*

The botanical portion of the study will be of more interest to the girls than to the boys. But they will like it, if you will help them to like it. As to the usual school term being at the wrong season of the year for experiments, I will suggest old crayon boxes and rich earth and the school stove at night. Not very long before they can see the many little roots that will come from a grain of corn, or a grain of wheat, when you take the sprouted grain out of the soil and gently wash it in water. And what would you gain by this? you may ask. The particular delicacy of the roots will suggest careful culture for the youngling plant, as a tender little lamb needs careful nursing. The pupils will get the idea, if you will go to the trouble to give it to them.

To teach agriculture in the public schools you need not have to leave off a single study. One study sometimes covers the field of studies. Every teacher knows this. If you are on foreign plants, locate the country in which they are grown. There you have geography. If you are discussing the weight of seeds, or the number of pounds to the acre you must sow, bring in your arithmetic. If you note a good sentence in your reading matter, call the attention of the class to it, and let them tell all about it; if it be the time of the discovery of a plant, note well the historical period associated with it, and teach history right there. You will learn the way, if you have the desire to carry on the work. The public-school teacher cannot be a specialist. If this be his desire and his bent, the college or university is his place. The country-school teacher must be an embryonic encyclopedia, in the list let agriculture not have the meanest place.

Somehow thus I would try to teach agriculture in the public schools, and it is my firm belief that nothing save good will spring from it, and maybe ere another decade passes by we will see many a waste place come to a bountiful harvest, and the boys and the girls that now we teach the happy owners of neat and well-cultivated little farms, their larders full, their granaries full, cider in the cellar, butter in the cupboard, and the glowing coals driving out the frost, and all as happy as honest labor backed by sound judgment can bring happiness in this world, where men must labor and women must wait till the great harvest time hereafter.

XVII

CHARLIE B—— *and* HIS YARNS

CHARLIE is truly quick-witted, as well as witty, and it is a dangerous matter to meet him in a battle of words, for his satire is as keen as a razor, and he uses it as if he had been lying in wait and thoroughly prepared for his adversary, even when the most unexpected attack is made upon him. There does not seem to be the slightest ill feeling on his part when he administers a double dose of sarcasm, but he does it in the most polite and apologetic manner, as if you needed it. You realize that there is not another word for you to say, and that your best course is to remain perfectly quiet and let the medicine do you good.

Not so long ago, Charlie was talking in a high key in the dining saloon of a steamer. He had his audience in a roar of laughter. Joke after joke was passed by him, and a right merry time of it were they having. In the midst of the gaiety the burly captain of the steamer came along, and in a very compromising manner (for he was of the kind who disliked to see others enjoy themselves, seemingly) said, "What is the matter with you, Charlie, making all of this noise in here? I will swallow you presently and be done with you." As quick as a flash, Charlie replied, "Well, Captain, when you have swallowed me you will certainly have more brains in your stomach than you have in your head, and the quality will be far superior also." The crowd yelled, and the Captain lost his appetite.

* * *

Charlie likes a "drop" occasionally. A friend went to him not long since and undertook to lecture him, and to caution him, and told him that he (the lecturer) and the rest of his friends would be forced to withdraw their intimacy if he did not mend his ways. This was given in the nicest manner and as if expecting tears to spring in Charlie's eyes. But not so with Charlie. With equal politeness, he replied, "Well, sir, when you and your friends see fit to withdraw your intimacy from me, please remember that 'the joy will then all be mine.' "

* * *

Charlie says his lack of education was due to the following: He was attending a country school in one of the Tidewater counties. He says his teacher was very good, but he was suddenly and very peculiarly deprived of his books, "Town's Blueback Speller," and a First Reader, and, being afraid of telling his parents that his books were gone, he never got any new ones. And this was the way he lost them: His lunch was of buttered biscuit, sliced ham, a bottle of country molasses, and green apples, when in season. He always put his "Town's Spelling Book" and his slate in the basket with his lunch, his First Reader being generally lost or left behind. One day he set the basket down while he was fighting a boy who had challenged him the day before. He says he was about to finish up the boy when he saw an old sow going off with his basket. He asked the boy to suspend operations until he could go and save his lunch and book. The hog willed differently. Round and round the grove she went, and Charlie right after her. When the hog was far enough ahead she would stop and eat the lunch. Finally the hog dropped the basket. Charlie ran up to it, hoping to save his book at least. But when he examined further he found that the hog had broken the molasses bottle and the contents had spilled all over the "Blueback Speller" and the slate. The hog did not mind eating slate and book, just so she got the molasses. So all, says Charlie, that he found was the rim of his slate and the empty basket. His teacher gave him a whipping because he missed *psalm* and *psalter,* and *saltpetre.* He says when his teacher asked him why he had not gotten the lesson "thoroughly *into* him" he told him, in reply, that the old sow had gotten all of the lesson, and the whole book to boot, *very thoroughly* into her, and there was no way for him (Charlie) to get it out. This closed his educational career.

* * *

One night, Charlie says, he was over in King and Queen County, Virginia, at a country store, where he had sold a bill of goods, as a drummer. He had no conveyance of his own, and the chance for hiring was very doubtful. He waited around for some hours, hoping that some one might come along and give him a ride to the next store, where he hoped to sell another bill and secure quarters for the night. It was very dark, and raining hard. He had about given up the hope of getting to the next store that night, when an old colored man came in, bowing and scraping in the way of salutation to the merchant and himself. "Zack," said the merchant, "this gentleman wants to go down to Mr. Courtney's store tonight. Can't you take him? You are in a buggy, aren't you?" "Yes, sir, I's got my buggy and hos, and I reckin I kin took um, if he ain't got too much to carry. Dat is, I kin take um as fur as I goes. I don't lib 'xactly at Mr. Courtney's, you know, but fur as I guine he kin go, too." Charlie clinched the bargain. Zack bought about as many little bills as he had brought eggs to pay for them with. Presently, as he put a big piece of tobacco into his mouth, he announced himself ready for the dark and muddy drive. Charlie quickly got into the buggy, took the reins, and away they went, the old man replacing his bundles and buckets so as to protect them from the driving rain. But the coal-oil can was his greatest concern, not having any stopper in the can. Charlie suggested to the old negro to put his finger in the place of a stopper, and this was accepted. Charlie knew every inch of the ground. But he thought it wise not to tell the negro this. He was in that buggy to stay until he reached Courtney's store, regardless of Zack's wishes to the contrary. By appearing to lose his road he might fool Zack and come out right at the desired store. But before resorting to this Charlie tried another scheme. "Uncle Zack, are you a believer in ghosts?" he said in a very serious manner, but with great politeness, as if having much respect for Zack's opinion on the subject. "Well, sir, I tell you, I hardly knows what I does b'lieve on dat subject. I's done sene strange sights in my life, but den I don't say dat any ob dese was ghosts." "But you are not afraid of ghosts, are you?" "I cuan't say dat I is 'xactly dat, but, still, I ain't looking for dem night nor day." "The reason I ask you, Uncle Zackiel—is your name Zackiel, or is it Zackius?" "I reckin eder will do, but dey most in ginerally calls me Zack." "You see, when talking on such a subject I like to be very careful. Well, as I was about to remark, Uncle Zackiel, I have lost a very dear friend recently, and I thought I would drive by the graveyard here at the old church and have a little talk with him if you did not mind." "Is he dead?" "Oh! yes, and has been buried several weeks." "Well, how you guine talk to him if he dead and buried?" "Ah, Uncle Zackiel, that is just why I was so considerate of your feelings and asked if you were afraid of ghosts. You see, I have great power over these poor wanderers of the dark and stormy night, and it helps me to call them up and soothe them with a friendly talk." Zack looked at Charlie as if he were an escaped lunatic. It was evident that Zack was trying his best to devise some plan to get rid of Charlie, and Charlie was working just as hard to dispose of Zack, that he (Charlie) might have that horse and buggy as far as Courtney's store. "By the way, here is the church now. I am glad of it. Poor Harvey, poor Harvey, how I have missed you!"

Zack gripped the mouth of the coal-oil can but the tighter, and felt the very sweat stand on his brow. He knew that it was his horse and buggy, but still he did not have power to assert his own rights. Charlie drove right along up to the cemetery gate, and Zack sat as quiet as a statue, freezing with fright. "Now, Uncle Zackiel, you have your hands full, I will tie the horse here for fear he might become nervous at the strange sight I now propose to present to you." Charlie knew it was safer to have the reins convenient to him rather than to Zack. "No, sir, no sir, Mr.—ah, what did you say your name was?" "My name? Why, Charlie, the charmer.' I had forgotten to tell you that." "But you, mister, ah, charmer, you—don't tie my hos dere. You gib me dem reins. You don't know dat hors, case when anything white comes 'round him he is a fool, I tell you."

"Hark! there he is! Perfectly quiet now! Steady, steady, not one word must be uttered. Your horse is safe and so are you if you keep perfectly quiet. One sound, and all is lost. Harvey, Harvey, come up Harvey! That is right. Come right along, Harvey Bowers; you know your old friend who loved you, Harvey. A little higher, a little higher, just a little higher. There you are, come to me, Harvey!"

There was a rush and a rattle and a bang and a tearing of old clothes, and the quickest disappearance from that buggy ever seen before. Zack went as hard as his old feet could carry him through the woods in a straight line for his home. Charlie stood and watched and laughed until he was sore. He got in that buggy and went on to Courtney's store in short order. He then sent the horse and buggy back to the old man and fully remunerated him for the use of the horse and buggy; but Zack says nothing in "dis wold would pay him for dat ghost coming outen dat grave dat night and for all de skin he scratched off hisself running through dem woods."

* * *

Charlie now and then becomes seriously (seemingly) affected by revival meetings. Not long since he was some distance from home, and after attending a series of meetings, he offered himself for immersion. There were many candidates for the sacred and the solemn and serious and beautiful rite. Charlie was doubtlessly in deep earnest, for the time, at least. The evening for the baptism arrived. Charlie, being away from home, had to provide himself with an improvised suit. The only pants that could be bought at the little country store were seersucker, and much too tight for Charlie. Shirt and pants and socks were the sum total of his garments when he entered the water.

As previously remarked, the pants were tight. Water followed by broiling sun-heat is bad for tight pants. The goods were not of the best. The buttons had been put on to show and not to use. The services went on. Charlie was the first to be immersed. He then took his place at the end of the line to assist the females and the boys as the minister tenderly administered the rites. The service was over. The choir, standing on the shore, rendered sweet sacred music. All except Charlie were moving along towards the shore. He held his ground as if anchored. He preferred deep water. The good old minister beckoned to him to come on out. Charlie tried to phone him by holding both hands beside his mouth to dismiss the congregation. He also pointed towards his pants. The truth of the matter was that the action of the sun upon Charlie's wet garments was very disastrous to buttons. In fact, he says, there was not one left, and he positively refused to march out of that water with tight seersucker pants on and no buttons besides. The old minister came out to him, and an explanation was made. Thereupon the congregation was dismissed, greatly to Charlie's delight. He says it was a difficult matter to continue in a religious frame of mind when those old buttons were popping off every time he moved to help some lady to stand up in the deep water. He says when he got ashore there was not a soul in sight. He called a boy and sent him to the hotel and had his satchel brought, gave the boy the suit, or such as there was of it, and jumped the first train he could get for home.

In one of the counties in Virginia there is a division into three parts known well enough by the people, but not mentioned by the maps. This county to which I have referred is divided into Texas, Chinkapin, and Boston. Now, Charlie has a little piece of land in Boston. He was in New York on one occasion buying goods. When his cash had run out, he asked for some concessions in the way of a long credit. The credit man was called in, and he asked Charlie if he had any property which might be subjected to meet this debt if the goods were sold to him. "Why, yes, sir, I have a Boston farm. And I am sure that is good for any bill I would make." "A Boston farm? What do you mean?" "Well, sir, is it possible you do not know Boston? I said a Boston farm. In the very heart of Boston. That is certainly good." The credit man looked around, thought awhile, cleared his throat, seemed puzzled, but presently said, "Mr. B——, you can have the goods." Charlie says that Boston farm was too much for them to stand. On another occasion, Charlie was hard pressed for means to meet a bill. He went to a member of the firm and, after a very tender greeting, asked him to endorse for him for a right large amount. "But, Mr. B——, you owe us now, and we are anxious for a settlement. Now you ask us to endorse for you?" Certainly, sir, that is just what I ask, and I want the money for you, don't you understand? For you, to pay this very debt. Nothing could be fairer." The note had been drawn, and was just waiting the endorsement. "You want the money for us, you say?" "Yes, sir, that very note for you." "Well, it looks fair. Very good." He endorsed the note and Charlie passed it over to him, saying that he was really sorry that he had made these gentlemen wait so long, but next time he would try to be prompt. "By the way, you had better send me down a lot of that best flour and two barrels of your double-A sugar and some sugar-cured hams. Let them come on this boat." And they came.

XVIII

AROUND *the* COUNTRY-STORE FIRE

THE good roads, the automobiles, the freight trucks and the mail-order houses are fast placing the old country store on the sharp decline, and in a few decades these very useful and convenient places of trade will be rare, if any at all are left. The country merchant is often misunderstood, and as often misrepresented—he does not charge all of those exorbitant prices and make all of those large profits. But he has to live, and he must make on his investment, or face the inevitable. Yet, there are still some left, these old-fashion country stores, where the neighbors come out at night and spend an hour or more in social talk. The city man has his club, the country man has his country store, with its nail-box and empty kegs and a broken-back chair or two for seating. And the old stove, ever needing to be replenished with fuel, but the fuel very near on the outside, and a good-natured colored boy handy to go out and kick the snow off and bring in an armful. Such is the country store at night. And who, pray! would have it fancy and fixy, robbing you of your freedom of movement, and hampering your conversation? There you may smoke your strongest pipe, eat peanuts, chew tobacco, open a can of sardines, have a stew of oysters, cuss out the entire community not personally represented, and tell all of the good jokes that come to mind, and relate your experiences, good and bad, for the last quarter of a century. Still, there is something fascinating about these gatherings. You come in contact with the real inner nature of the man—no semblance of airs, brag nor bluster. He would forthwith be called down.

There they sit, huddled around the stove, for I am thinking of a snowy night now, the weather that encourages sociability, and each in turn making his comments on the last year's crops, the whooping cough they had when he was a boy, and the winters for several decades past, whether good, bad or indifferent, and comparisons drawn with the present winter.

One big fat man said that the winters of late years are mere springtimes compared with those he used to experience. He then stated the following: The Rappahannock River was frozen across, and it is over two miles wide where I lived, and you could walk across with safety. Our wood was getting low, and we decided to sled some from an island not very far off. So we hitched a yoke of oxen to a big wood sled and drove up the river near the shore to the island. There was some snow on the ice, and this made the footing good—kept them from slipping, you know. Well, we continued to haul wood until we had a pretty good supply.

People had been walking across the river for several days, and the ice was thick and firm. I got to thinking about taking a sleigh-ride on the ice. I knew if it would hold a yoke of oxen and a heavy sled loaded with green wood it would hold a pair of horses. I had a nice pair of driving horses at that time, and they were pretty good steppers. They had been stabled for several days and needed exercise, anyway. So my brother Harry and I hitched them to the sleigh, and out we went, right towards the channel of the Rappahannock.

We then turned, and went straight down towards Bowlers Wharf, about five miles, I suppose. It was a very risky thing to do, but after we got started, those horses going at full speed, the wind cutting your face like a knife, and the horses having to jump over the big cracks in the ice now and then, almost lifting the sleigh in the air as they would jump, there was something thrilling about it, this going over the ice right where the big steamers generally went in following the channel, it was past thrilling. Well, we drove on down to Bowlers Wharf and rounded the pierhead and then we started for the shore. When within about fifty yards of the shore we found the ice covered with water; the tide, you see, had risen over it. And the nearer we got towards the shore the deeper the water was. We feared that any minute the horses would break through, and we with them, for we could not tell one thing about it, whether the ice had melted or not. So I jumped upon my sleigh seat and gave my horses the whip, for I determined to get as near the shore as possible. They went like mad, for they were not used to being whipped. I almost held my breath until they struck the shore. Man, it was a thrill as sure as you live!

Go back the way I came? No, sir, not for any consideration. Once was enough for me.

I frequently think of that silly trip when I am feverish at night, and wonder how I ever did such a thing as risky as it was. Still, it is something to hand down to my children, as an unusual, if not the only, feat of sleigh-riding over the channel of the Rappahannock. No, sir, I followed the shore on my way home; the snow on solid ground suited me better than snow on ice when there was twenty or thirty feet of water beneath it.

The fire was stirred up, and Ned sent out to get more wood. When he came in he made the remark that it was cold out "dare and snowing like de very debble." No one contradicted him, but all were ready for further talk. One gentleman alluded to the scarcity of game that season, and this led to hunting yarns. The fox hunts, the bird hunts, the 'possum hunts were all taken up in detail and fully described with all of the various and sundry items therewith connected. Presently a gentleman remarked that the strangest event of his hunting experience, though he had hunted in several counties in Virginia, in Arkansas, and in Louisiana, was on the edge of Loudoun County, near the Prince William line.

He said he and a doctor friend of his were bird hunting one day, having two dogs, Don and Pilot, and hunting somewhat apart, the doctor having Pilot, and he Don. He flushed a woodcock on the hillside, but failed to get a shot. The bird flew down to a little marshy place, and he followed, but failed again to get a shot, the bushes and briars being so thick. This time the bird flew to the opposite hillside, small pines and broom-sedge covering the hill. Don, he said, would not point a woodcock, but would indicate his near approach to the bird by stopping and wagging his tail, and by other signs known to huntsmen, such as turning around and looking at you as if trying to tell you that game was close ahead.

The dog did this, and he, the huntsman, walked up near enough to shoot the bird when he flew. Just then he saw Pilot coming to him at full speed, and, for fear that the dog would flush the bird before he was near enough for a shot, he yelled at Pilot to stop. Just as he called to the dog the bird flew up and he fired, the bird falling dead. As he approached to get the bird, to his surprise, the woodcock was lying on a rabbit, clearly indicating that both had been shot at once. He called his friend, Dr. Clifton Laws, of Maryland now, to have him as a witness to this most remarkable shot ever known to any huntsman. The doctor examined both the rabbit and the bird and saw that they were warm, as if killed but a few minutes before. The explanation was easy, for the flushing of the woodcock scared up the rabbit, both going up a right steep hill, and the huntsman being at the foot of it, his line of fire covered both bird and rabbit. It might not happen again in a hundred years, if ever. But it did happen just as he told it, he said. And the author of this knows it is true, for he is the man who shot the bird and hare at one shot.

After this story some one suggested an oyster stew, and all hands were agreed. Ned was sent over to the oyster house across the road, and soon returned with a full gallon of Bowlers Rock oysters, complaining as he came that it was "gitting sure 'nough cold out dare, and de snow gitting deeper and deeper." Evidently this was a fact. The big stew-pan and the fresh butter were soon gotten out, for this was not the first time they ever had an oyster stew in that store, and they knew what was needed. Ned was the cook, and he seemed to know how, as he did not stir the oysters, but let the butter melt in the hot liquor, and in this way go all through the bubbling stew, and the pepper and salt he added when the oysters were nearly ready to be served to the waiting group. Ned was a sailor-man and he knew how to cook. With crackers and soft drinks a-plenty, the feast was complete for those who really love oysters and know just how to prepare them best.

"Did you ever hear about Jim Turner turning white? Well, it's a fact; his skin just peeled off until he was almost as white as snow. It did not seem to affect his health at all, and none of the doctors knew what was the cause of it. He lived to be an old man, old man Jim did. He was a good old 'nigger,' and a good workhand." This brought forth much comment, and, to some, much surprise, but most of the crowd knew it was all true. "Speaking of turning white makes me think of old Mr. Simcoe. While he was already a white man, his hair was black as a coal, but in one night it turned snow white," said a gentleman who was enjoying his pipe after his supper. "And, strange to tell," he continued, "almost opposite where Mr. Simcoe lived old man Jim Burnett lives, and a strange thing happened to him. He had a heavy suit of black hair, for they say he is part Indian. Well, one Sunday morning as old Uncle Jim was combing his hair, getting ready for church, it began to come out, and the more he combed it the more came out, until he was as bald as a badger, and not another strand ever came back. I reckon he is one hundred years old now, and in good health. Always thought it strange that these two people, living so near to each other, should have had such experience with their hair."

A man from across the swamp asked if we had ever heard about the boys setting a regular bear trap for a young man who was visiting in their neighborhood. "Well," he said, "this young fellow used to come through the woods by a path that was narrow, and the woods thick. The bad boys in the neighborhood, a little jealous of the young man, perhaps, dug a regular bear trap right in the middle of that path—deep enough to bury a horse in. They covered it over with light trash so as to be hidden. That night the young man came along, tripping lightly and rapidly on his way to see the object of his desires. He had a way of throwing his head way back, and his line of gaze was way ahead. On he came and down he went, clean to the bottom, and there he stayed until morning, for all of his cries had failed to bring relief. This was really a cruel trick, but you can't help from laughing about it—a great, big fellow, all dressed up and going to see his sweetheart, yet caught in a regular bear pit. I have often wondered at just what that fellow thought when he began to fall, and if he ever did exactly realize where he was and what it was all about, anyway. Mad? He certainly was, but what could he do, and who would want to fight about being caught in a bear pit? He just had to endure it." The crowd laughed and wanted to know who was the party, but this was denied.

Another of the good-humored crowd remarked that one of the funniest, and yet rather startling experience, for awhile, was to find a maltese cat with her head hung in an empty salmon can, rearing and plunging all over his dining-room, one night. So rapid were the frantic movements of the cat that it was difficult to locate her exactly, for she would make a desperate plunge against some piece of furniture, fall back, spring up again, and just going all over the room. He said that he thought at first that a calf had in some way gotten into the house and into the dining-room, so much noise was made there in the dark. When a light was brought and the cat caught and held by means of a pair of tongs, and by strenuous efforts the can was pulled off, or, better, the head pulled out, the speed at which that cat moved has never yet been calculated, but she moved, that cannot be questioned. And now, to spoil the story, the ptomaine poison in that can killed the cat. He said he thought this was true, for he never saw the cat after her adventure with the can, and he felt sure that had the cat continued to run at the same rate of speed that it had when leaving his dining-room it would have reached the far and unknown parts of Kamchatca in a few days.

It was time to adjourn for the night, one of the party said, and it really was time, if the merchant was going to have his rest. "Cold out here, boys?" said one, and all agreed as they plunged in the snow and separated, going by groups, or pairs, or single, to their homes.

Like so many other things belonging to the old *regime,* the country store, with its coterie of friends and neighbors, will soon be gone, and I, for one, will regret the passing.

XIX

JIM ROBERT RHONE

PUZZLED ABOUT HIMSELF

James Robert Rhone was as good a piece of company as ever trod shoe leather. He was a gallant soldier in the Civil War, and a good citizen after the strife was over. His friends were many, for, indeed, it would have been unnatural to know him and not like him. He was the very soul of humor and fairly sparkled with wit. There never was a man who enjoyed a joke on a friend more than he, or who would go further to have his innocent fun. He was dreaded by the young men for miles around, for he would tease them about some girl whom they scarcely knew, and continue to do this until every one else thought it must be a fact, that the young men were in love with the girls, though perhaps they had never paid these ladies any attention in their lives. And he would laugh at these pranks and jokes in the heartiest old Virginia laugh until all around would catch the fever and laugh with him.

But, like other men fond of teasing, he never relished the joke on himself. And here is a good one on him. He had a brother who was a preacher. Twins are rarely more alike than these brothers were, in appearance, in general manner, and in voice. But Jim Robert, as his friends called him, was fond of something good to drink, and more than once did he go beyond the temperance limitations.

One night when he returned from court at a very late hour, and was under the hallucination of too many friendly "smiles," he felt that he would not be safe in making the trip from his yard gate to the house. So he called for help. Now during the day, while he was absent, his brother had come home on a visit. He thought that his brother was a hundred miles away. "Helloo!" he shouted in the loudest voice. The window to his room was raised and seemingly in the exact tone came back the word, "Helloo!" "Who is that in my room?" he called back. "This is Jim Robert," the voice answered. "No, it isn't," he shouted back, for I am Jim Robert myself out here on this horse." "Oh! no, you are mistaken. You are up here in your little room, warm and nice, and have been to sleep for hours." "No, I am not in my room, for I am out here on this old mare, freezing to death." "You are mistaken, for here you are up here." "Well, if 'm up there, who is it out here on this old black mare? That is what I want to know."

His brother, growing tired of his fun, went out and helped him to the house and then to his room, and put him to bed as tenderly as if he had been a child. Soon he was fast asleep and all of his day's adventures were forgotten. The light was turned down, but not put out. At a very late hour Jim Robert woke up and, to his astonishment, he saw that he had a bedfellow. He was himself again after many hours of repose. Well, he got up and raised the light higher and gazed into the face of the sleeper. There was his brother! And of all men on earth, Jim Robert had rather any other should have seen him in such a plight.

The whole thing came back to him, and he decided that he could not stand meeting his brother sober, when that brother had brought him into the house while he was *not* sober. He quietly donned his clothes, slipped downstairs and went out in the freezing night and got his faithful old horse and went away, no one knows where, and not a sound was heard of him until his brother had packed up and gone home. The story was too good to keep and from the two brothers the incidents of the joke were learned.

* * *

PERKINS *and the* CRACKER

Perkins was a good fellow and very fond of Jim Robert. He knew what an inveterate tease Jim Robert was, but, regardless of this, he would repose all of his secret troubles in him over and over again, though as many times Jim Robert would tell every word of poor Perkins' secrets just as soon as he got him before a crowd of mutual friends. Jim Robert had such a winning way and seemed so innocent that Perkins would trust him again and suffer for it the first time the boys in camp were ready for a hearty laugh. To tell Jim Robert a secret and have him promise, seemingly, most faithfully never to tell it was a dead sure case of having it published, provided there was a particle of fun in it, or, even if by adding to it a little, any fun could be gotten out of it.

Perkins had been ailing for several weeks, but not sick enough to be sent to the hospital. His diet was tea and crackers. Both were scarce. The commissary department of the South was not overflowing in diet for the sick in the last days of that sad and fratricidal struggle. Perkins' tea had given out, but he had three stale crackers left. One of these at a meal was all that he could afford. There was no counting on when another provision train might be captured or when some old Virginia tobacco might be exchanged for tea and crackers. So Perkins had to be economical to the extreme degree.

One evening as they were taking their horses to water, Perkins said, "Look here, Jim Robert, did you knew somebody has gone and stolen the last three crackers that I had?" "What!" said Jim Robert, "stolen three crackers at one time? That is the meanest thing I ever heard of." "Yes, and you know how sick I have been for weeks, and they were the only things I had that I could eat. I am so weak that I can hardly get along, and I don't know what in the world I will do now." "Perkins, old fellow, that was the meanest thing I ever heard of, and I am certainly sorry for you, and you have my sympathy." They went along together and watered their horses. On the way back Jim Robert said: "Perkins, that thing is on my mind all the time, and I cannot think of anything else. It was the meanest thing I ever heard of, and if you could only find the fellow who stole those crackers I would certainly help you to whip him well. It was such a small thing to steal three crackers." "Yes, I think so, too," said Perkins. "It was mighty mean. There is no doubt about that." They went along to their respective tents for supper.

Perkins had hardly sat down when some one called out, "Perkins! O Perkins! Is Perkins in there?" Perkins went out, and there was Jim Robert. "Look here, Perkins, don't you know that I could not eat my supper for thinking about that thing. It was the meanest thing I ever heard of, old fellow, and I am certainly sorry for you." "Yes, it was right mean. Won't you come in to supper?" "No, indeed, I am too much worried to eat. You go on back and finish your supper. Don't let me kep you out here." Jim Robert went on back to his tent and chuckled to himself.

In about an hour he again went to Perkins' tent. "Hello! Is Perkins in there? Perkins! O Perkins!" Perkins came out, but it was very evident that he was growing tired of being interrupted. "Is that you, Jim Robert?" he said as he poked his head out of his tent. "Yes, I came around here to see you a little while. Come out here a minute." Perkins went out and Jim Robert took him some distance from the tent as if he had a big secret to tell him.

"Look here, Perkins, I tried to go to sleep, but that cracker stealing is on my mind yet, and I came around here to talk to you about it." "Well, I tell you, Jim Robert, I am mighty sleepy and I had rather talk some other time." "All right, I will see you tomorrow or some other time. It was such a mean thing that I cannot help thinking about it."

About an hour later Jim Robert was back again, calling for Perkins. "Perkins! O Perkins!!" he shouted. This time Perkins was asleep, but one of his comrades aroused him, and out he went to see what was the matter. "Come out here a minute, Perkins, I can't get that thing off my mind, anyhow, for it was the meanest thing and the smallest thing I ever heard of, and—" "Look here, Jim Robert, if you say *crackers* to me I'll kill you. I wish I had never told you about it, and if ever you tell any one that I *did* tell you I will whip you on sight." And in his tent he darted, leaving Jim Robert laughing until his sides nearly broke. The threat was unavailing, for in a few days every member of the company knew it, and to say "crackers" to Perkins was enough to raise his ire to fighting pitch.

XX

PROF. ROBERT RYLAND BENTLEY

I CANNOT close this list of sketches without mentioning in brief some items in the history of this splendid type of old Virginia gentleman, involving so many of the characteristics of those we read of in the stories laid in the days of the old-time gentry of Virginia.

In a word, Professor Bentley was strictly in a class all by himself, if I may use such an expression, for I know full well that I have never known any man whom I might place beside him as a reasonably correct counterpart. He certainly was himself under all circumstances and at all times, save and except when he might have indulged too freely in what was not good for either his intellect or his decorum. Still, this was far apart from the real man, and short-lived. Yet some very amusing things happened when he had indulged, not too much, but sufficiently to make him even more entertaining than usual, and the best of it was he would relate in full anything amusing that may have occurred when he was celebrating, as he termed it.

But all of this is but a side issue when thinking of this excellent instructor, for indeed he was that. Of all the teachers I have ever known, there is not one among them who was quite as thorough in Latin and in mathematics as this splendid man. He had the way of going right down to the bed-rock of principles in his teaching, and brooked no short cuts—thoroughness was his watchword. In consequence, neither at Tulane University nor at Washington and Lee, his *alma mater,* was ever one of his students whom he endorsed found lacking in thorough preparation.

Professor Bentley was born and reared in this county, and where Mr. William Taliaferro now lives was his beautiful old home. He engaged in the educational work in his own county for several sessions, and later was in the same line of work in Kentucky. After this he went to Louisiana and almost immediately established himself as an instructor of wonderful ability. Following him, his brother, L. E. Bentley, now president of a bank in Bastrop, La., went to the same State, and then followed the late Professor Benjamin Junius Saunders, a grandnephew of President Monroe, and finally the writer of this sketch.

For years we three, a thousand or more miles from home, boon companions, in the same line of work, lived and loved each other as but few men ever do, and it was during these years, when in the classroom, or in the field hunting, in the social circles, or just when we three were together reviving in memory our boyhood days in old Essex, it was there during these years of intimacy, and the years following, when he had returned to his old State, that I knew him best.

Apart from his depth of intellect, his chivalry, his *keenest* sense of humor appealed to me most. His manners were perfect, and his address pleasing. I can see him now, walking measuredly along the street, when his daily task, which he loved, was over, with his big meerschaum pipe in one hand and his gold-head cane in the other, while his silk hat and Prince Albert coat completed the requirement of a well-dressed gentleman—it is as he was then that I love to remember him, *then* when his opinion on educational questions was the last word, for none dared to dispute him, and *then* when his salary was lucrative and his popularity unbounded.

He was a man of above-the-average height, heavy of build, and of unusual strength and activity. His hair was of that shade known as red in the sun and golden in the shade, and he had a wealth of it. His features were massive. His eye penetrating, even as if he were trying to look clean through you, to the very soul of you, and read it if he could. He had but little respect for the man who did *not* know, and was fierce in argument. 'Twas then I enjoyed him fully, provided I was not in the discussion. No attorney in his most heated attempt before a jury, even when his feelings had been ruffled by the opposing counsel, ever touched Professor Bob Bentley in his invective and bitter sarcasm. I suppose if he had been a lawyer he would either have killed or been killed, for he just could not stand opposition when he believed that he was right. But he was the very essence of kindness and gentleness when he felt that these qualities were needed. He was as brave as a lion. I mean just this, for I do not think that he ever felt the sting of cowardice in all of his eventful career. And how he hated meanness. I have never heard any one pronounce the word *mean* as he pronounced it and emphasized it. It would make you feel that of all high crimes and misdemeanors, *meanness* was the worst.

So I have drawn in this running manner a rough picture of this splendid fellow, and have him, as I write, in high-school work in the city of Monroe, La. And it was to tell some items in his history that prompted me to write the above, in order that the reader might form a better conception of the man and be better prepared to appreciate the little stories I may relate and see the amusing in them.

At the opening of a session we were very busy in grading the pupils, even from kindergarten to graduating classes, and all went fairly well, with the exception of ten boys who were not fitted for any grade in the school, seven of them, not fitted for any grade or any other place on this earth, or, maybe, below it. They were tartars, incorrigibles, or something else that may comprehend in full absolute worthlessness for educational pursuits. They had sense enough, for who ever saw the boy who roams the street from morning until night, watching and hearing, lacking in sense? But to this sense was added old-fashion meanness, the kind that Professor Bentley hated. But three of the boys were good enough and bright enough. There was a social club in the city called the "Original Fourteen." We named these boys the "Original Ten," and by that name they went. Just where to assign them was a serious question, for none of the lady teachers wanted them, and they had no business in the high-school department. They were *nondescripts*. They would have been most pleased had he sent them home. But we decided to keep them within the walls of learning, even if we had to tie them head and foot. Good-hearted Professor Saunders agreed to let them sit in his room, and promised when opportunity afforded he would try to teach them *something* at least.

These young gentlemen averaged about fourteen years of age, and were of size according. They had not been in that room very long before Professor Saunders came before the faculty and made bitter complaint. In brief, that those would have to quit, or he would, for a fact; that they were destroying the order of his classroom, and that he could not stand them. So, of course, they had to be placed in some other room or expelled. I came to the rescue, with the understanding that I might use my hickory switch *ad libitum*. I soon found that neither kindness, council nor whipping would do those boys any good, and I had to turn them over to Professor Bentley, he having the entire auditorium for his classes to meet him, with blackboards strung along the walls and room enough for a thousand. To the rear of this long hall he assigned these boys, the "Original Ten." There they sat, and there they concocted all the plans of deviltry known to the street urchins, objectionable and hostile, and annoying to a teacher. Much of what went on was unknown to Professor Bentley, sitting far to the front, and absolutely buried in his own work. It is probable that these boys recited about once a day and that in arithmetic.

It is also probable that some days they were entirely forgotten and did not recite at all. Then, again, he would take them up in detail after all the rest of the school had

Upper—"Hill and Dale," the Home of the Author
Lower—The Home of Miss J. L. C. Garnett, the Authoress

been dismissed. The delinquents he would retain until a late hour, trying to beat into their heads the rudiments of arithmetic. Well, one afternoon, when my classes and the rest had been excused, and the pupils had filed out orderly as usual, and gone to their homes, I walked into the auditorium quietly and took a back seat, having some school papers to look over.

All of the ten boys had been excused and gone on their way rejoicing, with the exception of one—Abe Kuhn by name, and known throughout the length and the breadth of the city—not for any serious crimes or delinquencies, but for a particular kind of cussedness all his own. Abe was at the blackboard as I entered; he was tossing a piece of crayon to the ceiling and dextrously catching it as it fell. He had one of the boards pretty well filled with ciphering, and was evidently awaiting to recite, when Professor Bentley roused up from his apparent sleep as he sat at his big desk with his face buried in his hands, evidently in deepest meditation. A meditation provocative of seriousness when over with. My coming had not aroused him, but it had suggested to Abe that he had better let Professor Bentley know that he had finished his task. So he said, "Professor Bentley, I am ready." There was no response and no change of pose. Abe repeated in a higher key, "Professor Bentley, I am ready." This brought the old teacher to full activity, with all of that peculiar but searching aspect, as if he was about to grind you to intellectual, or, better, non-intellectual powder. "You say you are ready, sir. Now, are you certain that you are ready, or do you just think that you are ready?" Abe said he was ready. "All right, sir, go ahead then and state your problem." "Do what?" said the boy. "State your problem; tell what I gave you to solve, sir; tell how you solved it and what was the result," said the teacher. "Do what?" said Abe. "What did I tell you to do, Abe, and what is your answer. Don't you understand that?" Abe then looked over the long array of figures, and then said, "You told me if my father was planting potatoes and needed a peck more to fill out the patch, and potatoes were worth two dollars and a half a bushel, and sent me up town to buy the peck, how much would I have to pay for them?" "You are correct, sir; that is exactly what I gave you. Now, Abe, how much did you pay for them?" At once the boy replied, "Eighty-one dollars and seventeen cents." "Eighty-one dollars and seventeen cents for one peck of potatoes!" the infuriated professor fairly bellowed. *"Abie,* they call you Abe, but I call you *Abie.* I can, by a stretch of my imagination, see why the good Lord made snakes, and lizards, and gnats, and mosquitoes, and all other seemingly worthless and annoying creatures, but why on earth He put you here, unless it was to torment me, I fail to conceive. Get out of here, sir. Get out of here." As Abe reached the street he was throwing his cap up in the air and catching it on his head as it fell. Abe was just as happy as if he had worked all of the problems in the whole book. Nothing as slight as that interfered with the even tenor of Abe's morbid cussedness; it was a part of his happiness. I said nothing, but I knew I would have in full the impression made upon Professor Bentley. Presently he turned and looked at me and said, "I have been trying, by using every conceivable arrangement of figures and performing every known method of permutation and by applying the simple rules of addition, multiplication, subtraction and division, to find out what that boy has on the board; I can see how by some unknown process he might possibly have gotten the eighty-one dollars, but where in the thunder he got that seventeen cents from is a mystery to me." I could not help him. And I am sure Abe could not had he been present.

At another time, when there was a public day, with all patrons and citizens in general invited, there was an oral test of the classes in the high-school department, and when all this was over Professor Bentley called up some of the "Original Ten," to show them off, so to speak. Aubrey

Haas was a bright boy, very nervous, always willing, and had given Professor Bentley but little trouble. Aubrey was at the board. He had been given an example in division of fractions. The little fellow ciphered away before that large crowd with all eyes upon him and not a word spoken, and after various and sundry calculations and much figuring, he announced that he was ready to recite. "All right, Aubrey, what did you do, and what is your result?" The child reported, and then the critical but kind instructor questioned the child's method and process in most penetrating tones. "What did you do, Aubrey?" "I inverted my divisor and proceeded as in multiplication," answered Aubrey. "You did what, sir? What do you mean by invert, Aubrey?" "I inverted the divisor and proceeded as in multiplication," again answered the then nerve-tried child. "But what do you mean by invert? is what I asked you. Come here, Aubrey. Now, sir, stand stiff, stand stiff!" and, saying this, he reached down and grasped the boy by his ankles and stood him on his head, saying, "Now, sir, you are *inverted!*" Aubrey, fully grown into useful manhood, says he will never forget that object lesson. That was Bentley's way. I must relate this instance in the history of this rare genius.

I have hinted that he would occasionally indulge too freely. Now, some sessions he would not taste a drop, but always felt privileged to celebrate during the vacation, when he would be up here at or near his old home. One session when he had been particularly temperate he was frequently at the Presbyterian church of which he was a member. The members were highly pleased at this, and one Sunday night Dr. Bowin, the pastor, told the professor that it was the wish of all of them that he should conduct the prayer-meeting the following Wednesday night. After much persuasion on the part of the members, and equally as much consideration on his part, he agreed to conduct the meeting as requested. Well, I knew nothing of this at the time the arrangement was made, nor for some days after the meeting had been held. I occupied a room in the high-school building, right near my boarding-house, suiting me for retirement, especially for violin practice under a master of that instrument, and for preparation of school work. But occasionally my friends would call around and while away the hours in pleasant conversation. Professor Bentley was, of course, among my number of callers. One evening he came and asked me where I would be the following Wednesday night, the very night, by the way, that his appointment for conducting the meeting had been made. I told him that I would certainly be in my roof if he was coming around to see me. He did not promise, but was very anxious to know that I would be at home.

Some time after that prayer-meeting he came to see me and told me what happened at the meeting and following it. He also told me that he was particular about knowing my whereabouts that Wednesday night, as he wanted to known that I would not be at the meeting, as my presence would embarrass him in his efforts to preside. He then told me that the meeting was a success; that he had given out some of the old Upper Essex Baptist songs and sang them with the congregation in full voice, and it was loud enough, I am sure. He said after the meeting was over the members just thronged around him and congratulated him on his successful conducting of the meeting. He said he was just elated over all of this fuss being made over him, and that he felt like celebrating his success, so he went on up the street, got with some of his old partners and got on the "biggest tear" he had been on for many a month. I don't think he was present at the next roll call at the prayer-meeting. Who else on earth would have done all this, and who else would have told it on himself? That was Bentley—honesty and he were mighty good friends.

One summer, after the close of his school in Louisiana, he was on his way home as far as Fredericksburg. There he found liquid refreshments to suit his desire. It was a fearfully hot day. In the afternoon he had gone down to the steamboat, awaiting her departure, and there he was hotter than he was uptown, for I do not think there is any place this side of Bagdad any warmer than a steamboat while lying at a wharf. Well, the whistle blew, the moorings cast off, and the boat went a-tripping down the stream, and with this a pleasant breeze sprang up, truly delightful to the perspiring passengers. Bentley had gone to the tip end of the upper deck, and with one foot on one railing and the other foot placed likewise on the other rail, with coat unbuttoned and thrown back, he was having the full effect of the delightful change. An old friend, who did not know he was aboard until he saw him sitting there, walked up behind him and said, "Hello, Bob, I didn't know you had come back." His only reply was, "Mr. Gresham, I am now celebrating the close of my school." And he *was,* in full force.

His maiden sister occupied the old home, and with her many a summer Bentley would spend. She knew him well, and was always lenient towards him. One summer she was expecting him most any day, and was prepared to give him both welcome and comfort after his strenuous year's labors. He came to Milford and drove over to his home. He was not exactly expected that day, but soon, anyway. When it was time to consider supper preparations, Bentley's dear old sister said, "Robert, what do you want for your supper?" "Oh, Sister Betty, just anything, don't you put yourself to any trouble on my account, just anything." "Yes, but, Robert, the girl and I don't generally have a hot supper, but we are going to cook for you just anything you want that we have in the house. I knew you were fond of salt herring, and I sent over to Lloyds the other day and bought a barrel of Potomac roe herring just for you." "Sister Betty," he replied, "you couldn't have suited me better." "Well, Robert, how many must we cook for you, because we don't eat them at night?" "Sister Betty, I reckon you had better cook about ten." And, being of the matter-of-fact kind, she carried out his instructions.

From his telling, I feel safe in saying that he celebrated a time or two before supper. Now, to use his own statement, "Garnett, I was hungry after that long drive, and I had whetted up several times before the supper bell rang. It was a delightful sound to me, that old bell that had called me to my meals hundreds of times. Well, sure enough, she had cooked ten salt herring. That yellow butter, those rich biscuits, that strong coffee, and those herring almost swimming in gravy, just made me as happy as a lark.

"Well, sir, I ate seven of them. That's a fact, seven. We talked a little while after supper and then I went up to my old room. I was soon asleep. I reckon it was about midnight that I waked up, and, sir, I never was as thirsty before in all of my born days. And, the worst of it was, there was not a drop of water in my room. Well, sir, I put on my shoes and crept downstairs, for I didn't want to wake Sister Betty up. I went down to the old spring, right near the house, and there is not a better spring in all the country, the moon was shining bright, but I could not find a cup or can, so I got down on all fours, cow-fashion, and I drank her dry. That's a fact, and it's a bold run, too. I could almost hear the water frying as I drank it, and never in all of my life did water taste as good as the water from that old spring that night."

So many things of an unusual character could I relate. But these must do, and maybe that I have said enough to give a picture of this unique character, the like of whom I may never even hope to meet again.

XXI

The WARE-HUNDLEY WEDDING

THERE was a beautiful marriage at Rappahannock Christian Church Tuesday evening at 8:30 o'clock, Mr. Burwell Ware, of Ware's Wharf, and Miss Pearle Garnett Hundley, of Dunnsville, being the contracting parties. The Rappahannock is an unusually large and handsome building, and with the graceful, tasty decorations, made with great banks of white chrysanthemums and festoons from floor to ceiling of the modest but lovely running cedar and flooded with lights from gilded candelabra and chandeliers, it was imposing and beautiful. The white and green color feature was carried out in every conception. Why, it was the whole thing. Your correspondent knows how to write a negro dialect story to beat tan bark, and he does not drop his quid in despair when it is a love letter for a heart-sick "coon" whose dusky maiden has gone off to Baltimore or "Jarsy," but, Saints alive, when it comes to describe a wedding with all of those costumes interlaid with French names and dressmaker's technicalities, he is bewildered, nonplussed, flat of his back with both skates off.

"Tell us about the wedding," they said as soon as we got back home. "Oh!! it was fine, beautiful, the prettiest country wedding we ever saw, and but few in the city can beat it!" we shouted all in one breath. "But the arrangement, the costumes, the designs, who was there, the music, how the bride looked, was the groom scared, did the children do their part well?" "Hold on there, for patience sake! and give us that in sections," we answered; "we are not charged with a phonograph. "But you are going to write it up for *The Free Lance;* why did you not take everything down?" "Couldn't do it. Too much for us. Just sat there and looked." But after we got away from all of those questions and sat down to solid thinking, this much of the occasion came back out of the labyrinth of the complicated, but beautiful, whole:

The platform in front of the sacred desk had been enlarged. It was snowy white, all but the borders of green. A dainty, soft-looking white cushion was in the center.

Festoons of green, doubled and tripled, swayed and shadowed the wall with shapes and fancies. The lights were brilliant, but there was a softness, perhaps a sacredness, in their white flames. We saw ribbons stretched and ushers busy. And the crowd began to swell and to swell until the seats groaned. And then there came from the organ a melody divine, soft at first, but growing louder and louder, with shrill treble, and trembling diapason, and pouring out its songs and its sighs until every nook and corner was flooded with the music. Then there came eight children in white and green and formed a sacred, living aisle of flowers. Then we saw the man of God walk in front of the sacred desk and stand. He was in black. His face told a serious mood. He knew that it was he who would strike the last wedge and launch a craft of hearts on the turbulent sea of dual life. We saw two maids of honor come and stand stately and queenly on each side of the aisles of flowers. And then there followed eight great, stalwart, broad-shouldered sons of old Virginia, and they marched with dignity and grace and stood near the maids of honor.

Two dames of honor (these were sisters of the bride) came and stood near the maid of honor. The bride came next. Her veil was caught with a brooch a hundred years old, and trailed along, dragging a bit of ivy leaf with it. Her necklace was once worn by her future mother, when she, too, was a bride. We saw her brother at her side, and in his hand we saw a sacred vellum "Marriage Vow." We saw her pause at the "Aisle of Flowers," and then steal away from her brother dear and join her lover, so true and tried in his love, and then together march arm in arm along the flowery aisle to go and seal their plighted faith with sacred vows. We heard the music grow soft and the prayer ascend, and the low, steady voice of the clergyman in questions serious, and the answers.

Then we saw the ring-bearer and her page trip along. We heard them promise their lives each to each, and then the benediction. The organ swelled, the procession reversed and outward marched, and then followed the crowd. The marriage was over.

Rev. J. T. T. Hundley, of Norfolk; Judge E. M. Ware, of Tappahannock; Dr. DeShazo, of Centre Cross; Mr. Maury Hundley, of Newport News; Mr. Preston Hundley, of Hampton; Dr. W. W. Hume, of Beckley, W. Va.; Mr. Charles Sale, of Tappahannock; Mr. Robert L. Ware, of Ware's Wharf; Mr. Muscoe Garnet, of Essex; Hon. William Campbell, of Essex, and W. D. Hoskins, Esq., of Dunnsville, were among the many gentlemen present at the marriage.

Miss McCarthy, of Richmond; Miss Warner, of Ware's Wharf; Miss Latané, of Westmoreland; Miss Jennie Croxton, Miss Della Wright, Mrs. R. C. Phillips and Mrs. George N. Anderton, of Tappahannock; Misses Campbell, of Campbellton; Misses Garnett, of Inwood, and Mrs. R. L. Ware, of Ware's Wharf; Mrs. Laura M. Garnett and Miss J. L. C. Garnet, of Cottage Park; Misses Newbill, Misses Street, Mrs. Kate Dillard, of Centre Cross; Mrs. R. G. Neale, of Bowler's, and Mrs. Hannah Hoskins and daughter, of Miller's, were among the scores of prominent ladies present. Miss Hundley is the youngest daughter of the late Professor J. T. Hundley, of Essex, and granddaughter of the late Judge Muscoe Garnet, of Ben Lomond, this county. Mr. Ware is a son of Mr. Robert L. Ware, of Ware's Wharf, and a grandson of the late Dr. James Latané, of Upper Essex.

The presents manifested the great popularity of the bride and groom. Mr. and Mrs. Ware left Wednesday by the Rappahannock Line of steamers for Baltimore and from there to Norfolk and there by Fall River Line to Boston. After December 1st they will be at home at Ware's Wharf.

Dunnsville, Va., November 4, 1904.

XXII

A RECIPE *for* SILENCING SOME AGENTS

NEITHER by nature nor by culture am I given to impoliteness, nor do I lack a reasonable supply of patience, but many a time have I, without lieve or license, or previous notice, been ushered into the realm of absolute, unmitigated boredom, and, unable to help myself, though I might have had in mind shotguns, pitchforks and all sorts of other implements to be used for speedy removal of the harmless but boring agent, for, indeed, when an agent is thoroughly filled with his prospect and keenly whetted for the occasion he generally has you bound tight and fast.

I love to see "green things a-growing," and during the summer I was in the field when not in my office. One hot day I was running a double plow in my stable lot, as it was called, and the land was not light. Still, the team were moving along with comparative ease. I was robed, not like Solomon in all his glory by any means, but in light garments, and old, suited to the weather and the work. I wore a very broad-brimmed, high-peaked felt hat, good in its time, but the worse for wear then. More to amuse my little boys than for any other purpose, I had stuck a lot of long rooster feathers between the band and the hat, Indian-fashion, for appearance. I was driving along very quietly when I saw coming across the field a man bearing a satchel in his hand, and as he got closer I suspected that he was an agent for the sale of some commodity, I knew not what. We exchanged salutations, and he at once proceeded to business. He had heard that I wanted to place slabs over the graves of my honored dead. This was correct, but that was not my time for entering into a contract. The weather was hot; the horses were hot; the land was hard and hot, and I, to be sure, was no exception to the general heat conditions.

He had a beautiful speech, I give this to him; the purity of the Grecian marble, the black Egyptian marble, the marble of Vermont, and of everywhere else that marble ever had been found, all of the history, all of the beauty, and all of the weather-resisting quality came fluently without catching a breath. But when he reached the Tennessee marble, of which his slabs were made, he rose to the highest pitch of oratory, and there was no possible telling when the end would be reached. I was leaning against my plow handles in closest attention. But I was plotting against him and only waiting for an opening.

Some years ago I had memorized a so-called speech made by an old gentleman who lived in one of our mountain counties, and for absolute conglomerated nonsense it cannot be surpassed. I watched him very anxiously, for I had determined to give him this speech.

He stopped to get a long breath, and I knew that was my only hope. So at once I began in loud tones, and with numerous gestures: "By the blood of the American eagle that whipped out the universal gamecock of creation, and now sits perched upon the electric telegraph of time's illustrious transmigration, let me encourage you to do better, sir! And the only way for you to raise yourself in the estimation of the people's minds in and around the vicinity of Dunnsville is to catch yourself by the fathomless parts of your boottops and to erect yourself to a zenith far above these people's understandings, and then to dip the holy pen of mediocrity into the golden bowl of superstition and then to write upon these men's foreheads the infallible rule of right conglomeration. Amen, sir."

He was sitting on his sample-case, gazing at me in openmouth wonder. I then asked him if he had any chewing tobacco "about him." To this he replied that he neither smoked, chewed, drank nor "cussed." I told him he was mighty poor company for me, then. He asked for instructions how to reach the village. They were not denied. And the last I saw of him he was ambling along, now and then turning to get one more look at me, and perhaps wondering then, as he wondered so many times later, but never able to reach a satisfactory conclusion, whether he had met an escaped lunatic or just a natural-born fool.

One day I was in my office at work. Without knocking in came a very nice-looking man, tall, well-dressed, but wearing no hat, nor did he have an umbrella, though it was raining a little. I asked him to take a seat, but he preferred to stand. Forthwith he drew from his pocket a bunch of tracts and began to give me the history of the Mormon church from the days of Joseph Smith, Brigham Young, and all the rest of the high potentialities to the present. I did not want to offend him, and in the same ratio I did not want to listen to him.

My opportunity came, and I gave him in full force the same dose I had administered to the tombstone agent. It was effective. I have tried it on range salesmen and soap sellers. It has great power and speedy relief for me.

XXIII

BOB *and the* PANTHER

About the time of the threatened struggle between the North and the South there was great unrest among the slaves, for they had heard there was going to be a war, and that they were going to be free. They had also heard that, could they get up North somewhere, they would be safe—in few words, a mighty stream of propaganda had been poured in among them, and their present conditions and their future prospects were often discussed secretly among themselves. Frequently there was talk of run-away negroes, and more than one den was found in the woods where some negro was in hiding. There is an old den in the writer's woods which was the home of run-away slaves during the Civil War. The owners, to prevent the negroes from leaving the farms at night and, maybe, preparing to escape, organized what they termed patrol bands to watch the negroes and to demand that their *pass* be shown, and if one was caught off of the farm and had no pass his punishment was pretty severe. Hence the origin of the old song:

> "Run, nigger, run! patterrol ketch you!
> Run, nigger, run! 'tis almost day."

Bob Turner was a good and faithful slave, but he was a part of the time separated from his wife by the broad Rappahannock, as his master owner farms on both sides of the river, and Bob's home was on the opposite side when this story begins. But on Saturday nights he generally got a pass from his master and then went to see his wife and children. In addition to the patrol bands to keep the negroes at home, there was widely circulated the report that panthers were in the woods, and many of them in the woods through which Bob's journey to see his wife lay. He was dreadfully afraid of these beasts, as well he might be, when the report carried with it that panthers made a specialty of feeding on negroes. But in spite of all this, Bob decided to make the effort to see his wife one stormy Saturday night. But let Bob tell his own story.

"You see, I hadn't been to my wife's house for ober two wicks, and I was jest bound to see how she and de chilltren was gitting along.

"'Twas a stormy night, let me tell you, wid de wind from de northwest. I had my own boat, case old marster 'lowed us oystermen to have our own boats and catch oysters to sell to de vessels dat came right up dare op'site de house, and paid us in gold for 'em. Ob course, I couldn't sell de boat, but I called it mine, case dat was de one I always used.

"We had to give old marster so much ob what we made and we kept de balance. Some ob de colored folks made right smart, and it has been said dat some ob 'em buried what day had, and it hain't nobody dat's ebber found it from dat day ketch dis.

"So I went down to my boat and got ready. Man, de waves was jest a-rollin', but I shoved her out from de sho' and struck for de other side. I was a man den, let me tell you, and 'twant a man on dat sho' could beat me rowing a boat. When I got to de channel de boat was jest a rearing like a horse. It was so dark I had to go by guess. You see, de wind was hitting me broadside, and she was shipping water sometimes, but I kept right on as hard as I could drive. I happened to see a light on de other side, and I knew de house de light was shining in. Well, sar, I got across at last, and got my boat up in a little crick and tied her. 'Twas a trip, sho's you born.

"Well, I started 'cross de field, going t'wards de big woods dat I had to go thru. All at once it come to my mind 'bout dem panters roaming round in de woods looking for colored people. De more I thought 'bout dem, de scareder I got. I had nebber seen a panter in all my life. But dey told me dese an'mals made dare libbin' eatin' colored people. I got to de woods and struck de path dat lead thru dem to a wide field. De wind was jest a-howling den. Sometimes a lamb would fall down off one ob de trees, and I thought ebbry time a limb fell 'twas a panter right arter me. I didn't lose no time, I tell you, gitting thru dem woods. Presen'ly I come to de fence jest 'fore you gits in de field, you know. Well, sar, I went ober dat fence in a hurry, and I was jest kinder feeling safer, when here come somethin' that knocked me sprawling on de ground. I jumped up and tried to run, but he had me agin' 'fore I could git away. I didn't hab no stick or nuthin' to fight him off wid. It was dark as pitch. I reached out and grabbed him by both his ears, and, man, we had a time!

"I weighed 'bout two hunnerd pounds den, and I was strong, let me tell you. He was a-rearing and a-charging to git hold ob me. He had his tongue out jest like he was hungry for me. I wanted to see what kind ob feet he had. So I let go wid one hand and reached down, but jest as I did dat he hit me full in de bres' and like to knock de very wind outen me. So I helt him wid both hands agin. I kept on backing t'wards de udder side ob de field. It tooken a long time to back 'cross dat field, but dat was de onliest way to save myself.

"Well, when I got in 'bout fifty yards ob de fence I let him go and ran for de fence. Man, I was a powerful runner in dose days, and when I hit dat chestnut rail fence I was almost flying, I tell you. I tried to jump ober it, but I hit de rider rail and fell a-sprawling on de udder side. Neer mind dat, I got up a-running, and soon I could see de light in my wife's house. I was nearly outer wind when I got dare, wid my hat in my hand, a-sweating like a horse. Man, I flung myself gin dat door and off she come. I picked it up and put it back on de hinges quick as I could and was trying to prop it when de old lady says, 'Bob, what is de marter wid you? You scared us all nearly to deth, de way you come in de house.' I told her 'twant no time to talk den, case a panter was right arter me. I nailed up de doors and de winders, and we hardly slept enny dat night, 'specting dat panter all de time.

"Arter de old lady had done cooked som'in' to eat next morning I thought I would go down dare whur I jumped ober de fence and see if I could find de panter's tracks out dare in de field. Well, bless de Lord, I hadn't more den gotten ober de fence den here come a littl runt two-year-old bull dat had been turned out dare. 'Fore I know'd it, here he come and butt me sprawling on de ground. 'Hi,' I says to myself, 'you is de panter dat was arter me last night, is you? Well, I'll fix you, sho's you born.' So I went back in de woods and cut me a long hickory switch dat would reach from his head to his tail. I got back ober de fence and here he come. I grabbed him by his tail, and if I didn't lay it on dat bull it was a caution. Round de field he went, jest a-bellowing, and I laying it right on him. I told him he wan no panter. No, indeed. Pren'ly we come near de fence, and dare stood de old lady dat had come dare to see 'bout me. 'Hi, Bob,' she said, 'dat hain't no panter. Dat's jest Marse Robert's little bull. De chillen larnt him to butt likt dat. He was jest a-playing wid you.'

"I told her, 'Yes, and I's jest a-playing wid him now. He won bother me de next time I comes 'cross dis field, play or no play,' and he never did."

XXIV

MARSE FRANK

DID I know Marse Frank?" said Bob. "How come I didn't know him, when I b'longed to his mammy and was born and fotched up right dare on de same place? Ob course I knowed him. I was a leetle older den Marse Frank, but he growed faster den I did and soon kotched up wid me. Old miss kinder put dat boy in my charge for playing and doing.

"I 'members one day old miss had done fixed Marse Frank up in a white suit, and he looked mighty fine. She told him to come out in de yard to play wid me, but he mustn't git no grass stains on his white pants. We played around, and arter a while Marse Frank asked me to go down de meadow wid him. Well, 'twas muddy down in dat meadow, and dare was a right deep little crick dat ran 'long it. So we-all played around dare and Marse Frank slipped up one time and down in de mud he went. He was a sight. Ha, ha, ha! I 'members it. Yes, sar, he was mud from head to foot. So I kinder helt him in de crick to wash him off. Dis didn't do no good, for he was jest streaked when he come outen de crick. So I knowed we had to go back arter awhile, anyhow, and we jest well go den. When old miss seed dat boy she was a-raring. And she axed me what I had done wid her chile. I told her I hadn't done nothin' 'twas de mud dat did it. She told me to come to her. I went. She had an old cowhide switch. Man, she like to have worn me out, and when she let me go I went out in de yard and bellowed louder den I did in de house. She come to de door and told me if I didn't stop dat fuss she'd give me somin' to cry about. I thought I had 'nough den.

"Arter while Marse Frank come out in de yard wid a whole pie in a tin plate; half un it, he said, was mine. I stopped crying right away. I used to go to school wid Marse Frank when he had done grown up to be a right good-size boy. I mean I went long wid him to take his books and snack. He allays saved me some ob his snack. De teacher certainly did talk funny. Day say he was a Yankee. He called me a little *rascal* one time when I made some fuss outen dare waiting 'round. If he had been one ob our kind ob people he would have said *roscal.* Dey tells me dat *rascal* means de debble, but *roscal* is jest kinder funny, like when you playing wid somebody and call 'em dat. Well, sar, one night old miss called me 'bout 12 o'clock and told me somin' was arter her fowls. I was a right big boy den. I allers sleeped in de big house on a little pallet. Well, dat night I ran as fast as I could fly, and when I got dare to de henhouse ebrything in dare was just a-squarking and a-cackling. I had a stick in my hand, and I opened dat door. I was barefooted, and soon as dat door was open here come sumin' a-crawling ober my feet. I shot down on it and kept on beating on it. 'Twas a snake, man, dat what 'twas. De biggest black snake I ebber seen since I was born. But I kilt him, yes, sar, I kilt him. Old missus was sartin'ly proud case I had done kilt dat snake. De next day she told me to hang him up a tree, case we was having a drought and dat would make hit rain, so I hung him up, and dat night, sho 'nough, dare came up de heav'est storm we'd had in many a day. De ditches and de gullies was all filled up. So Marse Frank didn't go to school dat day, and old missus said we could play in de house and 'muse ourselves.

"Ha, ha, ha! Lordie, we sho did 'muse ourselves dat day. We went up in de garret, whur we had nebber played 'fore in our lives. Dare was a great big old clock put up dare, jest to keep it outen de way. She was one ob de kind dat ran for a week 'thout winding agin. I don't know when she had been winded up, but when Marse Frank got to projecking wid de works, man, sar, she started, and you nebber hearn sich a fuss since you was born. Seemed like she nebber guine to stop. Old missus come to de foot ob de hall steps and axed what in de world we was doing, making all dat noise in her house. I told her 'twant we-all, 'twas dat old clock. It stopped presently, and I was glad un it. We got to foraging around in de garret, and way ober in one corner dare was a bag dat had 'bout a bushel ob walnuts in it. De old bag must hab been left dare for years. Me and Marse Frank dragged it to de head ob de steps so we could 'zamin it, and, bless de Lord! soon as we got it dare de old bag busted and down de stairs, clean into de very bottom hall, dose walnuts went a-pouring. I knew dare was guine be trouble. We kinder helt our breath. Soon old missus hollowed up dare, and axed what on earth we was up to den. I told her 'twant we-all, 'twas de walnuts. She made us pick dem all up and fling dem away, case, she said, day was too old to be fitten to eat.

"Well, we got our dinners, and old missus said it had dried off right smart, so we could go outdoors and play. Dat was good news for we-all, I 'members it mighty well. Marse Frank said for us to go down to de barn and play. When we got down dare, Marse Frank said dare was a great big brass bell inside de barn, and dat it had a strop and a buckle on it, and let's we-all go and put it on a calf dat was stopped up to keep him away from his mammy. He was a good-size calf, but he had nebber hurd a bell ring since he was born. So we went in dare whur he was in a stall, and I helt de tongue ub de bell whilst Marse Frank buckled it on him. Well, sar, I let go de tongue, and Marse Frank he let go de calf. He made a break for de door and outen he went wid his tail sticking out straight behind him, and jest a-bellowing as loud as he could, and, don't you know, 'twant no whur else in de worl for dat calf to go but right t'wards de front yard, whur old missus could hear him and raise de debble 'bout what we-all had done done. Round and round de house he ran jest a-raising de headest fuss, he and de bell, you ebber hueard. De calf's mammy hueard him bellowing, and here she come a-trotting and a-calling to him. 'Twas a time in dat yard dat day. And den here come all de cattle outen de pasture, for day had done broken out. De yard was jest full ob cattle, and all ob dem was bellowing like dey does when dey smells whur a beef has been kilt. But dat bell made more fuss den any ob dem.

"Old missus came outen de house wid dat old cowhide switch in her hand. She came straight to me, and said, 'Now, you come here, sir, I cannot stand this any longer.' Jest as she grabbed at me, and I was 'specting to be nearly kilt, here come dat calf around de corner ob de house jest a-flying, and a-bellowing, he and dat bell. Well, sar, he hit old missus plum in de back, and down she went in a puddle ob water in de walk. She couldn't git up and jest kinder rolled around in dat mud and water. She was a big 'oman, old missus was, and 'twas hard for her to git up anywhur. Lordie! how I wanted to laugh, but I dasn't. She told me and Marse Frank to come and help her up. When we got her on her feet she said, 'Now, just look at me, and see what you have done.' I told her 'twan't me, 'twas de calf. She was certainly a sight. Then she said, 'Now, you go and tell the hands to come to de house and take all ob this stock out of my yard.' I went fast as I could, but, somehow, arter I got away from old missus I couldn't laugh a bit. Was you ebber in dat way?

"But don't you know she nebber did do one thing to nuther one ob us. She was a good 'oman, she was, and she know'd we was sorry. Yes, I reckin I did know Marse Frank, and his pappy, and his grandpappy 'fore him. Yes, indeed."

XXV

BAYLOR *and the* BULL

IN old Virginia it is not uncommon for those who have highland pasture to trade the use of their pasture certain seasons of the year with those who have salt-water pasture. This refers to Tidewater Virginia, of course. In the early spring, when the young and tender marsh grass is like a green carpet all over the newly burnt marshes, the stock get rolling fat. But later the grass is tough, and flies and mosquitoes molest the stock so that they suffer. Then it is that the farmer with his upland pasture can return the favors extended by his lowland neighbor earlier in the season, when the grass had not hardly started to grow on the hills.

Be all this as it may—for I mention it simply as a matter of local history—but not long since I had made arrangements with a good neighbor bearing the time-honored and very popular name of Jones to take a two-year-old red bull from his marsh to my pasture. In order to drive the aforementioned bull from Jones' pasture to mine, I secured the services of Baylor, an overgrown colored lad of, perhaps, eighteen summers. Baylor was dressed in a pair of white pants, very tight in the legs, and fully six inches too short. He wore a high collar and a very long coat. This garment was also white, but not bearing any seeming relationship to the pants. His stockings had fallen down and were hanging about his legs in an exaggerated golf style. He wore a cap with a very long brim, and this was turned back, imparting a kind of devil-if-I-care air about the ensemble of Baylor. He announced himself ready to go after the bull. I took in the make-up of Baylor very thoroughly as he stood before me costumed for most anything else rather than driving a wild young bull from a muddy marsh. He is particularly long of limb, awkward in his general movements, wears about a ten and a half shoe, and slow enough at all times, unless the music of the mouthharp falls on his musical ear, and then he is as agile as a cat and as quick as a flash in his dance movements, bending his lithe body almost to the floor as he backsteps and claps his broad hands.

We soon reached the house of good neighbor Jones, and after he had given Baylor full and very minute directions as to finding the cattle, and just how to get them off the marsh he and I went into the house. Now, be it remembered that in this marsh there are divers and sundry muskrat holes. These creatures perforate a marsh as worms and moles perforate the higher land. In fact, some marshes are so cut up by the works of the muskrat that thy are unfit for grazing, as the cattle mire in the soft and deep mud. This marsh was literally infested with the rats. This had not entered into Baylor's mind, however, when he was making his toilet for the bull driving.

Mr. Jones and I talked on various subjects for an hour or more. We had lost sight of Baylor in our thoughts. After a while Mr. Jones said, "Look here! I wonder what has become of that negro. He must be lost out there in the marsh. My cattle are as gentle as they can be, and he should have no trouble to get them up."

We went down to the barn, and in a few moments here came the cattle, coming lazily along, and Baylor, armed with an immense stick, came plunging after them. I did not make even a rough estimate of the number of muskrat holes in that marsh, but it is safe to say that Baylor had formed a very intimate acquaintance with a large percentage of them. He was muddy from head to foot, and especially from the top of those white pants to the bottom seam thereof. In fact, the color line had disappeared. There was a grimness and a determination evidenced on Baylor's face never noticed before. He was clearly ready for any fate before him. A sad but powerful resolution. The cattle were easily driven into the pen. Mr. Jones then began to give me the pedigree of the bull. He was a great mixture. I really believe the bull knew as much of his family history when friend Jones was through as I myself did. But he was *in parte and in toto* a very well-bred animal. Still, I cannot say he was much for looks. At least, not at this time. The mud and the flies and the marsh grass had not been factors along the beauty line. "Well, give me the rope, Baylor, and I will tie him for you. He is perfectly gentle. My little son can drive him anywhere."

Baylor did not seem to agree with Mr. Jones. He had one arm slung over the fence and was standing in a very loose-geared manner. His eyes were fixed on that bull. The bull's eyes were fixed on Baylor. They were mutually impressed. I stood by the bars and watched the proceedings. There was some fun ahead. I could feel it in the very air. The bull objected to the rope being put over his horns, but while his eyes were very strongly centerd on Baylor, Mr. Jones caught him unawares and placed the rope just as he wanted it. "All right, now. Take hold of the rope and drive him right along. You (addressing me) can pull down the bars and let him come."

Baylor advanced cautiously, took hold of the rope as directed, and signified to the bull that it was time to move. The bull did not budge. As Baylor walked around in the course of his attempts to make the animal start, the bull managed to turn his head so as to follow Baylor with his eyes. Mr. Jones said, "Never mind! I can start him. You just hold the rope. That is all that I want you to do." He caught hold of the obstinate animal's caudal appendage, gave sundry twists and jerks and a kick. These did the work. He started, and the start was all sufficient. I gave him full right of way.

Here he came! His tongue was out, his tail was straight and on a level with his back. His eyes were wild. He bellowed with the force of some terrorized wild animal. Baylor was to him the devil and the deep blue sea combined and hitched close to him. There were roads leading from the barn. But none of them seemed to suit his course of rapid departure. There was a field of ripe tomatoes. This lay in a straight line from the bars. A mad bull and a fast-following negro boy at the end of a rope are not helpful to the market value of ripe tomatoes. This patch was Mr. Jones' pride. He had worked hard and long on this crop. Next day they would be taken to the market. Some of them were destined otherwise. Right through the best of the field the bull flew. The faster he ran, the louder he bellowed. Baylor struck the ground at intervals. Mr. Jones watched silently. He had pronounced the bull gentle. There was now nothing to say. The ripe fruit as well as the vines were flying in every direction. Baylor clung on heroically. On they went, cutting a regular swath through the patch. Presently Baylor's foot hung in a large tomato vine, and this, with the force he was going through the air, completely tripped him. Down he came broadside, seemingly nearly bursting himself open and causing the bull to turn a complete somersault. Mr. Jones and I ran as fast as we could to hold a probable inquest. But when we got there both were alive, if breathing hard. They were lying flat, but the bull had so squirmed around that his eyes were still fixed on his tormentor.

When we reached the scene of the disaster the first thing that Baylor said was, "Never mind, suh, but I got you." It was a matter of doubt on our part whether Baylor had gotten him or that he had gotten Baylor, for indeed the darkey was a sight to behold, for the tomato juice had not been any improvement on the marsh mud, of which Baylor had a bountiful supply before the race through the tomato patch. I feel safe in saying that he was not in fit condition either for attending church or to appear at luncheon among full-dressed guests.

We helped the bull to rise. And then, seemingly with conquered spirit, he was led along with no trouble, and thus ended the episode, perhaps one of the most amusing ever it was my good fortune to be somewhat a part of, for, since it was not attended by fatality, it all may be considered from the humorous point, and it was, of a truth, humorous to my neighbor and myself, but Baylor might not agree.

Some years have passed. Baylor is now in charge of a restaurant in Baltimore, and, I trust, doing well. But as long as his memory holds true, he will not forget his adventure when he raced through Mr. Jones' tomato field behind a terrified young bull.

XXVI
OLD UNCLE ROUZIE GREY

I WAS returning from my boarding-house to my lodging one beautiful Sunday morning, and observed an old negro sitting on the handles of a wheelbarrow right in front of my gate. The contents of the wheelbarrow were varied and numerous. I noticed some old garments, a basket of newly cooked food, a pile of bones in one corner, some old scrap iron in the other, a half-worn home-made hamper filled with jugs, bottles, several dilapidated umbrellas, an old coffee pot and a lot of empty fruit cans. As I stood looking curiously at the loaded hand vehicle the old man was rising by degrees, bowing as he rose, hat in hand, and repeating over and over again, "Morning, sur; morning, sur. Nice morning, sur." Where negroes are as thick as mosquitoes almost in that section of Louisiana, I had really noticed the wheelbarrow more than the man who was pushing it. But as he spoke so politely, I turned to him and said, "Well, old man, how are you getting along?" "Poorly, sur, poorly, I tell you. My back is all kilt up wid de rheumatiz." "With the wheelbarrow, you mean," said I. "No, sur; no, sur, dat ain't nutting! Hit's my back." I told him that I thought that load enough to break the back of a Texas mule. And I then asked him where on earth he got such a mess, and what he intended to do with all of it.

By this time he was as straight as I ever saw him afterward. And this means to say that he was very much in the position of a K reversed with the perpendicular omitted, unless an imagined elongated condition of his hickory stick, which he held behind him with both hands as if to prevent the aforementioned back from snapping, would supply it. "You see, I goes 'round ebbry Sunday mornin' and does little things for de ladies and gemmen, and dey gibs me dese things to take 'long home wid me. You know I cuarnt wuk now like I uster could. My back is all broke up and all dat, and I's gitting old, too. Yes, sur."

As he was delivering all of this information concerning himself I noticed every word he uttered, every gesture, every rise and fall of his voice. And when he was over with it, I said, "Look here, uncle, where are you from?" "Me, sur? I's from up here on de ribber [he meant the Mississippi, for that in Louisiana is always "*The* River"], but I's ben libbin' in dis town for some years now." "Do you mean to say that you were born and raised on the Mississippi?" "No, sur, no, indeed! Dat I want raised dere. I was fotched dere, dough, by de man who bought me. And I libbed up dere on his place for years and years, tell de war was all ober and de colored folks was free, and den I comed to dis here town, and here I's been off and on ebber sence."

"But where were you born? Where did your Louisiana master buy you? This is what I want to know." "Oh! he bought me in Richmond, Furginia. Dat's de place. But I wasn't raised dere, neder." "Well, where were you raised?—*that's* the question." "In old Essex County, Furginia. Now you got it, ain't you? I was born right nigh Lloyds, Essex County. I came outen de Rouzie 'state, and de Grey 'state, and libbed wid de Greys in a town dat dey called Toppohonnock, right on de Roppohonnock ribber, ten times bigger den ebber de Mississippi ebber was in her life, in de purtiest town in de State, where all de big men in de worl was borned and raised—de Croxtons, and de Farlands, and de Mi-koos, and de Gordans, and de Wrights, and de Rhones. But, bless de Lord, mister, I cuan't talk 'bout all dat now. Hit's 'nough to kilt me jest to *think* ob hit all." "I knew it, old man; I would have bet my last penny you were a Virginia negro. You haven't lost your pronunciation if you have been among the French for forty years and more." "No, sur, I ain't loss it, and I don't want to lost it, neder. But how you know I ain't loss hit? Whur you from?" "I live right here, too, and have charge of the schools of the city." I did not propose to let him know my home just then, for I wanted to hear him tell unrestrictedly more of a section that was near and dear to me. So I said, "Tell me more about that old country, uncle." "Tell you more 'bout it? Dere is ebbrything to tell. De fish and de oysters, de great houses, de old-fashion cooks and de eating dey could 'pare, old mistus, and old marster, and all ob de young marsters and mistussis, and de horses, and de cows, and de hunting wid de packs ob dorgs, and all ob my 'lations dat is up dere—I cuan't tell you 'bout dem, no, sur, I cuan't." Like a flash, it all was written.

I saw before me a thriving city. We were standing near one of the greatest trunk-line railroads in the country, over which the "Sunset Limited" flew, with but few stops between New Orleans and San Francisco. I saw the beautiful Berwick Bay silvered, save where the great steamers were troubling its sheeny bosom. I saw great tropical plants in bud or in flower and the bees gathering their sun-kissed sweets. I saw the song birds of rich plumage nesting in the semi-tropical trees and heard them sing to their mates. I saw the scarlet-throat lizards basking in the sunshine. I heard the Catholic bell, in powerful tones, call hundreds to "late mass," and the great trembling diapason of the organ, followed by "Te Deums" and "Sancta Marias" in full and splendid chorus.

I saw great fields of cane promising tons of sugar. I saw the live oak trailing its wayward branches in placid lakes, and fish dart upward and turn their silvery sides to the sun. I saw, in the distance, forests, where deer and wolves and bear roam temptingly for the sportsman. I saw the distant prairie lands, where purple plover pipe and the plump partridge whistles to his mate. I saw the mighty swell from the gulf come and meet the laughing ripples on the shallows. And I saw stately mansions beside the classic rivers, where Evangeline had sat and wept and thought of home. I thought of the wealth and the growth and the splendid future of this God-given land, whose soil is deep and rich, whose waters are peopled with fish of scale and of shell, whose climate offers work the year round, and whose forests could shelter millions and build railroads across the continent when their growth of oak and of cypress is given to the woodsman's axe, and whose nether veins were bursting with oil to light the student and to drive the engine—I thought of all these things, and yet before me I saw an old and feeble negro, whose heart was stoned against the wealth and the beauty of his surroundings, dying away slowly but surely, longing, tenderly longing, for old Virginia, the home of his childhood.

The old folks he had known (old when he left them, forty years and more ago) were still right there as he last saw them. The ashpone and the buttermilk, the old cook and her great chimney with its open fireplace, and the pot hooks, and the crane, and the boiling ham, and the little negroes standing around the kitchen door, daring not to trespass upon Aunt Diana's sacred domain, and the hickory fires in the parlor, and the old country-distilled applejack, and the crowds of "ladies and gemmen dat was staying at our house."

It was all as it used to be with him. His memory had lapsed over the cruel war, the graves of "marster" and of "mistus" had not been wet by his tears, nor had the favorite flower been taken from the garden and placed over them to grow and to scent the sacred air and drop its petals amid the soft dews and the evergreens.

He had heard that the war had devastated property and crimsoned the soil. He knew that the old slaves had been somehow fashioned into citizens. But his old mind could not grasp these things. I wondered if it were not better for me to let him remain in his blessed ignorance. But I did tell him who I was, and that from my old home I could look out upon that very old Rappahannock River, and that

I knew many of those great men (if not the greatest in the world, none greater in the love and in the respect I held for them), and that I had eaten those fish and oysters, and had watched Aunt Diana, or Aunt "Somebody," just as good a cook, with her great dishpans and her broom-straw home-made broom, and her big pots and kettles, and had eaten her best and richest and rarest cooking, time without number. That I had "whooped" to the dogs as they made the welkin ring with their great glory cries in chorus of deep-mouthed basso and tenor-shrieking clarions. That I had one time slept with "soft content for a pillow and never waked but to a joyous morning." That I knew every hog path and cross-road which he had mentioned. That, in fine, I was born and reared in the very county in which he had been born and reared. That I loved every grain of sand and every pine tag in it. That the flowers were not half as sweet to me anywhere else as the old home flowers. That the very water was wetter and cooler, and more fire-"squenching" than any other water that ever bubbled in well or burst from bank. That the birds there had a different song and a different melody in that song. That the very sun, moon, and stars had a kinder light at that old home than they could give me here or anywhere else on the top side of earth.

When I had finished my outburst of what came straight from the heart, the old negro's eyes were streaming. With his hat off, his poor old body bent, his nappy hair mixed with black, and sorrel, and gray, he said, "I knows 'tis de truf, chile! 'Tis de Gouard-Omighty's truf!" I suppose that this meant a perfect sanction of my sentiments. "Now, Uncle Rouzie, would you really like to go back there and see your old home. For if you do, I will try to help you."

"Go back dere? Me go back dere? Lord, mister, I would be so glad dat I 'spects 'twould kill me. I couldn't stand it! In course I would go, if I had de money to go wid. But dat is de trouble."

I told him to leave that to me; that I knew many of those in the town whom he had said were his friends, and that I would speak to them about it. He thanked me kindly and after many grunts and groans and many parting words, he raised the handles of his old wheelbarrow and pushed it slowly along. I went to my room and ran over the bass solo I had promised to do for the choir that day, and then repaired to the church. But amid the sermon, and amid the singing, and the organ swell and the happy faces before me, old Uncle Rouzie was not forgotten. The human was in that story of his too strong to be driven out of mind all at once. I kept my promise and talked to his friends. They responded very willingly (for there are not on this earth a more charitable people than you may find in Louisiana), and soon there was a purse raised quite sufficient to meet the poor old negro's expenses. But when he had thought over the matter (perhaps owing to the wise judgment of some one else) he decided that he would be like a stranger among those who had years ago been his own. So they let him keep the amount raised and this and the many other little presents given him I trust were all sufficient to make poor old Rouzie even happier than he would have been had he come back up here to find himself a stranger in a strange land. The river still flows on, and the old town still rests beside that lovely river, and the fish trouble its waters, and the oysters lie on its shelly bottom, and some of the old houses still stand on the hills; but the old folks have ceased to sing their evening songs, and old "marster and old mistus" have gone the way of their fathers. The old times, too, have gone. The new *regime* has bloomed and fruited in another generation, different in some respects from the old, but still a great and a progressive people, and just as true to their State as ever their fathers were, but they would not know poor old Rouzie and he would not know them. So we will let him rest where he is and may his last thoughts of this earth mingle the land of magnolias and sugar cane with the land of his home, the land of old times and good old negroes.

Upper—PROF. BENTLEY'S METHOD OF TEACHING THE DIVISION OF FRACTIONS
Lower—ONE OF MY JEWELS

XXVII

BOB BEAZLEY SHOOTS AT *A* "FLOCK" *of* DOGS

Bob has not lost any of his story-telling powers, if he has grown a little older since his big coon-hunt in the snow, a few winters ago. He was standing in a very loose-jointed position, and seemingly lost to his surroundings. The store was crowded. The country store in old Virginia is a royal place for negroes and stories. The ice a few years ago was yards thick. The wild pigeons used to come by millions and break down the forest trees. Old hares and coons were once as thick as English sparrows; and goblins and ghosts roamed the big woods. Such topics meet with specific orators, and the rest are as attentive as though a heavy fine would be imposed for breaking the silence.

This night dogs seemed to be the favorite subject. Some of the crowd were eating sardines; some pricing eggs; some trying to read their papers; but all were throwing in a word on the dog question. They could not have pleased Bob better. He was evidently preparing his speech. The whites of his eyes rolled as he turned towards first one speaker and then the other. He suddenly straightened himself up to his full height, pointed his finger in true oratorical fashion, and thus delivered his experience a few nights ago.

"Taxing dogs is not right. Now, I says dat pintedly! Kin I not keep a little dog and hunt him in peace? Got to pay a tax on him when he are not wof one cent cept to me? And he ain't wof dat less he is huntin' or somin' like dat. No, sar, I like dogs and I specks to keep dem, tax or no tax. My dog kin run to de woods and 'tect himself when de dog-killer comes around. My old marster didn't pay no dog tax and he was a *man,* I tell you! You 'spose I guine to even try to out-do him? No, sirree! Yes, I lubs dogs, but dare is such a thing as gitting too much ob eben what you lub. Just like night 'fore last. I was tired dat night, sho.

"I had been oystring all ob dat blessed day and come home late. I sot down dere by de fire and got good and warm and den etten my supper. I smoked a little while, I did, and den I went to bed. I had hardly dropped off to sleep before somethin' hit against my house, 'brim!' like 'twas guine tear ebrything to pieces. 'Hi!' says I, 'what is dat hitting 'ginst dis here house like dat?' I kinder listened and held up my head so I could hear. Here it come agin, and den dere was de headest dog-fight right under my house dat ebber you did hear in you life. Looked like dey was guine tear de very sleepers up. 'Gimme my gun,' says I, 'I wont stand habbing my house prized up from de ground for all de dogs in de county.' I went out wid old 'Lucy' in my hand. She was loaded wid number fours, and I knew she was guine wake dem dogs up. I giv a little yell and out dey come from under my house and jes as dey kinder bunched up as dey started across de yard, I cut down on 'em. Man, sir, de very air was libe wid flying dogs. 'Twas so unexpected, you know. Some jumped my paling fence, like 'twant no fence dare. Some busted through the palings like de heads was as hard as a ram's. But I thought I had laid out fully a dozen from de yells and howls dat came from de yard.

" 'Bring de light,' I said, 'and let me see how many I's got.' When de light done come, dere was but one. He was stretched out like he was dead as a stone. 'Hi,' says I, dis is old Pinter, if 'taint, I hope I may die!' Yes, sir, 'twas my *own* dog. And I wouldn't had taken fibe dollars for him any time. Dey helt de light closter and he seemed to hab some life in him. I made dem bring me a bucket ob water and I flung dat on him. Up he jumped! But, sir, his tail was shot clean off. 'Twant one inch long! Well, sir, how I shot into dat flock ob dogs and only kilt one (for you jess well say he is kilt, wid no tail,) is a mystery to me; and de worst ob it all is *'twas my own dorg,* you see."

XVIII

A CORN-SHUCKING BEFORE *the* CIVIL WAR

DID you ever go to an old-fashioned corn-shucking, with the corn piled high ready for the husking, and the moon at its full, a crisp November night, and the negroes full of song and—no, I did not say that they were full of anything else, but "old marster" always had a supply in his cellar, just as all the other "old marsters" had, and these were the times when apple-trees flourished and the product was not wasted? Well, you have missed something, something you can not possibly see now, for the "old marsters" are nearly all gone, and the old-time negroes nearly all gone, and the corn; well, there is yet some corn made, but the shucking is done by piece-meal, with few hands to help, and then there is no song, no rollicking laughter, no wrestling, and boxing, just as so many other things have changed, so has the saving of crops, and the old-fashion corn shucking is gone for good.

Ned was tall and as black as he was tall, and broad of shoulder, and as strong as he was broad. He was the king wrestler of the plantation, and no man could maul more rails or cut more wheat than Ned. He was good-humored generally, but not always. And when he was bad he was very bad, to say the least of it. He liked a dram occasionally, and sometimes took too much. But on the whole, Ned was not mean. Ned was the leader at the corn-shuckings in the songs, and boasted that he could shuck more corn than any other man on the farm, and that there was not a man in the county who could "dirty his back" in a wrestle. He was long of limb, and wiry in his actions, whether jig-dancing or boxing. Now, this was Ned as I can write him.

Old Kingston was the head-man. The rheumatism had crippled him up so that he did not work very much at this time, but he was still recognized as the head-man and held in high respect by the hands. The corn from the "flat-iron" field had all been gathered and placed in a long and high pile. The hands had been notified to be out ready for work as soon as they got their suppers.

Lucindy was Ned's wife. She was one of the washer-women at the 'great house," and a favorite of "old missus." Many a pound of brown sugar, and many a peck of flour did Lucindy take home when the day's washing was done. Lucindy was neat about her cabin and "old missus" had sometimes called by to see her and sat a while. "Lucindy, I'm going to give you a set of cups and saucers, and some knives and forks, and a table cloth, so you can have your table looking neat, and this will teach your little boy, Sam, and little Nancy to be neat. I want all of my servants to be tidy and careful." That was old missus' way in the house and out.

Lucindy had come back from her day's work, bringing her little children with her, for they always went along with her to the "great house" on wash days, and picked up the sticks in the yard, and hunted for eggs for "old missus," and many a treat of cake and preserves she gave them. The fire was blazing away in the broad fire-place, and Lucindy had made up her dough for the ash-cake, and was only waiting for the hearth to be really hot, and the coals ready to put on the cake after she had put a cabbage leaf at the bottom and then another on the top and piled on the hot ashes for the baking. The meat was all sliced ready for the skillet, and the tea-kettle singing a cheerful song, so the coffee would soon be made. The bucket of buttermilk was handy, for this was another one of old missus' provisions. A right good supper seemed in store—better, indeed, than many a one of the old negroes of that day ever have now, I fear. Lucindy was tired. She sat in an old, but comfortable, rocking chair for a few moments waiting for the fire to burn a little more that there might be coals in plenty. She began to rock, and as she rocked, she began in her high tenor to sing, "How tedious and tasteless the hours," but before she had reached the second verse, Ned came in. "Lucindy, is my supper ready? I's a hongry man, I is, and I's been wukking hard dis day. I wants my supper soon's I gits home from my wuk. Dat's what I want." Ned had persuaded old Uncle Kingston to give him a portion of the brandy that he had stored away in the barn for treating the negroes that night at the shucking. It may be that Ned had taken too much. He was crusty at any rate.

"You hain't wukked a bit harder den I is dis day. I knows dat." Ned did not agree with her and continued to grumble and complain, and wound up by saying: "I knows what I's guine to do. I's guine quit you right away. If I cuant git my supper when I comes home from wuk I's jest guine quit." "How you guine quit? You knows old marster hain't guine let you go no whur." "I don't kere if he won't, I's guine quit any how." Lucindy raked more coals on the ash-cake, poured the boiling water in the coffee-pot, and put on the meat to fry. Ned was quiet. Lucindy went over to her clothes-press and got out a white apron and put this on, and then reached up and got her Sunday bonnet. The little children, one on one side on a cricket, and the other on the other side on his cricket, were watching their mother's movements, for they did not think it was a time for visiting. Ned was watching his wife's actions, too. Lucindy, arrayed in her best bonnet and white apron, threw her head back and went out of the house. Ned rose and followed her. "Whur is you guine, Lucindy, dis time ob night?"

"Whur's I guine?" she replied. "I's guine to git me another man, dat's whur I's guine. You say you guine to quit, so I'm guine to git another man, better dan you is."

"Who is he, and whur you guine find him?" said Ned. "Ne'r mind 'bout you, I kin find him, and I haint guine tel you nuthin' 'bout him." "You better not tell me, case if you did I'd beat him to death dis here night." "Whur you guine beat him for? You said you guine quit me." Just at this juncture, one of the little children opened the door, and called out, "Mammy, de ash-cake is done and a'buning on top." "Lordie, 'pon my soul and body!" she said, as she darted back into the house. It was not long before the supper was all ready, and a little table drawn out to the middle of the floor; a chair for Ned, a chair for Lucindy, and a bench for the two little children. The coffee-pot and the tin sugar-dish at the head, the dish of fried meat with its gravy at the foot, the ash-cake and buttermilk in the center, formed enough to satisfy the appetite of the hungry family. "Ned, hain't you guine say grace?" Ned bowed his head, but no man knoweth what he said in thankfulness. The supper over, Ned arose and started towards the door. "Lucindy," he said, "I's jess guine to the shucking. I ain guine quit you sho 'nough." "I knowed you wasn't all de time," said Lucindy. "And I jess wanted to skeer you up a lettle, case I don't want no udder man, long as you 'haves yu'self."

Old Kingston called the hands together and placed them around the corn pile. "Now, boys, dare is 'bout twenty-five barrels ob corn in dis pile, case dat is what de flat-iron field most in generally makes. I's got a plenty for you all to drink, but I hain't guine gin you too much."

There they were, great, husky fellows, twenty-five or thirty of them. I can see them now. There was Caleb, broad-breasted and tall; there was Titus standing near him; there were John and Anderson and Roy—all brothers, that powerful Lindsey family. And old London, almost white, but a negro just the same. And Tom Lee, one of the dining-room waiters, just to enjoy the fun.

Old Kingston hobbled around and gave each of the men a drink of home distilled apple brandy. "Don't fling any corn in de shuck-pile, boys; wuk 'long steady."

The men went to their work in earnest. After a while, Ned, who counted himself the leading singer, jumped up on the pile and began to walk up and down, shucking and singing as he went. He would lead with a line or two, and the crowd would respond in full force. One of his songs ran this way, without rhyme or reason, in parts, but good for the shouting:

"Miss Sallie libbed on de Eastern Show,
And I hurd her sing in Bortimo,
And, ah hey, John, ah hey!
Round de corn, Sallie.
Oh, Sallie gal, I did not a' think you'd a' treated me so,
And hey, John, a' hey,
Round de corn, Sallie."

This and very much more they would shout and you might have heard those powerful and musical voices for a mile or more that crisp November night, as the chorus rose and fell in its majors and its minors, typical of the negro melodies, inherent, perhaps, and born in them generations ago, way back on the Guinea coast. No white man can fully imitate a negro in song—it can't be done, it is a part of him, as his laughter is his; his hair, his foot, his nose and his broad mouth with its broad smile. All his, and cannot be imitated, save in apology for the real negro.

After the jug had been passed around a time or two, Ned felt like starting something exciting. So he began to boast of his prowess. "Dare hain't a man on dis plantation kin put my back on de ground. Dare hain't one dat's guine try me, needer. And dare hain't a man I cuant whip. You knows dat. You needn't be looking at me, Jack, for I kin eat you up in a hurry." Little Jack wasn't so small, but smaller than Ned. He was strong and active and full of nerve. Ned held a grudge against little Jack, and was anxious to get even with him. It seems that Ned had hidden a bottle of brandy in the hollow of an old apple-tree back of the tobacco barn, and Jack had seen the operation. One night when Jack was poorly, or thought he was, he had gone and drank most of Ned's brandy. Ned had found it out, and the bad-feeling followed with many a threat. So when Ned gave his challenge personal to Jack, from the corn-pile, Jack felt then and there was the occasion to settle disputations.

Jack replied to Ned's insults by telling him that if he, Ned, wanted to eat him up, he could come right along and do so then. Hearing this, Ned jumped down off the pile, and, waving his hands and boasting and shouting, he ran towards little Jack. Jack was on his feet in a second and the "issue was joined." Old Kingston came hobbling along, and told the men that they had to box fair, for "dere hain't guine to be any kicking and biting and chokin 'lowed." There was one accomplishment which Jack possessed not mentioned in old Kingston's bill of exceptions—he was an expert *butter,* and it was said that he had butt down several cabin doors just to prove he could do it, and said if "Old Marster would give him 'mission', he could butt down the barn door."

I don't think Ned knew anything about this pugilistic item of attack. In fact, it does not appear that Jack had thought of it on this occasion, so busy was he in dodging the powerful blows of the big fellow aimed at him. But he could not dodge all, and those he received were fast telling on little Jack. Jack's friends saw this, and feared that he would not last much longer. One of these friends, knowing Jack's butting power, passed close to him, and whispered, "Butt him, Jack! Why don't you butt him?" The advice was savory and just in time, for Jack's wind was nearly gone. The little fellow watched his chance, and when Ned's arms were high, with his body exposed, Jack ran back a few feet, and then came like a battering-ram full force and unexpectedly square on Ned's stomach.

The effect was instantaneous and final, for Ned fell like a struck beef at full length on the ground. Jack's friends cheered powerfully. Old Kingston came hobbling along, and, leaning over Ned, he said, "Ned, is you hut? Is you hut much, Ned?" Ned was breathing hard. He replied to old Kingston, "No, I hain't hut so much, but I hain't got nö bruth left inside ob me." Cold water thrown in his face, and old Kingston's jug brought Ned to his feet, but not for a fight, and as he passed near little Jack he sulkily remarked, "Ne'er mind, sar, I'll fix you yit." But it does not appear of record that he ever did.

The shucking went on, and the singing went on, and ere chanticleer had sounded his midnight horn, the pile was all shucked and the men all gone to their cabins. And to their eternal homes long years ago, and it is pleasant to me to think and to hope that their rest is peaceful and a fulfillment of the visions and dreams they had cherished all of their lives.

XXIX

ARCH JOHNSON

The NOTED FIDDLER

OF all the old-time violinists I ever knew, there was not one equal to Arch, for truly he was an outstanding figure among the violin players of Eastern Virginia, and was known far and wide for his excellent dance-music, for, really, a ball in the country without Arch was a mere apology for a ball.

Arch was owned by the Motley family of King and Queen; and he had a musical atmosphere from his first breath, for his father was a great fiddler, and three of his young masters performed on the king of instruments, also. It was handed down that Arch's father's violin was buried in the coffin with him. I question this, however, and a member of the family told me it was not true. Whether true or false, the father did not bury his talents, for these fell in very strong and wonderful force on his son, who improved them fourfold and more.

Arch was left-handed. This was quite a handicap to the little black boy, who was trying so hard to play the fiddle backwards as the strings belong on the bridge. Some one came to his rescue and taught him to string the instrument in reverse order, and, of course, use his right hand for fretting the strings and his left for the bow. He soon caught the idea, and, with his wonderful ear for music, was soon playing simple tunes by memory, for Arch never knew a note in music—it was all by ear. Arch was a pet in the family and was allowed many privileges.

He soon was able to play with his young masters, and from them he learned all the tunes that they could play. So rapid was his development, that soon he was employed to play at public, as well as private, dances. When one had danced by Arch's music, he was not satisfied with any other. He became known from the Greenbrier White Sulphur to Old Point Comfort. His bow action was simply superb; from frog to tip his bow would go with perfect ease. In fact, he handled his bow as thought he were indeed playing with it—no frowning, and turning, and twisting of the body. He was the master, and the fiddle his willing slave, and a lovely service it gave him. Arch was of over the average size, maybe 5-10 in height, and weighing, say, 175. He was dark; in fact, nearly black. His countenance was open and his smile never to be forgotten; how could it be, when you had ever seen him while playing at his best, and those snow-white teeth shining like pearls, as he showed his delight at the dancers moving so gracefully to his music. Every tournament ball, every fish-fry, every political meeting, and any other occasion where music was expected, there was a call for this fiddler. His manners were perfect, and he was as graceful as a Chesterfield. So polite and so well known was the negro that many of the ladies would have Arch to come into the parlor and play for the guests, as some lady would play his accompaniment on the piano. He always knew his place, wherever he might be. Arch was never spoiled by his popularity. I remember a dance, when Arch played, that stands out in looking back to the long-distant past, that is fairly clustered with radiant flowers. On the bank of a broad and beautiful river there is a house bearing in every detail some history of the long, long ago—those large rooms, wainscoted, carved mantels, and spacious halls. And the large lawn where the lindens, and the maples, and the beech give their classic shade. An ideal house for a dance, an ideal lawn for the promenade, and an ideal river with the moonlight silvering it.

The guests had arrived from town and country. The extra touch on the ladies' cheeks had been made, and the extra polish on the gentlemen's boots was all done. They had come down from their dressing rooms, and were eagerly awaiting for the dance to begin, and it could be heard all over the room, "Has Arch come yet?" "Has Arch come?" They did not have long to wait, for presently the gentleman of the house made the announcement that the noted fiddler was there.

The guests were all waiting in one of the spacious parlors, while the other, robbed for the occasion of its massive furniture and ancestral portraits, with polished floor, was ready for the dancers. The sliding doors were drawn back and there stood Arch, with violin in hand continually bowing to the room filled with the guests, and addressing those he knew best: "Good evening, Marse Lal; good evening, Marse Junius; how are you, Marse Tom? Good evening, all of you, ladies and gentlemen." He then announced that he was ready for the grand march. When this was over, he called out, "The first set will be a quadrille. Please get your partners. That's right, just one more couple on the side. All ready now. Please listen to my calls and keep time to the music. I shall play 'The Ladies of Lloyds'." This was Arch's own composition.

Then followed "A Trip to Richmond" for the next figure in the set, and "Billy in the Low Grounds" for the last figure, for there were always three figures for each set for the square dances in those halcyon days. Arch tapped the back of his violin with his bow, which was always his notice that the set was over. Soon he called out, "The next will be a waltz. I shall play, 'The Voice of Flowers'." And he played it. I can see the dancers now gliding in measured grace over that polished floor. Not the hopping, and the bobbing, and the twisting and turning they have now, seemingly regardless of the music, but an expression of the poetry of motion. To be a graceful dancer was an accomplishment for any lady, and the men strove hard to deserve a compliment of the same merit. On they went, square dance, polka, waltz, schottische and galop, but the old square dance, so treasured by the old folk, was the most popular. Louder than Arch's violin, and louder than the gay laughter, was an ancient and venerable sound—the supper bell. And the gentleman of the house announced that there was room for twenty-five couples. And what a supper it was, with its boiled ham, roast pig, stewed oysters and so many other dishes, both tempting and gratifying. Arch was not forgotten. At a side table in the kitchen the spread before him was copious, and it would not be a vague stress of imagination to think that the master of the house, in the goodness of his heart, had offered Arch something rich and rare, which was not refused, maybe, even a second offer taken did no harm, for ten-year-old apple brandy, even in those days, was not often refused.

When Arch came up after supper he announced that by request he would dance a flat-foot jig, and play his violin at the same time. Side-shuffles, back-steps, and all the rest of the intricate and, to me, tangled and twisted movements, he executed with perfect ease and grace, while he played "Money Mosk" or some other tune equally as difficult to play, and as well suited to his wonderful movements. The ladies and gentlemen gave him a hearty cheer, and he deserved it.

For some time the dance went on. I can close my eyes and draw the picture vividly, and a beautiful picture it is stamped on my memory. Captain Roane, gallant soldier, tall and handsome; Junius Saunders, the leader of the dance, and the sweetest singer in all the country round; George Croxton, big of body and big of heart, and almost as handsome as his father; Waller Faulconer, moving with the rest, but not given so much to "the light fantastic;" Taylor

Woodward, smiling as he danced; Ernest Wright, ready for a joke; and so many others gliding along, as I recall them in my memory picture. But the ladies—well do I remember them, too, for the beauty and grace of the town and county, and the capital city, as well as another State, was represented in that gay and happy throng.

The dance went on—set after set—and continued pleasure. But it was already among the small hours of the night.

Arch tapped the back of his violin with his bow, and said, "Ladies and gentlemen, the next will be 'the Old Virginia Reel.' Please get your partners for the reel." I knew this would be the last. And may I say here that many who were in that happy crowd have long since gone the way of all the earth. Sad to recall, but true.

The lindens and the beechen trees still wave their branches among the other beautiful trees in that lawn, and the grass carpets it over as before, while the river is often silvered by the moonlight, and the birds build and sing undisturbed, and the flowers offer their perfume as of yore, but the host and hostess are not at the threshold to give their welcome. And Arch—well, he lived out the measure of his days. And don't you know it comes to me that a soul filled with nature's sweetest melodies here, and happiest when surrounded by those who loved music as he loved it, must be happy hereafter?

Yes, Arch has gone, and the old-fashion tunes are gone, and even the old fiddles must be gone, too, for they are not often seen or heard. The new day is upon us, with its new music, but do you think it is better, or that it touches the heart as the old and well-loved tunes of the past? I doubt it.

XXX

The HISTORY *of the* VIRGINIA MAD-STONES

REGARDLESS of pathological investigations to the contrary, there are yet many who believe, intuitively, if not logically, or experimentally, in the mad-stone, and it is not uncommon to hear of some one going miles and miles to have one of these stones applied when he has been bitten by a dog thought to have the rabies. It may be a matter of absolute *faith* in the curative powers of the stone, rather than the stone itself, but it is none the less a fact that few, if any, who have had the mad-stone applied, have ever suffered any ill-effects afterwards from the bite of dogs or poisonous reptiles. There is a bit of history connected with the old Virginia mad-stones which may be of interest to the reader of these simple, but true, sketches. Mr. Edward Tyler, of Loudoun county, owns one of these stones, and he gave me the following history of the mad-stone as it had been handed down through his family: "My grandfather, on my mother's side, Captain James Smith, was a Scotchman by birth, but came over to this country when quite young, and settled in Virginia. This was in the year of 1785. His first residence was in Richmond. His brother came over with him and remained in this country until he was seventy-five years of age and then returned to Scotland. My grandfather moved from Richmond to Dumfries, Va. It was quite a shipping port at that time, especially for tobacco. Captain Smith used to make long sea-voyages—going sometimes to Australia and the East India islands. On one of these trips he saw for the first time a mad-stone.

It was this way: He was lying near a little island of the East India group, and went ashore to trade with the natives. Among other things brought with them were some little blue, or dark-green, stones; flinty, and irregular in shape. Captain Smith asked the use of the stones. They replied by an object lesson. One of the men had a scorpion, and another held a cat. They made the reptile bite the innocent cat and in a few moments the creature rolled over in agony and soon after died. It had all of the symptoms of hydrophobia. Disgusted at such conduct, Captain Smith could scarcely prevent his men from doing violence to the natives for their cruelty. The situation was relieved, however, by one of the natives letting the scorpion bite him on the fleshy portion of his arm. At once this stone was applied. It stuck tight. After a little while it ceased to adhere. They then removed it and washed it. Again it was applied. And again it stuck. This process was continued for half an hour or more. When it finally refused to stick, the native whose arm had been bitten by the scorpion looked at Captain Smith very composedly and smiled, as if to say he had shown them what the use of the stones were, and how valuable they were. The astonishment of Captain Smith and of his men knew no bounds. They wanted to know where the stones were found. The natives told the sailors and Smith to follow them, and soon pointed to a place along the shore and told them to dig. To their delight a large mad-stone was unearthed. But it was found out later that this was only a trick, for one of Smith's men saw a native hiding a stone in the sand. Upon close questioning it was found that it was contrary to the law of their tribe to tell where the stones came from. But Captain Smith succeeded in buying some eighteen or twenty of the stones and brought them back with him to Virginia.

The legislature was in session at the time, and he gave some of them to his friends in that body, and the remainder he reserved for his relatives. This stone is one of that number. One of them was taken to Arkansas by the

Armistead family. Another is in Richmond in the King family. There is one in Washington. And my brother, who lives in this county, has one. There is also one in Essex county in this State. I can locate nearly all of them. And I know all of them to be of the number brought over here by my grandfather, Captain James Smith. As to the value of this stone, I could give several instances. There is not one particle of doubt on my mind that it will draw out poison of any kind. It does not matter whether it is a mad-dog bite, or a snake bite, or poisonous insect. It is a regular little suction pump for poison. I will give one instance: Jerry Jackson, a colored man, now living, and strong, and well, was bitten on the arm by a copperhead snake. I was sent for. When I reached the negro his arm was swollen to twice its usual size and then swelling rapidly. His sufferings were intense. I took my pen-knife and scratched the wound until it bled freely. I then placed this stone right on it. To my delight, it stuck fast. So soon as it was charged with poison it fell off. I put it in milk-warm water and you could see little bubbles rising and bursting as soon as they reached the surface. I think this was the poison. When it was cleansed I placed it back. It adhered as before. Well, I continued this process for eight hours, and when that stone failed to stick to the wound, Jerry's arm was its natural size, and he felt no inconvenience from the effects of the poison then, nor has he ever complained since. He is at work in the blacksmith shop now. You can ask him. Then I have known several persons not to use the stone, having no faith in it, and they died in the agony of hydrophobia; these persons were bitten by the same dog that had bitten others, who did apply the mad-stone and got well. I tried it to a finish test on a rattlesnake bite. That should satisfy any one. Nothing was used but this stone.

A colored child and a white child were bitten the same day by a mad dog. The colored child had the stone applied and recovered. They would not let the stone cure be used with the white child. What was the result? The little thing died of hydrophobia. I prize it as an heirloom as well as for its virtues. It cannot be faith alone. There must be some property possessed by the stone which is a strong absorbent of poison. This is not impossible. Just as a chalk pipe sticks to the lips when there is no moisture, this stone sticks to a wound when there is mad-dog poison or snake poison in the wound. I do not know why. But a fact is a fact. And this stone will surely draw out poison."

XXXI

SORA SHOOTING *on the* PISCATAWAY

Now that the rigid quail law will soon be out and the eager huntsman is counting the passing moments gleefully as he pets his best dog and cleans up his last season's gun for a three months' chase of the gay and festive Bob White, we are reminded of the more popular, in this section of Tidewater, if not so fascinating, sport of sora shooting. Though not widely known, there is, perhaps, no hunting ground in the South equal to the marshes along the creeks and small rivers tributary to the Chesapeake during the early Fall. The Piscataway Creek, which flows into the Rappahannock just above old Fort Lowery of limited Civil War fame, during the month of September, is a sportsman's paradise. While summer or woodduck are found in considerable numbers, sora or rail shooting is the chief source of amusement.

Just whence the sora comes and whither it goes is a question as yet unanswered by sportsman or ornithologist. But that these marshes are suddenly alive with them the latter part of August, when but a few days before not one can be found, is a fact; even thousands of them on a few acres of this saltwater marsh, with no seeming decrease in their numbers when thousands of them have been bagged by the eager huntsman. This continues until the first killing frost. Clap your hands or slap the water with your paddle during an incoming tide, and seemingly hundreds of their shrill cries will answer you, but on an ebbing tide not one note will they utter. Now let the frost come, and every bird will disappear in the most mysterious manner. Some say they bury themselves in the mud and hibernate there; others that they take their flight, all of them, in a single night; while the old-time negroes firmly believe that they come from frogs and back to frogs they surely go just as soon as the cold weather sets in. This sudden departure at night theory might seem good to one not fully acquainted with the habits of this pride of epicures, but the flight of th sora is short at best, even when hotly pursued, and at the time of its disappearance the bird has grown so fat from its unstinted feeding on the rich wild oats, beaten down by the autumnal winds, that it could be easily captured could one follow it afoot.

The sora belongs to the snipe family, and when standing or wading it much resembles a jacksnipe, but on the wing it is quite different; its legs hang danglingly and its flight is slow and short; fifty to one hundred yards it awkwardly flies and then drops suddenly, as if wounded or dead. And strange, too, that no one has ever seen or heard this mighty flock as it moves off to parts unknown. So their habitat before and after the six weeks' season remains an open question.

The equinoctial storm in September is the time longed for by every sportsman, would-be and real, and then, armed with anything from the single-barrel muzzle-loader to the latest improved hammerless, they flock to the creek. A long ducking canoe, light and strong, a stout negro who knows his business, to shove your boat, an easterly wind bringing in its full tide, and you are fixed for a day of sport royal and unique.

There live along the Piscataway a class of people somewhat resembling the "Georgia crackers" and the "dirt eaters" of North Carolina. These Chinkapinites, as they are called, are *sui generis,* however, in dialect and habits. But they are splendid fishermen and huntsmen. Be a good fellow with him, and a portion of his early green tobacco and a bunch of his fish are yours; but put on airs and be "citified" around him and documentary evidence as to the distribution of your estate had best be speedily arranged. One of these Chinkapinites, if you are on the good side of him, will give you the best hunt. The negro shover is a little shy of going into the thickest of the fight, even when armed with fighting whisky. For when we say that on a piece of marsh the size of a block of ground in the city it is not unusual to see from fifteen to twenty boats hunting and as many shots fired in a few moments, it is quite evident there is risk enough, especially where the grass is so high that you cannot see ten steps away. A charge of small shot, which was intended for the bird, may be received by you or your pusher at any moment. "Mind where you shoot," is heard on every side, and often before you have time to offer an apology or an explanation for your own careless shot, here comes a load of No. 10's rattling against the side of your boat, or perhaps against you and your pusher. At this time, if it happens to be a negro who is doing your pushing, he will duck his head, drop his pole and say: "Look here, boss, dis is mor'n I kin stan'. I knows a piece of ma'sh dat's jist as good as dis one is, so let's we all go dere." But if you like the excitement and do not mind the risk, and happen to have a thoroughbred Chinkapinite to do the pushing for you, then you can stay; for when he gets a sprinkling of small shot his blood mounts to fighting pitch, and in a voice shrill and funeral-breeding, he yells out, "Mind whur you is a shooting, pleague take your hide of you! Cuant you see nobody? Got dey same rights in dis ma'sh dat you has, and I ain't agoing to leave it, neither. Do you hear that? You take my gun, mister, she's loaded with No. 4's, and drap that open-at-both-ends thing of your'n. She will do the work for him!" And he holds his ground.

As high as two hundred and fifty of these birds have been killed on a flood tide, and only one bird at a shot, by a single huntsman. The expertness of an old hunter in finding the dead birds among the weeds and grasses is very clever, and when one falls crippled none but the most practiced eye can find it, for the sora dives as readily as a duck, and to get the air will poke just the tip of its bill above the water.

The bony structure of the little birds is so slight that when properly boiled one can eat "bones and all." To pluck them is a task. The old negro cooks singe the downy feathers, which are too fine for the fingers to pull, and this adds to the flavor, it is thought. Many pronounce the sora superior to the canvas-back duck in delicacy of flavor.

Years ago, many of these mysterious visitors to our marshes were killed by torch-hunting, using a paddle to knock them down as they were blinded by the light. A remnant of an Indian tribe on the Mattaponi River still hunt them in this manner. They are thought to be better for the table when thus killed, for their flesh being so tender, they are frequently mangled by the shot, though of the smallest size. A queer bird is the sora, but surely there is none other which furnishes more sport, short-lived though it be, and a more dainty dish than this long-legged, green-billed visitor to our marshes in the early fall.—W. C. G.

XXXII

A NEW REMEDY *for* ALL ILLS

THE country is safe. The freeze may kill out some, and some may sink out of sight in the mud which will follow, but to those who survive, health, happiness and a celebration of their one hundredth birthday will come. I know that something would be done as soon as the railroad was built, but scarcely hoped of any great development before the completion of it. Yet, "coming events cast their shadows," etc. Winter Wright, a colored man, fired by the mere hope of what is to follow when this section is aroused from its sleep and the clatter of machinery frightens off the goblins of hard times, has formed a joint-stock company to buy machinery and operate the same for the purpose of extracting sassafras oil. One merchant in Dunnsville headed the subscription list with $100; other citizens, Winter says, will be as encouraging. The plant will cost $500. The product will insure every one who uses it to live to be 100 years old and to be free from ills and pains, fleas and toothache and all the rest of the things annoying in this life during the interval. Three drops will keep a barrel of cider sweet all winter, and the mere presence of the oil in barn or cellar will cause rats to vacate spontaneously, and stray cats to follow thereafter. Here I have been grubbing and cutting sassafras bushes for forty years or more, and hating their presence in my alfalfa field as I would snakes among the goslings, and never dreamed of any worth or merit in them, save for spring tea when boils were in evidence. And now I feel like the "ancient mariner" and think of them killed as the albatross shot with my crossbow, and fancy the spirits of thousands of modern Methuselahs rising up against me, and enough cider, soured and spoilt, to flood a creek. But I do not know. "Duffey's Malt Whisky" will retire, and "Parrine" will never more trap the unwary reader into a story "ad." Winter hears only loud peals of thunder and the dinner bell, and like most deaf people, he talks rather low. He is a respectful kind of a colored oddity and no one cares to offend him, but when he "hitches on to you" to talk the merits of sassafras oil you had better be surrounded by book agents and lightning-rod men, for he is literally deaf to all refusals as well as to all unsavory remarks on your part. He declares by the powers that he will run his plant and cure the people *nolens volens.* Whether he will join the Standard Company or not doth not yet appear, but mighty things we may expect, even that when sassafras roots give out that "sour mash" or a barrel of hard cider may form a quasi substitute; and then, indeed, folks might imagine that they would live 100 years for a brief period, but beg piteously to die forthwith ere the spell had vanished.

XXXIII

A LITTLE BOOK TALK

FOR years I had heard of the novel, "George Balcombe," by Tucker, and made strenuous efforts to find it. From what I heard, it was laid at "Bathurst," the old colonial home on the Piscataway Creek, and having George Balcombe as the hero, and Lady Bathurst as the heroine, surcharged with valuable local history, such that a writer would fairly go wild with delight to have. I enquired of those who had old libraries and were supposed to be "bookish," and I solicited the aid of the query column of a paper and of a book store to locate a copy. I learned of one second-hand copy which might be bought for the modest sum of seventy-five dollars. I didn't order. Well, by good luck a lady connected with the State Library called to see me along the line of some family history, and through her I learned that a copy was in the library, and upon her endorsement the book was loaned to me for two weeks. So I have the long looked-for "George Balcombe," and never in my reading experience have I been more disappointed. The author, Nathaniel Beverly Tucker, I presume, was a lawyer. I also conclude that he was familiar with the English and American poets, as he always introduces his chapters with a stanza of poetry. The book was laid in about 1825. The story begins in Missouri, but after various and sundry adventures, and the very unreasonable meeting with Virginians, and the successful search on the part of a sub-hero to find George Balcombe, the hero, the whole "shooting match" come back to King and Queen County not only to straighten out a will but in pursuit of the villain in the play, Edward Montague. All who were in the grasp of love seem to have found their mates, and all property restored which had been surreptitiously detained, Montague killed, and a kind of "All's well, ends well" for the close. Not a word of Lady Bathurst, not a line of Lord Bathurst, not a line to give the conditions of those times, save in a very general way, as far as my reading admits; no history at all, for the descriptions are unnatural. I do not question the author's ability as a lawyer, for I do not know. Nor do I question his general knowledge of this section, but novel-writing was not his calling by a long shot. His plot is poor, his characters, for the most part, weak, and his scenes unreal and badly pictured. The name of Tappahannock is mentioned three or four times, and this simply in passing. And Fredericksburg is mentioned as a place his party stopped at while in pursuit of the villain, Edward Montague. No, I did not send the seventy-five dollars for the second-hand copy, and now I would not send seventy-five cents for it. For being a very poorly written book, it is of no value as an addition to the library, and of no historical value to me, at least.

But there is another volume loaned to me from the library. And this is those noted lectures by James M. Garnett to the pupils attending his wife's boarding school. The little book is handsomely bound, excellent print, and well preserved. The style is of that day, say, 1825, and in strictest accord with the English writers of the time. These lectures, as may be supposed, are largely moral, just about what every good mother would tell her daughter. Mr. Garnett was evidently a man of method as well as one of culture, and thoroughly interested in the educational development of the State. The work was most heartily and prominently endorsed by Chief Justice John Marshall, Professor Leroy Anderson, Rev. William F. Armstrong, Rev. Richard Channing Moore, De Witt Clinton, Rev. John H. Rice, Rev. Frederick Beazley and William Wirt, Attorney General of the United States. What a group of intellectual giants! Did they leave their shades, or did they with prophetic vision see the coming of the moneyed period when the high intellectual would be subordinated to wealth?

Another work which I value highly is on my table—"Service Afloat," by Raphael Semmes, the commander of the ill-fated Alabama. This is the most interesting sea story I have ever read, and all true. Semmes was as brave a commander as ever sailed the seas, and his one ship did more damage to the Federal shipping than, perhaps, the rest of the Confederate navy. By the way, he pays a handsome compliment to Commodore Maury.

In brief, he says that with Maury's sea charts in hand you can follow the ocean paths as easily as a pioneer can follow the blazed path through the forest. And why, pray, were Maury's geographies discarded from our school book course? Out of date? Well, a few pages of correction consequent upon the World War would have remedied the deficiency. Maury's Physical Geography of the Sea is a grand work, and of itself would entitle him to long-lasting fame. But it had to go along with the many other excellent discards. You may wonder why Essex with her schools and teachers has not contributed more to literature, especially with such a background of educated forebears. In fact, our contribution is almost *nil,* and but for one lady who has published several books, it would be just that as to the last fifty years, so far as I know. But this excellent contribution by Mr. Garnett, mentioned above, of itself holds up our intellectual along the line of letters, and to my surprise and great pleasure I find that an Arithmetic by Richard Cauthone, of Essex, is in the State Library, and so much valued that it is kept in a glass case. How would I like to have that book. But it is not for loan save in the library. James Muscoe Mathews contributed much to the legal literature by his digest. These three contributions are all that I know of, and they are decidedly of the far past. It is to be devoutly hoped that with all the money spent in schools and for teachers that some product will come to place Essex along the line of writers from other sections of the State. Why not? NOW AND THEN.

Dunnsville, Va.

XXXIV

JUST *A* LINE *from* DUNNSVILLE

THERE is scarcely ever seen a more beautiful marriage than was celebrated at Ephesus Baptist Church, Dunnsville, at high noon on Saturday, the 22nd inst.

Miss Lillie Maxwell Gaines, of Centre Cross, and Mr. Eugene W. Phillips, of Tappahannock, were the contracting parties.

Rev. G. Y. Bradley, the pastor of Ephesus, performed the ceremony. After the marriage a luncheon was served by Mrs. George B. Kriete, a sister of the groom. Mr. and Mrs. Phillips left by the Norfolk steamer Saturday night for Old Point and other places of interest and pleasure on an extended tour.

To mention by name all of the ladies in attendance would make a list too long, but the beauty and grace of old Virginia stamped the assembly of gentlewomen; and a list of all the gentlemen would be equally as long, though the chivalry of the State did not suffer with them as its representatives. This community wishes the couple all of the happiness, all of the prosperity, all of the friendship, and all of the love they, themselves, could ask. Mr. and Mrs. Phillips will make their home in Tappahannock, at which place Mr. Phillips is now engaged in the mercantile business.

The old-time colored people will soon live but in legend and in brief written history, but to me they are ever a source of interest, and the unique way in which they tell a story is often as graphic as it is free of grammatical correctness. But the thought is the very essence of description, and no grammar, and no dictionary, and no rhetoric and no praxis will make a weak thought a strong one, nor paint a poor thought a pretty one.

Let's try to follow without notes the account this old colored man gave of this beautiful marriage. See if he did not draw the picture of what went on, and the picture is the sum and substance of all descriptive writing:

"Yes, sar, I seen it from start to finish. Ebry bit ob it, and ebry word of it. De old lady and myself has been going to de margis ebber since we could 'member. You see, I knows dese young folks. I kinder feels an intrust in dem. I knowed Mars Josh Roan jest as well as I does you.

"He was dis here lady's grandpa. And her ma, she was named Miss Lula Rhone, you see. Den she married a Gaines. And her grandma was a sister to Dr. Chris Newbill and Dr. Willie Newbill and all of dem. Now you see how 'twas. Dat's how Mr. Frank Newbill ob Cuarter's Crick was dare, and Miss Kit Newbill ob Norfolk and all de Streets, and de Newbills who was dere. Den I ben knowing de Phillips fambly all ob my life. I knowed dis here Mr. Hugene's grandpa and his grandma too. She was a Clarkson, Mars John Clarkson's sister; and his ma too 'fore she was marriad; she was a Jeffries fromb 'cross the ribber. And as to his pa, I couldn't help knowing him, case I almost fotched him up.

"So I says I was guine to dat marige whether or no. And I went. Well, sar, when I got up dat galry, de church was in a blaze, and broad day time too, outside. Why, honey, I says to myself, if dey ain't gone and turned de berry day into night right here at 12 ob clock. Dare was sebenty-five candles all burning at onct, and de pulpit was like de woods at night, for dey had gone down into de depths of de forests and hauled de ebber greens and sot dem up dare behind candles. And I was setting dare athinking 'bout what it all meant, and how it seemed jest day 'fore yistiddy dat Mr. Hugene was a curly-headed baby.

"All at onct fromb de corner in de bottom ob de church dey struck up a thune on de orgin dat was de solemest thune dat I ebber did hear. It kinder kotched me up wid it and carried me 'long wid it floating out somewhere or nuther. I didn't kere where. I jest shot my eyes and went 'long. I saw purty sights and sad sights all mixed up, and I saw purty little angels and little sad-looking children running 'long 'gether, and dere was lubly houses, houses jest filled wid fine ladies and gemmen, and de tables jest a-breaking down wid de food for dem to eat, but on the outside dere was dose little angels and dose little sad-looking chillun a-trying to git in de house, as if dey was hungry.

"You could hear de water running 'long de streams, and de very flowers seemed to grow as de music went floating 'long by dem. Says I to myself, 'Jest hush your mouth! I don't kere where dey goes, I's guine to follow dis day.' Up de hillsides and down de valleys dey went, dose little chillun and de angels wid dem. Presenly seems dat de little chillun got used to de angels and 'gan to laf wid 'em, and play and skip and all dat. 'Hallelujah!' says I, and 'bout dat time de old 'oman, she kotched me by de shoulder, and says, 'Why don't you wake up, Bob!' 'I ain sleep, Nancy, but I is jest a-dreaming in de daytime.' Den de music stoped. And de gemmen pranced 'round de pulpit to see lights was all right. Den de orgin struck up a diffunt thune. Dis was loud, like de soldiers march by. 'Hush your mouth,' says I, 'for now dey is a-coming sure.' Dere was a gemman marchin' on one side and a lady marchin' on de other side.

"Here dey come, jest as slow, and as quiet as if dey had all ob de day before dem. Den here come another couple, and another, tell de pulpit flatform (negroes never say platform) was jest libe wid 'em. And here come de lady herself wid Mars Jack Rhone, and Mr. Hugene wid his brother Syd. De all had de headest 'zanthemums pinned on 'em dat ebber I did see, and de lilly ob de valley dat blooms in de springtime was a blooming in de fall ob de year. Dey was flowers, dey was! Den de music hushed up so you could hardly hear it, and Brother Bradley, he began his ceremony. Dis was solemn, sure. All dem flowers and dose candles a-burning, and dose ladies all dressed like dey was going to be married demselves.

"Dat was a purty sight fore de world. I heard de preacher ask her if she would obey, and she said she would. And den I touched Nancy. And she drew up kinder stiff-like, and got furder from me. I saw 'em when de ring was put on, and I hurd ebrything dat was said. And when de preacher 'nounced de benediction dey all turned round and moved out. Dis time Mr. Hugene had his bride. And Mars Jack Rhone he had some udder lady wid him, cause he had done gib up Miss Lillie to Mr. Hugene at de altar. Dey marched on out and de music kept on playing, and dare I sot tell de last one was out.

"When I got down Nancy had gone home. But Mars Wilton Phillips, he was dare, and he said, 'Come on over to de house, old man, and git your dinner.' Went? Ob course I went. I stayed outside tell dey called me, and, being dere was no one else in de room to eat, cause de white folks had finished, I had de room to myself. So dey put me at a side table and filled up two plates, one ob sweet things and one ob stantials, and fotched dem ober dare to me. All I could say was, 'De Lord be praised!' Dat was a dinner like dey used to have when I was a boy. Dere was ebrything dare to eat dat de mouth ob man could ask for. But, sar, I finished dem two plates, and 'fore I could git outen de house dey had done fixed up some for de old woman, and some ob de gemmen gave me a cigar, and den I went home rejoicing. So you see I saw it all from start to finish, and 'twas de finest marriage and de greatest dinner I'se seen since de war."

And the old colored man pretty nearly had it right in the judgment of many others. ONCE UPON A TIME,

W. C. G.

Upper—THE YOUNGEST AND ELDEST OF A HOUSEHOLD
Lower—READY FOR SCHOOL

XXXV

"A FOX-HUNT 'FORE DE CIVIL WAR"

NOT long since I was riding leisurely along over the "White Oak Swamp" road on my way from a village in the lower portion of Essex County, Va., to the county seat, and coming at a very easy gait was an old horse pulling a kind of mongrel vehicle, neither sulky nor road-cart, but known as a "jumper," while in it was an old negro man looking as contented as you please.

When I met him he very politely and, to my surprise, quite gracefully raised his hat and said:

"Morning, sir, morning! How are you this morning, sir?"

I replied that I was in the best of health, but in need of information, and, seeing that he was disposed to talk, I reined up my horse and, turning half-way around in my saddle, asked him how far it was to Tappahannock. While saying this I took in the contents of the vehicle: bundles and bags, and bottles and buckets, and a big bunch of fodder tied on behind. On one of the bags I noticed the familiar lock which accompanies Uncle Sam's mail service, and at once decided that he was the mail carrier.

"Well, sir, it is not so very much further now. If 'twant fer dem trees up de road dere you could see de town. But it hain't so fur to Mr. Jones' gate, from dere you kin see de town, but, ob course, you has to cross de bridge 'fore you gets dere. Yes, sir."

He had a good face and a genteel manner, both pleasing and attractive in their uniqueness, to me. He evidently belonged to that class of "old-time," well-raised negroes which bring back memories of better days in Virginia, a class rapidly thinning out now. Small in stature, but compact and as full of vehement gestures as a Frenchman. I told him that I was a stranger in that locality, but had spent four years in the State some twenty-five years ago, and this very much against my wishes.

"You was in de war den, sir, I suppose. On de other side, 'cause I know you ain't no Furginian by your voice. My name is Tom Banham, sir, and I carries de mail way down to Montague's and back ebry day. Dese here bundles and things, sir, dey belongs to de folks long de road, and dey pays me a little sumthin' to bring them to um from town—Hush!! What's dat? Don't you hear um coming?"

"Hear what?" I asked.

"Man, it's de dogs! Hush! Don't say a word; dey's coming dis way as hard as dey can drive!"

I halted my restless horse and faced the other way, and, sure enough, they were coming. 'Twas a beautiful morning, crisp and bracing the air, and the frost just melting, and every note seemed to echo doubly as a pack of some ten or twelve hounds came dashing through the woods on the right.

"Dere he is! Dere he goes! See him? See him? Don't say a word! Keep right still! Dere he goes!"

At that moment a fully grown gray fox cleared the pine rail fence and crossed the road and with increased speed disappeared into the woods, running straight in the direction of the river. Not two hundred yards behind came the dogs, "all in a bunch," to use a fox-hunting phrase, and as they struck the hot scent on the melted frost in the woods, their notes seemed even louder and sweeter than before. On they went, seemingly sweeping everything before them. At this moment, the old man, unable to contain himself any longer, stood up on his jumper seat and gave such a yell as I had never heard come from human lungs before:

"Hark up! hark! Hark him, boys, hark! Whoop, hark him, h—a—r—k!"

My horse, unaccustomed to such demonstrations, nearly jumped from under me, and I did not take him in for fifty yards, and when I did succeed in stopping him he wheeled around and looked at the old negro and gave a snort as if he had been suddenly turned into a bear. Standing there on that seat with his hat in one hand and his whip in the other, his bald head shining just above an immense overcoat collar, his eyes fairly bursting out of his head in his wild enthusiasm, I thought he was enough to frighten the devil himself, and quickly forgave my horse his unusual capers.

"Dat horse ain't no hunting horse, sir. No, sir; I can tell um ebry time. He don't like de music. Hark him, boys, hark him! Whoop, hark him! Hark!! Dey is certanly pushing him, I tell you!"

I told him if he did not quit his yelling he would frighten my horse to death.

"Lord, marster, it makes my very blood bile when I hear de dogs run. 'Minds me, sir, of de fox-hunting 'fore de war. But you didn't know Marse Raz Wright, and de Guarnetts from Careline, and de Sanderses, and all of dem. Dey was fox-hunters, dey was. Sometimes dey had mor'n a hundred dogs when dey got dem all together for a big hunt, and you never seed such times, sir, in all your life as dose men had. And de eating! Well, sir, dey used to make 'rangements for weeks ahead when dere was gwine to be a 'gethring,' sir, as dey called it. De cook was a rubbing de pots and skillets and baking up bread for de dogs, 'nough to feed a regimin,' and missus, do she didn't like dogs, used to fix up de things 'bout de house and have ebry room clean and de furniture rubbed jest as bright as glass, and when dey all got dere and had done locked up de dogs ('cause makes no difunce how well strange dogs will hunt together in de daytime, dey will fight in de night and git cut up so dey ain't fit for to run, if dey ain't stopped up), dey would go in and warm up 'fore de fire in de parla and den Marse Raz would warm dem up wid some of dey old-fashion Furginia brandy stilled right dere in de neighborhood. Ebery one ob dem had de 'bes' dogs, ob course, and dey certainly would brag on dem. But, Lord, sir, dose dogs dey used to bring wan't nothing to Marse Raz's old Ben. You see, I driv de kerridge ebry Sunday, but week days all induring the season, I had to start de fox, and Marse Raz's dogs knowed me better den dey did him. Marse Raz used to ride a big white horse, and, sir, he could clear any fence in de country, and if he did knock down a few rails, Marse Raz would go 'long 'bout his business, and Tom, dat's me, sir, had to stay dere and put it up agin.

"So you see, I knowed old Ben, and when he couldn't beat fair he'd cut, sir, and get ahead, and so nobody knowed de difunce, for he always done his cutting in de woods. I'd go in de house to put wood on de fire and always tooken a long time to fix de fire, 'cause I wanted to hear dem gentlemen talk. Marse Raz said one night as I went in de parla wid wood, he says, 'Here is Tom, gentlemen,' and dey says, 'Well, Tom!' Marse Raz says, 'And I'll bet you Tom dat old Ben cleans up de pack tomorrow in special if we starts a red.' And one ob dem says, 'I'll carry Tom home wid me, 'cause Tariff will come in two hundred yards ahead.' I says to him, 'No, sir; Tom ain't gwine nowhere, fur dere ain't dat dog born yit can beat old Ben if he ain't sick, or nothin' tall like dat.' Den dey would go in to de supper, and dey Cuarter's Crick oysters dat dey would eat was a sin, sir. Marse Raz says, 'Boys, don't let's set up too late tonight, for I am gwine to have ebry one ob you up at five o'clock in de morning. Tom, get my dogs from the mill fuss, and make a big fire for all dese gentlemen, 'cause de mornin' is gwine to be cold!"

"Next morning, when I blowed dat horn for de mill dogs, de whole place was in a charm, sir. You could hear dem coming and howling as dey come, so glad dey was gwine, and all de other dogs was howling to git out, and de horses was jest as glad as de dogs, for dey knowed what was coming. I took Marse Raz's dogs on ahead 'cause dey knowed de country, and I knowed it. But when dey started de fox dey all got in, and, sir, 'twas 'nough to make the very hair stand on your head, dis paticular morning I's thinking 'bout! 'Twas a full cry all de time and dey neber did lose him. Dat was a hunt, dat was! No, sir, dey don't have no dogs, and no horses neither, like dey use to have in dem days, nor people, neither, no, sir. 'Stresses me powerful to think ob dose happy times. Dey is all gone now. Marse Raz gone, de horses dey is gone, and de dogs, too!"

"But which dog beat the chase?" I ventured to ask, for I had become interested.

"Beat? Old Ben, ob course! Bound to beat! Old Ben got flung out once, but I harked him in, and de next time dey seed him he had gone cut a quarter ob a mile ahead. I must be a-going, sir, or I'll be late." and with a gentle jerk of his reins the old horse aroused from his rest and jogged on at the pace which I had interrupted.

Memories of happier days come to us all; may they soften the pillow of poor Uncle Tom, and may the grass grow green over the grave of Marse Raz.

Dunnsville, Va. NOW AND THEN.

XXXVI

BOB'S 'COON HUNT

You don't know Bob Beazley, do you? Well, you have missed something. Bob does not lay claim to one drop of Caucasian blood in his veins; thoroughbred is he, and fully endowed with every instinct, aspect and tendency of his race. He can swing his cradle through the ripened wheat field as gracefully as he can cast his baited line to the eager trout, and woe be to the straggling gobbler when Bob deftly imitates his mate, with his muzzle-loader ready for action.

But wheat-cutting, and fishing, and turkey hunting are but side issues in Bob's fund of *amusements*. A starry night, a bundle of fat pine and two well-trained coon dogs, true to the scent and never to bark unless there is a varmint on trail or up tree—these conditions measure Bob's paradise earthly. Badly fares the King's English with Bob, but his poses, his gestures, his cadences would become a senator when his enthusiasm over his last hunt prompts him to his native eloquence in detail of recital. "Yes, sar, coons does eat old huares. I knows day does. 'Case I knows what I is done seen wid dese here ver' eyes I has got in my head right here now. Day does eat 'em. I jes knows day does. Some people has told me dat day only eats frogs and corn and things like dat, but dis is not true. Dey eats old *huares*, I tell you.

"How does day ketch 'em? How come I know how day ketch 'em? I does not know how day ketch 'em, still day does do it. Dat's pintedly true. 'Case I kin tell you what I is done seen right down yarnder in Misser Macon Ware's woods. 'Twas a terrible snow 'pon de groun,' for de ver' bushes and de stumps and de big piles ob briars was all kivered up. 'Twas a terrible time for varmints in de woods.

I had done walked myself nigh to death dat day hunting and a-doing in de woods, but I hadn't kilt one thing. 'Twas gitting late, and gitting colder, too, and I was kinder on my way home. All at once I seed some 'coon tracks on de snow, right by a heap ob brush and stuff. So I called old Bounce and showed him de tracks, but he couldn't smell nuthin', he nor Tip neither.

"De dorgs looked at de tracks, and den looked up in my face at me. I told 'em day was de headest fools I'd ebber seen, 'case dose certainly was not my tracks. I knowed dat pintedly. So I shoved dem outen de way, and I got to looking round dat brush pile. I seed a little hole whur som'in' had been a-crawling in and a-crawling out. Seemed like dis had been guying on for some time, but dare wan' no fresh tracks dat I could see. So I got me a forkit stick, and I punched hit in dare, I did, kinder under dat big pile ob brush and briars and stuff, jes as far as I could. Dare seemed like a sorter lead like dat went under de groun', so I kept on a-shoving and a-pushing and a-twisting dat forkit stick tell bymeby I felt summin' soft, I did, and den, sur, summin' snapped at de end ob dat stick and come nigh jerking it outen my han'. Says I, 'Hi! what is dat, anyhow, a-snapping at dis stick? ' Old Top and Bounce was both a-standing right dare looking up in my face jes like day didn't hab one single bit ob sense. I nebber dit un'er'stan' what was de marter wid dem dorgs dat ebernin', nohow, a-standing dare looking at me so hard. Day mus'er thought I was kinder crazy down dare on my knees a-punchin' an' a-twistin' in dat hole wid dat stick. I punched in dare agin, and dat time I felt him, yes, sar, I felt him, kinder soft-like. I twisted and twisted, and when I pulled dat stick out I had de hind legs ob a old huar, and den I kept on a-punchin' and a-twistin' and a-pullin' tell I drugged out five old huars, 'case I could tell how many day was by de parts I had done gotten outen dat hole. Well, sar, I didn't know what to think on hit, 'case som'in' had sartinly been a-snappin' at de ends ob my stick, an' I knowed pintedly dat hind legs ob old huares couldn't snap at nobody's stick. I knowed dat.

"De nex' time I shoved dat forkit stick in dat hole I huerd som'in' growl. 'Hi!' says I, 'dat is a coon, sho' as you lib.' Me I got to thinkin' dat if I couldn't twist him out, I'd try to shoot 'im outen dare. So I took old Betsy, dat's my gun's name, and I shoved her in dare jes as far as I could. Well, sar, I hadn't shot her off dat day, 'case I hadn't found nuttin' to shoot at. You know dat biggest boy ob mine, don't you? Well, he had done loaded dat gun sense I had it last time. He's de headest goose 'bout loading a gun in dis worl. He don't know how much is a load, let me tell you. Dat day he musten had ten fingers in dat old long gun. She was a kicking gun, anyhow, eben with a reg'lar load. But when you ober-loaded her, man, don't you say a word. Well, I poked her in dat hole far's I could. I didn't hab my shoulder ginst de stock like you giner'ly has, but 'bout six inches from de stock. I pulled de trigger, an' de Lord hab mussy! 'twas a 'splosion, show as you lib, I tell you. Dat gun come'd back ginst my face like I was hit wid a maul, and knocked me flat as a flounder down in de snow an' brush an' stuff, right 'mong de dorgs, and here come de biggest coon I ebber seed in my born days, right on top ob me, all singed up by de powder, and den de dorgs jumped right on me and de coon. 'Twas a time in dis worl! 'Twas dark, man, and de blood jes a flowing from my mouf and nose so I couldn't see a wink—all mixed up down dare wid de dorgs and de coon, a-fighting and a-making so much fuss de couldn't hear nottin' I said, an' day couldn't a-tell me from de coon. Old Top, a grand roscal, kotched me by my lef' leg once, an' was jes a-grinding down on it 'for I could kick him offen me. I wan't no coon to be chawed up by my own dorgs. I kicked and hollowed tell I gotten outen dat pile ob dorgs an' coon an' got on my feet. Man, 'twas a fight in dis worl! But day kilt him, yes, sar, day kilt him. An' he was de biggest coon dat I ebber seed in my life. He was a bouncer, sho' as you lib.

"Yes, sar, coons does eat old huares. Dat's pintedly true, I tell you."

Bob bought a piece of tobacco, straightened himself to his full height, bowed and went on out of the store, and then to his wife's house, as the old-time negroes delight to call their homes. With the passing of Bob and a precious few others, the negro as I knew him in the good old days before the Civil War will be an unknown quantity—the dialect will be gone, the singing will be gone, the ashcake and the cabin will be gone, and not for long will the writer have these very pleasant talks from the good old negroes for whom there is and always has been, a tender spot of sympathy and respect, for there is very much of the negro which we of the South know and value that is unknown to those who have not been intimately associated with him as servant before the days of his freedom and since as a neighbor, but always knowing his place.

Many more years for old Bob, and may his "dorgs" remain true to the scent, and his biggest boy never overload his old Betsey again.

XXXVII

An ADDRESS *by the* AUTHOR *at* *A* MEMORIAL MEETING*

Mr. Chairman, Ladies and Gentlemen:

I am proud that I am among those who are called upon to express a word of sorrow and a sense of deep emotion on this memorial occasion; and I would indeed be glad, could I, in befitting terms, voice my sentiments as I contemplate the scenes enacted in the city of Buffalo on the 6th day of September last.

So much has come from eloquent tongues, and so much has fallen from gifted pens, bespeaking a feeling of horror at the foul deed done; so much of the life and the character of the noble victim fallen; so much of sympathy for the fond and noble woman widowed, that it seems to me that I scarce can say a word more that would add a greater cause for grief, or a deeper call for sympathy.

But as an American citizen, enjoying the life and the liberty vouchsafed in the "goodliest land that the sun ever shone upon," under the best and the strongest government that is on God's green earth, I am too full to remain silent, when you say that I may speak, though I tell an oft-told tale to you. Warburton, the romance historian, says that the life of a nation is like the life of an individual. As there are sharp corners in the life of the average man, which mark his course of success or of failure, so we may note the same in the life and the growth of a nation.

---

* Delivered at Morgan City, La., upon the occasion of the death of President McKinley.

Long before the Mecklenburg resolutions had been framed, or the streets of Boston had been wet with American blood, a few of the citizens of old Westmoreland (as the legend runneth), met at Leedstown, a mere hamlet on the banks of the Rappahannock, and raised a solemn protest against British tyranny (an event deemed insignificant beside a greater event in '76), but then and there was kindled a flame which, fanned a little later by the magic eloquence of Henry, and, growing as it went, until it became as a mighty prairie fire of patriotic enthusiasm, thirsting for freedom of representation, and freedom of conscience, until it, in its onward sweep, broke the first bands at Lexington and the last at Yorktown, and launched this mightiest republic on the tide of time. A corner was turned and a sharp one indeed.

Long before John Brown had his visions of freedom and planned his frenzied raid; and longer before the signal gun at Sumter had aroused the South to action; several of the congressmen, then at a dinner-party in New York, agreed that all of them present should rise at once when congress assembled and claim the floor, and thus by force of numbers overpower the opposition and secure the speaker's recognition, that a certain measure might receive immediate attention. At that critical time David Wilmot did with those many rise, and through him was offered that proviso known as the "Wilmot Proviso," and while it failed as a measure, through it was kindled another flame that, in its terrible fury later on, burnt to the very vitals of that republic, the *saddest* and the *bloodiest fratricidal strife* known in the history of the world. A sharp corner, indeed, and one that made us pause and ponder long.

But when the congress of these United States voted fifty millions of dollars to be placed into the hands of William McKinley, to be used as he saw fit, that we might rid that "Queen of the Antilles" from the hand of Spanish oppression, *the Civil War closed,* and the Blue and the Grey rallied around the proudest flag that floats on the breezes of heaven, marched to the same drum-beat, sang America in unison, and stretched the Monroe Doctrine to the very isles of the sea.

A united people, indeed; proud, powerful, progressive. And now, my friends, when peace reigns, when commodities are borne to and fro most lavishly, when factories hum day and night, when the working man greets his children with a smile, when the farmer smokes the pipe of peace with the capitalist, when in the midst of joyful celebration, when great cornucopias of wealth, prefiguring the plenteousness of this land and people, appear on every side and the badge of honor is offered by millions of men to their sovereignty true, and the smiles of joyous people meet his smile, a red-handed exponent of lawlessness takes the life blood of the head of this government, we mark another *sharp* corner, and it is time that we "turn us about" that we may look into this matter, eradicate, yes, annihilate, that diabolical pestilence that has insinuated itself into this country, militating against the peace and security of our government. This much for the dead, and of the man we have but words of kindness and of praise. He was a typical American citizen. He arose from the humble walks of life and by dint of brawn and brain, he overcame the obstacles in the pathway of fame and reached its highest pinnacle, higher than the throne of any prince or potentate in all the world, and honored there by the unimperiled voice of the noblest people beneath the sunlight of heaven—the chief executive of the greatest system of laws, the commander-in-chief of the mightiest patriotic army that the world ever saw.

He was a man of his own convictions, and fearlessly followed them, and with a steady hand and a mighty grasp he steered the grand old ship of state through the perils of war, and through the greater perils of opposing parties. When at the zenith of his power, when his manhood's hour had scarcely passed its noon, he fell. Not as imperial Caesar on the fatal Ides of March, stabbed by the hand of cruel jealousy, which the very vastness of his success and power had brought upon him; nor as the mighty Napoleon, banished to a lonely island with his hands behind him, gazing out on that sad and solemn sea which mocked the vastness of his fallen fortune, and dreaming of empires won and lost, but in the midst of loving hearts and in the flood-tide of his glory, and in the enjoyment of Heaven's best gift, he fell, struck by no party hand, but by the hand of blood-stained anarchy, and died while a flood of tears were shed around him, and as the flags of every nation drooped in responsive grief for "Old Glory," and the badge of mourning reached from the frozen peaks of Alaska to sunny Florida, from the Aristook to the Rio Grande. He fell, the President of the United States. Our president to honor and protect when living, to honor and bemoan untimely dead.

His political creed was not the same creed that was followed by many millions over whom he presided, but they honored him as a man, and, as their president, they answered when he called, and followed the grand old flag from the Occident to the Orient, and whether soldier or civilian, they took his hand in friendly greeting when he passed among them.

Harsh criticism, like slander, pauses at the grave; and the error, when error there was, is lost in good, and the eye of sympathy drops a watering tear on the modest immortelles. Peace to his noble ashes, and may his life, and the success thereof, inspire the youth of our land with noble impulses, and tell them that merit wins at last, whatever may betide.

"A king once said of a prince struck down,
'Taller, he seems in death,'
And this saying holds true, for now as then
'Tis after death we measure men."

W. C. GARNETT, *of Dunnsville, Va.,*
At Knights of Pythias Hall, Evangeline Lodge, No. 23,
October 9, 1901.

XXXVIII

MY SHIP

I longed for my ship so ardently,
And I waited, and waited so patiently
For my ship from way over the sea.
Her captain was royal, and her crew were all loyal.
And the treasure she bore was a treasure for me.

I leaned on that treasure so heavily,
And I built with that treasure extensively,
So great was the treasure from over the sea;
My plans were all royal and my motives as loyal
For the treasure in trust borne safely to me.
In dream I saw her once distinctly,
And I cheered, and cheered her heartily,
My ship coming a'booming to me;
Her colors were all flying,
And the distance fast dying
'Tween me and that ship on the sea.

I spent of that treasure, but not profusely,
I gave to the poor, but gave to them wisely;
That treasure a trust placed safely with me.
They thought me so royal
And my motives so loyal
As they shared that treasure from way over the sea.

I woke from that dream so dazedly.
And I thought of my loss so seriously,
A phantom, it was, and no treasure for me.
Her captain was a braggart, her mate was a laggard,
They had stolen my treasure far out on the sea.

Now I think of my loss quite soberly,
And hope for the best continuously,
And find the treasures vouchsafed to me;
My home is right loyal,
My friends all royal,
And these are my treasures on this side the sea.

XXXIX

An ODE *to* NATURE

I have given my soul to the herd on the lea,
To the rocks and the rills down the glen;
They'll keep my soul right safe for me,
Ere long I'll find it again.

I have given my soul to the birds and the trees,
To the field and the fallow on the hill;
'Twill return to me on a summer breeze,
I'll know it when all is still.

I have given my soul to flowers and to song,
To love and to laughter and to lambs at play;
"We'll return your soul, 'twill not be long,
We have kept the faith," I hear them say.

I have given my soul to the star-lit night,
To the clouds at the passing day;
I know 'tis safe for its winged flight,
And as pure as the sun-sent ray.

I have given my soul to the forest kind,
To the dove a'moan near her nest;
My soul some day I'll safely find,
They'll keep my soul as they know best.

I have given my soul to the winding stream,
To the shells and the sands on its shore;
I have seen it there in a quiet dream,
In peace and love, content and pure.

I have given my soul to the wild wind's blast,
To the snowflakes a'dance and a'glee.
In trust they'll hold it safe 'til the last,
Then my soul will come back to me.

—W. C. G.

INDEX

A Guide to Commissioners in Chancery, 51
A Review of Judge Black's Novels, 70
A Trip to Richmond, 204
Abrams & Kerr, merchants, 40
Acree: Walter, Prof., 89
Acts of Assembly, 23
Adam, 131
Adam's land: warehouse established, 28
address by the author, 234
agriculture in public schools, 131
Ainslie: Charlie, 46; Peter, Dr., 45, 46
Akers: Henry, 98, 99
Alaska, 237
albatross, 215
alfalfa, 14, 45, 133
An Ode to Nature, 239
Anderson, 43; Dr., 40; John Fretzall, Dr., 40; Leroy, Prof., 218
Anderton: George, 52; George N., Mrs., 169
Angel's Visit (Colored) Church, 41
Angel's Visit Church, 42
apple brandy, 112
apprentices: liable for military duty, 35
Archie, 123
Aristook, 237
Arkansas, 147, 208
Armistead Family, 209
Armstrong: William F., Rev., 218
as Indian village, 105
ashcakes, 197
ashpone, 190
Atkins: W.O., 44
Australia, 207
Aylett: Wm. R., Col., 58
Bacon's Rebellion, 24
Bagdad, 165
Bagwell: John, 24, 25
Baird: Edward R., Capt., 60, 70; Willie, 70
Baird home (Epping Forest), 60
Bake-House Creek, 97
Balcombe: George, 217
Baltimore, Md., 37, 45, 170
Banham: Tom, 226, 228
Bank of Essex, 58
Baptists, 63
Bareford: Henry, 88; Howard, 94; Willie, 88
bathing, 80
bathing shores, 13
Bathurst, 45, 101, 217
Battaill: John, Capt., 26
Baughan: E.E., 93; Webb, 97
Baylor: Mr., 182, 183, 184, 185, 186
Baylor Family, 61
Beal: John, 34
Beale Memorial Baptist Church, 105
Beale Memorial Church, 52
Beaufort: new town at Laytons, 31
Beazley: Bob, 193, 230; Frederick, Rev., 218
Beckley, W.Va., 45, 169
Beckwiths: Misses, 72
Ben, 228
Ben Lomond, 41, 60, 101, 169; (photo), 64
Benjamin Syms School, 64, 65
Bentley: L.E., 158; Prof., 192; Robert Ryland, Prof., 60, 157, 158, 159, 160, 161, 162, 163, 164, 165
Bentley Family, 60
Berkeley: William, Gov., 65; William, Sir, 64
Berry: Mrs., 125, 126
Berry Hill, 48
Bestland, Va., 75, 82, 83, 89
Bethany College, 45, 85
Betsey, 232, 233
Betty, 165

Beverley: Robert, 59
Beverly: Robert, 33; Robt., 34
Bibles, 79, 131
Billy in the Low Grounds, 204
Blakey: Thomas Evans, Hon., 58, 102
Blandfield, 59
Blanton: Joe, 48; Mr., 95
boats, 20, 23, 77
Bob, 128, 129, 130, 176, 233
bob whites, 211
Bohannans, 83, 99
Bohannans Wharf, 83
Booker: Lewis, Capt., 62
Booth: John Wilkes, 62
Boston, 144
Boston, Mass., 32, 33, 170, 235
Boughan: James, 26
Boughton: Tom, 90
Boulware: Thos., 34; William, 61
Bowen's Geography, 29
Bowers: Harvey, 141, 142
Bowler's, 41, 169
Bowler's Ferry: warehouse established, 28
Bowler's Rock oysters, 14, 41, 149
Bowler's Wharf, 147
Bowling Green, Va., 62
Braddock's defeat, 30
Bradley, 224; G.Y., Rev., 221
bran, 134
brandy, 200
Braxton: Carter, 99
Bray: Charlie, 46; Fred P., 83
Brays, Va., 48
bricks, 117
bridge keepers, 47
brigs, 87
British tyranny, 235
Brizendine: Tom, 115
Brockenbrough: John, 34; Mr., 101, 106
Broky: Robt., 26
Brooke Family, 61
Brookes: George T., 93; Irving, Prof., 93; Marion, Mrs., 93
Brookes Family, 92
Brooks: George T., 48; Sarah, Mrs., 29
Brown: John, 235
Brown's old mill swamp, 90
Buffalo, N.Y., 234
Bundy: Stephen, 47
Burnett: Jim, 149
Bush: Silas, 55, 56, 57
buttermilk, 134, 190, 196
Byron Park, 78
Caesar, 236
cake, 196
cakes and pies, 122
Cambridge, 121
Campbell: Alexander, 46; Miss, 169; William, 43
Campbellton, Va., 169
Cannon: G.G., Hon., 92
Care: Fanny, 61; Mrs., 61
Caret, Va., 59, 128
Carlton: I.G., 88
Caroline County, 13, 227; line, 14
carriages, 121
Carruthers: Elmer J., Prof., 108
Carter: John, Maj., 23
Carter's Creek, 222, 228
Caslett: John, Capt., 26
Catlett Family, 61
Cauthorne: Bob, 90; Maj., 42; R.T., 53; Richard, 70; Richard, author, 219
Center Cross High School, 46
Center Cross, Va., 41, 88, 89, 91, 169, 221
Champlain, Va., 59
Chancellorsville, Va., 101
Chapel Grove, 71, 72
Charlie, 138, 139, 140, 141, 142, 143, 144
cherries: tartarian, 43
Chesapeake Bay, 19, 37, 211
Chesterfield, 203
chewing tobacco, 128
Chickann plantation, 22
Chinkapin, 110, 144
Chinkapinites, 111, 112, 113, 116, 117, 118, 212, 213
chinquepin bushes, 110

chub fishing, 15
Church of England, 26
churches, 27; and town hall, 50, 106; Angel's Visit, 41, 42; Beale Memorial, 52; Beale Memorial Baptist, 105; destroyed after the Revolution, 29; Ephesus Baptist, 43, 221; Howertons Baptist, 85, 95; Lebanon Methodist, 72; Lower Piscataway, 27; Mount Zion Baptist, 59, 92; Oak Grove Baptist, 83; Rappahannock Christian, 45, 79, 80, 167; St. Johns Baptist, 94; St. Luke's Episcopal, 41; St. Paul's Episcopal, 48; Trinity Methodist, 48; Upper Essex Baptist, 164; Upper Piscataway, 27; Vauter's, 29; Vawter's Episcopal, 61; Vertis, 91
Cicero, 100
cider, 215
Civil War, 45, 54, 57, 61, 63, 66, 67, 68, 69, 70, 71, 72, 82, 83, 92, 101, 112, 118, 119, 152, 174, 195, 211, 225, 235; homes destroyed, 44; negroes, 11
Clarkson: John, 222
Clarkson Family, 222
Clemens: Mace, 48
clergy, 29
Cleveland: Grover, Pres., 57
clothing, 182
clover, 78; German, 14
Clyde Side, 45
Cockburn: Rear-Adm., 37
colleges, 16
Colson: Wm., clerk, 26
Columbia University Library, 64
Confederate monument, 50
Congress, 101; first in Philadelphia, 34; representatives and senators, 38
Continental Congress, 34
Cook: Howard, 53
coon hunting, 230, 232
coons, 193
corn, 14, 53, 83, 132, 134, 137, 195
corn shucking, 195
Cottage Park, 46, 169
Cottage Park (photo), 160
cotton, 87
country stores, 145
courthouse portraits, 101, 102, 103
courthouses, 50, 52, 54, 105; courtroom, 100, 101, 102, 103; first in Essex, 59; jury room, 54, 56; marriage licenses, 55; monuments, 117; records, 103; records relocated, 54; repairs, 103; tablets, 41; tree at site of first, 128; tree marks location, 59; trials, 55
Courtney: Mr., 92
Courtney's, 140
Courtney's store, 140, 141
Covington: Capt., 84; Rich., 26
cows, 127
crabs, 15
crackers, 154, 155, 156; Georgia, 212
Craig's Ford, 101
Cralle: A.A., 58
crayon boxes, 137
crickets, 197
crops, 14, 83, 132, 135
Crosby: Mr., 58
crossbows, 215
Croxton: D., 88; George, 54, 205; George T., 59; George Thomas, 94; Jennie, 169; Miss, 53; Thomas, 58; Thomas, Hon., 48, 49, 53, 94, 102
Croxton Family, 188
Croxton's Mill, 59, 94
Crutchfield's Store, 59
Curlette: John, home (photo), 32
Dabney: Dick, 87
Daingerfield: William, 36
Dale: Sir Thomas, Gov., 22
Dangerfield: George, 51; Harry, 58; Harry, Hon., 102; John, Col., 37
Daniel: Robert, 45
Davis: Grigg, 84; Jimmie, 86
Deep Landing, 99

Demosthenes, 18, 99
deputies appointed, 34
Derieux: George, 52
Desha, Va., 94
deShazo: John Newton, Dr., 88
DeShazo: Dr., 169
deShields: H.C., mayor, 51
DeWitt, 218
Diana, 190, 191
Dickens: Charles, author, 124
Dillard: J. Harvey, 89; Kate, Mrs., 169
Dillard brothers, 89
Diocletian, 135
Dix: Walter, 49; Walter A., 92
dog bites, 207, 210
dogs, 29, 193, 228, 229, 233; hunting, 148
Douglass: Bob, 89
Douglass' Shop, 89
Downing Bridge, 17, 44, 51
Dragon flats, 82, 83
Dragon Swamp, 13, 89
drum fish, 14
du Pont: Alfred, 103; Alfred, Mrs., 108
Duffey's Malt Whisky, 216
Duggar: Prof., 136
Duggar's Agriculture for the Southern Schools, 133
Dumb Priest game, 121
Dumfries, Va., 207
Dunbrooke High School, 93
Dunbrooke, Va., 49, 75, 92, 93, 94
Dunn: H.W., 44, 76, 79; James A., Rev., 45; Mr., 76, 79, 92; Muscoe, 86
Dunn Family, 92
Dunnsville Grammar School, 46
Dunnsville, Va., 12, 44, 45, 53, 79, 84, 89, 101, 167, 169, 170, 215, 220, 221, 229, 237; history, 75, 76
Durham: T.T., 62, 84; Willie Frank, 84; Willie Frank, Mrs., 84
E.M. Ware, Jr. & Co., 44, 76, 89
East India Company, 32, 33
East India islands, 207
Eastern Virginia, 18, 202
Edmondson: James, 33, 34
Edmundson: Thos., 26
education, 16, 64, 66, 67, 68, 69, 70
eggs, 115
Egyptian marble, 172
Eldorado, 39
elections, 27
Ellis: Garnett, 46
Elmwood, 60; school for girls, 69
Emerson: James, maintaining soldiers in prison, 30
Emperor of Rome, 135
employment, 15
England: fleet from, 21
English sparrows, 193
Ephesus Baptist Church, 43, 221
Essex County, 19, 225; bar, 58; Board of Supervisors, 44, 55; court records, 107; divided into parishes, 26; established, 25; first courthouse, 59; formation, 52; military district, 35; overrun with briars, 30; population, 13; School Board, 40, 48; schools, 67; size, 13; Superintendent of Public Education, 48; Superintendent of Schools, 60, 68; treasurer, 44, 76
Essex County Court, 25, 26
Essex Grist Mill, 80
Essex Mill, 82, 87, 96
Essex Mill pond, 86
Essex troops, 37
Eubank Garage, 42
Europeans, 21
Evangeline Lodge No. 23, 237
Evans: Mr., 89; Rev. Dr., 71
excelsior mills, 15
fairs, 27
Fall River Line, 170
Farland: Joe, 53; Z.S., Rev., 53; Zebulon Skinner, 53
Farland Family, 188
farm work, 16
farmers, 53, 59
farming, 136

Faulconer: John Waller, 58; Waller, 205
Faulconer home (Little Egypt), 58
Fauntleroy: Moore, Capt., 23
ferries, 27, 44, 51; public, 29; public, established, 29
Ferry: Dr., 48
ferry bridges, 83, 99
fiddles, 120
fires, 53, 79; Dunbrooke High School, 93; Lombardy Grove, 84; Richmond theater, 101
fish, 13
fish and oyster industry, 14
fish fries, 60
fish traps, 14
Fisher: Ella, 46
fishing, 54, 80, 98, 230
Fitzhough: Mr., 61
Fleetwood Academy, 68
Florida, 237
flour mills, 49
Fogg: Elza, 84; Mrs., 84
Font Hill, 60
Font Hill (photo), 32
Fort Lowery, 44, 211
Fort Monroe, 17
Fort Sumter, 235
Fountainbleu treaty, 30
fox hunting, 225, 229
France, 19, 57
Fredericksburg, Va., 14, 30, 164
French and Indians, 30
French broadcloth, 119
frigates, 37
frogs, 212
fruit trees, 14
furniture, 117
Gaines: Bernard, 26; Lillie Maxwell, 221
Garnett, 166; Billy, 73, 74; David States, Dr., 79; Ella, 53; Henry, 34; Henry Wise, 11, 18; J.L.C., 46, 160, 169; James, 28; James M., 218; James M., Hon., 60, 69; Laura Fleet, 46; Laura M., 169; Lewis Henry, 58, 102; Manie Leroy, 46; Miss, 169; Mr., 219; Mrs., 69, 70; Muscoe, 33, 34; Muscoe Russell, Hon., 60, 69, 101; Muscoe, Hon., 41, 53, 58, 64, 101, 169; Richard Brooke, Gen., 101; Robert S., Gen., 101; Taylor, Hon., 40; Thomas B., 40; William Care, 12, 237
Garnett Family, 227
Garnett home, 160
Garnett's boarding school, 218
Garnett's Ice Cream Parlor, 89
Garrett's barn, 62
General Assembly, 22, 23, 24, 25, 30, 35; divides colony into districts, 35
George, 112, 113, 114, 115, 116; William, Dr., 42
Georgia crackers, 212
Georgia negro dialect, 12
German clover, 14
Gettysburg, Pa., 101
Gloucester County: military district, 35
Gordon: Bowler, 96; Dr., 53; Jane, 53; Mr., 96; Thomas, 25
Gordon Family, 188
Gordon's Mill Swamp, 95
Gouldman: Francis, 26
Gravatt Family, 61
Gray: Mrs., 68, 107; Rouzie, 107
Gray's Boarding School, 107
Gray's School, 68
Great Britain, 30, 31; imports and exports, 32; merchants and manufacturers, 33; persons not removed to, 33; war with, 24, 36
Grecian marble, 172
green peas, 14
green tobacco, 212
Greenbrier, White Sulphur Springs, 122, 203
Greenwood: James, 62; Parson, 85
Gresham: Ashby, 59; Henry, Dr., 47, 48, 58, 68; Misses, 58; Mr., 165; Willard, 58
Grey: Rouzie, 187, 192

Griffin: Mr., 89
Griffon: John, 28
Griffon's land: warehouse established, 28
Guinea coast, 199
Gulf of Mexico, 107
gum trees, 15
Gustavus Adolphus, 19
Haas: Aubrey, 163
Haile: John, 48
Hall: B.F., 40; Maggie, Mrs., 53; Prof., 53
ham, 122, 190, 205
Hampton, Va., 64, 65, 169
hares, 193
Harris: Joel Chandler, 12
Hayes: Monroe, 45
Hell Bottom, 110
Henley: Len, 51
Henry: Patrick, 30, 31, 235
hens, 115
Henshaw: John, 34
Hermitage, 88
herring, 14
high schools, 16; Center Cross, 46; Dunbrooke, 93; Howertons, 84; Rappahannock District, 88
highways: Richmond to Tappahannock, 17
Hill and Dale (photo), 160
Hipkins: Mr., 53
Hipkins Folly, 53
Hobb's Hold, 52
Hobbe's Hole: changed to Tappahannock, 27; established, 25, 26; warehouse established, 28
hogs, 111, 139
holly, 134
Honolulu, Hi., 70
horsecakes, 57
Hoskins: Hannah, Mrs., 169; W.D., 169; Willard, 45
Hoskins Creek, 13, 49, 105
Hoskins Hill, 45
House of Burgesses, 22, 25, 30
Howertons Baptist Church, 85
Howertons Church, 95
Howertons High School building, 84
Howertons, Va., 62, 71, 83, 84, 86, 96
Hudgins: Mr., 48, 95
Hugene: Mr., 223, 224
Hume: W.W., Dr., 169
Hundley: Andrew, 45; Deane, Hon., 44, 76, 87, 96; Hervy, Rev. Dr., 41; J.T., Prof., 169; J.T.T., Rev., 169; Jack, Dr., 40; John T.T., Dr., 45; Maury, 43, 169; Maury, Prof., 84; Pearle Garnett, 167; Peyton, Dr., 88; Preston, 169; Tom, Dr., 40
Hundley Hall (photo), 96
Hunter: R.M.T., 101; R.M.T., home (photo), 32; R.M.T., Hon., 60
Hunter's Mill, 60
hunting, 230, 232
hunting dogs, 148
Hustle Road, 60
Hustle, Va., 60
hydrophobia, 210
Ides of March, 237
Illinois, 64
imported goods, 25
importing tea, 32
imports to and exports from Great Britain, 32
Indian girls, 108
Indian towns, 21
Indians, 20, 105; attacks by, 21; hostages, 49; massacres, 22, 30; Rappahannock, 21, 23, 105, 109; Topponock, 52; war with, 23, 24, 30
Ingelow: Jeane, 40
Inwood, 169
Iraville, Va., 61
Irish potatoes, 14
Italy, 57
Jack, 200, 201
jacksnipe, 212
Jackson: Jerry, 209; Stonewall, Gen., 101
James I of England, 19, 64
James River, 22

Jamestown: settlement of, 19
Jamestown, Va., 22
Jeffries: Ella, Mrs., 46; Mr., 48; Orville, 42, 43; Wm. George, Dr., 46
Jim, 112, 113, 114, 115, 116, 117, 118
Jims: Mrs., 117
Johnson: Arch, 202, 203, 204, 205, 206; Francis, 87; Mr., 92
Jones: Mr., 58, 182, 183, 184, 185, 186; Mr., gate of, 225; Robert, 28
Justices of the Peace, 26
Kalamazoo, 40
Kamchatca, 151
Kentucky, 158
King and Queen County, 13, 37, 68, 88, 140, 202, 217; line, 14, 48, 72; military district, 35
King Family, 209
King George III, 31
King of England, 19
King William County: military district, 35
Knights of Pythias Hall, 237
Kriete: George B., 44
Kuhn: Abe, 161, 162
labor, 135, 137
Lady Bathurst, 218
Lady Bathurst of England, 45
Lancaster County: formation, 23
land tax, 30
Laneview, Va., 40
Latane: Allan, 51; Allan Douglas, 71; James, Dr., 169; Lewis, Rev., a Huguenot, 27; Miss, 169
Laws: Clifton, Dr., 148
Laytons: new town named Beaufort, 31; warehouse established, 28
Lebanon Methodist Church, 72
Lee: John, 33, 34; Robert E., Gen., 68
Leedstown: causeway through marsh, 29
Lewis: James M., Hon., 51; Noel, 73
Lightfoot: Mr., 117; Willam B., 61
Lincoln: Abraham, Pres., 62
Lindsey: Anderson, 198; Caleb, 198; John, 198; Roy, 198; Titus, 198
liquor, 76, 77, 82, 83, 86, 149
Little Dragon Swamp, 72
Lloyds, Va., 59, 60, 89, 188
log cabins, 118
Logan, W.Va., 97
Lombardy Grove, 84
London, 198
looms, 111
Lord Bacon, 18
Lord William Boulware, 61
Loretto, Va., 61
Loudoun County, 147
Louisiana, 60, 147, 158, 164, 188
Lower Piscataway Church: now Marigold, 27
Lucindy, 196, 197, 198
Lucy, 194
lumber, 15, 88, 117
Lumpkin: W.R., 45
Lumpkin's Store, 42
Lynchburg College, 45
Maddox: William Arthur, Dr., 64
mad-stones, 207, 208, 209, 210
mail service, 225
Major Bob, 119, 120, 121, 122, 123
manufacturers, 15
Marathon, 18
marble, 172
Marigold, 27
Marse Frank, 178, 179, 180, 181
Marse Lal, 204
Marse Robert, 177
Marse Tom, 204
marsh grasses, 182
Marshall: John, Chief Justice, 218
Maryland, 72, 148
Massachusetts, 38
Mathews: James Muscoe, 50, 219
Mathews County, 40
Mathews Family, 50
Mathews' Digest of Criminal Law, 50
Mattaponi River, 214

Maury: Com., 219
Maury's Physical Geography of the Sea, 219
Maximian, 135
McCarthy: Miss, 169
McKinley: William, Pres., 234, 235
Meade: William, Bishop, 29
meat, 196
Mecklenburg resolutions, 235
Merigold, 74
Methuselah, 215
Micou: Edgar, 95; James Roy, 54, 55; James Roy, clerk, 53; Kitty, Mrs., 95
Middlesex County, 13, 37, 58; military district, 35
Milford, Va., 165
military: male teachers exempt, 66
military service: age 16 to 50, 35
militia, 30, 37
mill creeks, 87
Miller's, 169
Millers Road, 84
Millers Tavern, Va., 48, 96
mills, 42, 87, 106, 129; Croxton's, 59, 94; Essex, 82, 87, 96; Essex grist, 80; flour, 49; grist, 72; Hunter's, 60; Waring's, 59
Minor, Va., 48
Minter: Charles, 97
Mississippi, 188
Mississippi planters, 107
Missouri, 217
Mitchell: Herbert, 49; Winburne, 71, 72
molasses, 89, 139
Monroe: James, Pres., 158
Monroe Doctrine, 236
Monroe, La., 159
Montague: A.J., Gov., 45; Andrew, Prof., 92, 101; Edward, 217, 218; Howard, Rev., 85, 86, 92, 101; Robert L., 58
Montagues, Va., 40
Monument Hotel, 58, 106
Moore: Augustine, 34; Richard Channing, Rev., 218
Moratticick Creek, 23
Morgan City, Ala., 234
Mosely: Wm., Capt., 26
Motley Family, 202
Mount Clement, 48
Mount Landing, 59
Mount Landing Creek, 13
Mount Zion Baptist Church, 59, 92
Muse: General, 74; Hunter, 74; Jim, 74; Lallie, 74; Mrs., 41; William, 74
Mussel Shell Hill, 96, 99
Mussel Shell Swamp, 96, 97
My Ship, 238
Nancy, 196, 224
Napoleon, 237
Neale: R.G., Mrs., 169; Sam, 41
Ned, 147, 148, 149, 195, 196, 197, 198, 199, 200, 201
negro cooks, 214
negro dialect, 11; Georgia, 12
negro quarters, 29
negro shovers, 213
negroes, 82, 89, 118, 140, 175, 178, 179, 180, 181, 183, 188, 190, 193, 209, 210, 215, 221, 223, 225, 233; Anderson, 43; Civil War, 11; London, 198; Nina, 90; Page, 85, 86; punished with lashes, 86; Sampson, 43; Venus, 90
New Jersey, 91
New York, 235
Newbill: Charles E., Hon., 88; Chris, Dr., 222; Christopher F., Dr., 71, 72; Frank, 222; Henry L., Hon., 40; Kit, 222; Miss, 169; William Jeffries, Dr., 71; Willie, Dr., 222
Newport News, Va., 40, 169
Newton: Isaac, Sir, 133
Newtown, Va., 61, 89
Nina, 90
nine pins game, 62
Noels, 49
Norfolk steamers, 221
Norfolk, Va., 76, 169, 170, 222
North American Review, 70
North Carolina, 212

North Farnham Parish, 27
North Pole, 131
Northern States, 16
Northern writers, 11
Northumberland County: formation, 23
Northwestern Territory, 36
Norway pine, 120
Oak Grove (Colored) Baptist Church, 83
oak timber, 15
Oak-hill flats, 90
oats, 14, 134
Occupacia, 18
Occupacia Creek: warehouse established, 28
Occupacia District, 14
Old Kingston, 196, 197, 199, 200, 201
Old Point, 221
Old Point Comfort, 203
Old Virginia Reel, 206
Oliver: Capt., 43
Original Fourteen, 160
Original Ten, 160
Osborne: H.S., Rev., 108
Owen: John, 84; John Ritchie, 84; Morton, 84
oysters, 122, 205, 228
Ozeana Colored Academy, 16, 41
Ozeana, Va., 41
Page, 85, 86; Thomas Nelson, 12
Paris, Fra.: School of Medicine, 48
Parker: Jim, 47, 125, 126, 127; Jim (photo), 96; John A., Col., 70; Waller, 59
Parrine, 216
parsonages, 44; Methodist, 71, 72
Passagaluppi: John, 57; Willie, 50
Paul's Cross Roads, 95, 96, 97
Pendleton: Bob Lou, 48; Robert Louis, J.P., 95
Perkins, 154, 155, 156
Peyton Family, 61
Philadelphia, Pa., 49, 61, 83; first Congress, 34
Philip, 18
Phillips: Eugene W., 221; R.C., 46, 53; R.C., Mrs., 169; Sydnor, 53; Wilton, 44, 224
Phillips & Powers, 53
Phillips Family, 222
Piankatank River, 13
pianos, 203
Pigeon Hill, 106
pine timber, 15
Piscataway Creek, 13, 45, 47, 80, 83, 87, 95, 97, 99, 101, 211, 212, 217; warehouse established, 28
poetry: *An Ode to Nature*, 239; *My Ship*, 238
poisonous reptiles, 207
poll tax, 30
Poplar Spring, 48
population, 13, 15
population census, 37
Port Conway, 62
Port Royal, Va., 61, 62
potatoes, 134
Potomac River, 22
Potts: William, 24
poultry yards, 72
Pratt Family, 61
preserves, 196
Prince Albert coat, 158
Prince William County, 147
public ferries: established, 29
public free schools, 64
public schools, 16, 66
pumpkins, 134
rail shooting, 211
railroads, 132, 135, 189, 190, 215
Ransone: A., 44, 78; Mr., 80; Ryan, 44
Rappahannock Christian Church, 45, 79, 80, 167
Rappahannock County: divided, 25; levies, 24; named, 23; overrun with briars, 30; prisoners, 24; troops furnished, 24
Rappahannock County Court, 25, 26
Rappahannock District, 14, 88

Rappahannock District High School, 88
Rappahannock Indians, 21, 23, 105, 109
Rappahannock Line of steamers, 170
Rappahannock River, 11, 13, 14, 17, 20, 22, 23, 32, 41, 44, 49, 51, 54, 87, 88, 91, 105, 108, 174, 190, 211, 235; exploration of, 19; ferries, 27, 29; frozen, 146, 147
Rappahannock Times, 71
Rappahannock towns, 23
Rappahannock Valley Association, 15, 16
remedy for all ills, 215
Rennolds: Alfred, Capt., 101; Ben, 59; home (photo), 64; Robt., 34; William Gregory, 88; Wm. G., 64
resolves, 31
Revolutionary War, 29, 36, 65, 235
Rexburg, Va., 59
Rhone: Jack, 223, 224; James Robert, 152, 153, 154, 155, 156; Lula, 222
Rhone Family, 188
Rice: Evan, Col., 97, 101; James, 88; John H., Rev., 218; Mr., 89; Rob, 41; Will, 88
Richelieu, 19
Richmond Beach, 49
Richmond County, 27; established, 25
Richmond County Court, 25
Richmond Enquirer, 65
Richmond Highway, 48
Richmond sportsmen, 47, 86
Richmond, Va., 41, 45, 53, 80, 90, 96, 117, 169, 188, 207, 209; road to Tappahannock, 17; theater fire, 101
Richmond-Tappahannock Highway, 95
right to dispose of property, 31
Rio Grande, 237
Ritchie: Archibald, 33, 34; Mr., 101, 106; Thomas, 65
Ritchie Home in Tappahannock (photo), 128
Ritchie place, 50
Riverside Hotel, 58
roads, 42, 88, 95, 118; Hustle, 60
Roan: Josh, 222
Roane: Capt., 205; Lawrence B., Capt., 102; Mr., 101, 106; Thos., 34; William, 34
Roanoke, Va., 45
roast pig, 205
Robb Family, 61
Robinson: Prof., 41
rockfish, 14
Roman Forum, 100
Rome, Italy: early days, 69
Rouzie: Mr., 128, 129
Ruffner: William H., 68
Rumford College, 64
Rural New Yorker, 135
rye, 14
Sadler: John Ferdinand, 72; Tom, 47
Sadler's landing, 98
Sale: Charles, 169; Charlie, 52
Sale Family, 61
Sallie, 199
salt fish, 89
Salvation Army, 125
Sam, 196
Sampson, 43
San Jose scale, 14
Sand Landing, 99
Sanders Family, 227
sassafras oil, 215
Saunders: B.J., 59; Benjamin Junius, Prof., 158, 160; Junius, 205
sawmills, 15
school buildings, 66
School of Medicine, 48
school subjects, 133
school topics, 137
schools, 16, 64, 67, 68, 70, 84, 218; agriculture in, 131
schools for girls: Elmwood, 69

Scotland, 207
Scott: A.F., Rev., 43; Bunny, 83; David, 83; Francis H., Rev., 45
Semmes: Raphael, 219
servants, 29, 233; liable for military duty, 35
Service Afloat, 219
settlers, 18
Seward: Hamilton, 40
shad, 14
Shearwood: Charlie, 51
sheep, 29
sheepshead fish, 14
shingles, 117
ships, 83, 106; Alabama, 219; grifate, 37; man-of-war, 37; sloop, 37
silk-worm industry, 62
Simcoe: Mr., 149
Sisson: Mrs., 92
slaves, 29, 37, 41, 83, 110
Smith: Benjamin, Jr., 72; George W., Hon., 101; Harry, 90; James, Capt., 207, 209; John, Capt., 11, 19, 20, 21, 52, 105, 208; Joseph, 173; Lawrence, Maj., 24; Meriweather, 34; Meriwether, 33, 36; Mr., 41; Sam, 96; William F., 72, 73; Wm., 34
snake bites, 209
soldiers in prison, 30
sora hunting, 211, 212, 213, 214
sora shooting, 15, 97
South Farnham Parish, 27, 33; divided, 30; history, 29
Southworth: Harrison C., 51; Harrison C., clerk, 102, 103, 107
sportsmen, 212
spotfish, 14
Spotswood: Gov., 27, 28
St. Anne's Parish, 27, 33; history, 29; letter from Gov. Spotswood, 28; part from South Farnham, 30
St. Johns Baptist Church, 94
St. Lawrence River, 91
St. Luke's Episcopal Church, 41
St. Margaret's Episcopal School, 16, 104, 105, 106, 107; grounds, 108, 109; gymnasium, 103
St. Paul's Episcopal Church, 48
Stamp Act, 30
Standard Company, 216
steamers, 138, 146; Norfolk, 221; Rappahannock line, 170
Stewart: Benjamin, 72
Sthreshly: Thos., 34
Stiff: Frank, Dr., 88
storehouses, 76, 79; Bestland, 82; Tanyard, 46
stores, 72, 76, 86, 88, 129, 140; country, 145; Courtney's, 141; Dunbrooke, 92
Strawberry Hill, 42
Street: Miss, 169
Street Family, 222
Surry, Eng.: River Wye, 27
Sweden, 19
Taliafero: Francis, 26; John, 26
Taliaferro: Phil, 59; William, 60, 157
Taliaferro home (Oakalona), 60, 157
Tanyard Storehouse, 46
Tappahannock, Va., 15, 42, 44, 46, 47, 48, 53, 57, 65, 70, 83, 88, 93, 94, 169, 188, 221; an Indian town, 52; area increased, 29; as a port of entry, 27; as suburb of Richmond, 90; businesses, 52; courthouse, 50, 54, 100; courthouse tablets, 41; death at town hall, 76; exploration of, 20; first courthouse, 52; Gray's Boarding School, 107; junta, 101, 106; Monument Hotel, 58; Mrs. Gray's School, 68; name mentioned, 218; preventing hogs at large, 29; Riverside Hotel, 58; road from Richmond, 17; St. Mararet's Episcopal School, 16; St. Margaret's Episcopal School, 104; streets in, 28; town hall, 49, 106;

wooden chimneys prohibited, 31
taxation, 31
taxes: increased, 30; teacher salary from, 65
Taylor: Crawford, 41; Peter, 116
Taylor's Creek, 116
teacher salary from taxes, 65
teachers, 132, 136, 137, 139; males exempt from military, 66
Temple: Christian, 45
Tennessee marble, 172
Terrapin Forest, 110
Texas, 27, 144
Texas mules, 187
The American Citizen, 100
The Free Lance, 167
The Ladies of Lloyds, 204
The Secret Causes That Led to the Civil War, 70
The Voice of Flowers, 204
Thoreau: Henry David, 134
Thornton Family, 61
Tidewater, 211
Tidewater Inn, 44
Tidewater Trail, 15, 73, 83, 88, 91; Washington, D.C. to Fort Monroe, 17
Tidewater Virginia, 182
tobacco, 25, 87, 207, 233; as export and currency, 28; chewing, 128; green, 212; inspection, 28; Virginia, 154
Todkill: Amas, 20, 49, 51, 105
Tompkins Family, 45
Topponock Indians, 52
town hall, 106; former church, 50
Town's Blueback Speller, 139
trade, 32
trapping, 15
Treaty of Ghent, 37
Trible: Austin, 101; John Meredith, Rev., 85; John S., Dr., 85; John S., Rev., 45; Miss, 85
Trinity Methodist Church, 48
trout, 14
Tucker: Nathaniel Beverley, author, 217
Tulane University, 157
turkey, 122
turkey hunting, 230
Turner: Bob, 174; Jim, 149
Twain: Mark, author, 124
Tyler: Edward, 207
universities, 16
University of Virginia, 100
Upper Essex Baptist songs, 164
Upper Piscataway Church: now Texas, 27
Upright, Va., 71, 72, 73, 74, 83
Upshaw: Forest, Capt., 30; John, 31, 33, 34
Urbanna, Va., 37
Urquhart: Charles, Dr., 62; Louisa, Mrs., 61
Vauter's Church: built, 29
Vawter's Episcopal Church, 61
Venus, 90
Vertis Church, 91
violin practice, 164
violins, 202, 203, 204, 205, 206
Virginia: size of state, 66
Virginia mad-stones, 207
Virginia State Library, 69, 70, 217, 219
Virginia tobacco, 154
Vorhees: Daniel W., 100
Walden Pond, 134
walnut tree at Caret (photo), 128
War of 1812, 36, 106
Warburton: Will, 234
Ware: Burwell, 167; Catesby, 45; E.M., 45; E.M., Hon., 58, 169; Edward Macon, 76; Edward Macon, Hon., 102; H.H., 44; John, 44; Judge, 76; Macon, 230; Mr. & Mrs., 170; R.L., 44; R.L., Mrs., 169; Ritchie, Rev. Dr., 45; Robert L., 169; Robert L., Sr., 44
Ware's Wharf, 44, 76, 167, 170
warehouses, 28; established, 28
Waring: Lowery, 76; Thos., 34; W.L., 44; William L., Dr., 76
Waring Family, 61
Waring's Mill, 59

Warner: Charlie, Dr., 52; Miss, 169
Warren: Adm., 37
Washington: George, 30
Washington, D.C., 11, 14, 18, 40, 62
watermelons, 14
weapons, 77, 79, 126, 212
weddings, 167, 221
West Indies, 32
West Virginia, 53
Westmoreland County, 91, 169, 235
wheat, 14, 53, 83, 134, 137
white guineas, 90
White Oak Swamp, 225
White Sulphur Springs, 122, 203
Whitlocke: Robert, 94
Whitlocke Estate, 94
widow glass, 117
William & Mary College, 53, 67
Williams: Mr., 61
Williamsburg, Va., 34
Williamson: Jack, 53
Wilmot: David, 235
Wilmot Proviso, 235
Winder: Mr., 128
Wirt: William, Attorney General, 218
Woodland, 46
Woodward: Taylor, 206
World War I, 219
Wright: Della, 169; Ernest, 58, 206; Raz, 227, 228, 229; T.R.B., Hon., 50, 104; Thomas R.B., 102; William A., Hon., 49, 51; Winter, 215, 216
Wright Family, 188
Yankee ingenuity, 132
Yeardley: Sir George, Gov., 22
York River, 22
Yorktown, Va., 235
Young: Brigham, 173; Wm., 34; Wm., clerk, 34
Zack, 140, 141, 142

www.ingramcontent.com/pod-product-compliance
Lightning Source LLC
LaVergne TN
LVHW050615100826
845148LV00011B/1593

* 9 7 8 0 7 8 8 4 2 6 1 5 5 *